GUITAR RIGS

CLASSIC GUITAR & AMP COMBINATIONS

A classic tone generator: Jimmy Page with a Les Paul into a 100-watt Marshall stack.

GUITAR RIGS
CLASSIC GUITAR & AMP COMBINATIONS

Dave Hunter

GUITAR RIGS

CLASSIC GUITAR & AMP COMBINATIONS

Dave Hunter

A BACKBEAT BOOK
First edition 2005
Published by Backbeat Books
600 Harrison Street,
San Francisco, CA94107, US
www.backbeatbooks.com

An imprint of The Music Player Network United
Entertainment Media Inc.

Published for Backbeat Books by Outline Press Ltd,
Unit 2a Union Court, 20-22 Union Road, London, SW4 6JP, England.
www.backbeatuk.com

ISBN 0-87930-851-6

EDITOR: John Morrish
DESIGN: Paul Cooper Design

Origination and Print by Colorprint Offset (Hong Kong)

05 06 07 08 09 5 4 3 2 1

CONTENTS

Introduction

Guitar players have chased the sounds of the stars ever since recording – or world tours – existed. For many, the lure is like a siren's song, drawing us ever onward to purchase this 'custom shop' guitar or that vintage amp, try a new germanium-transistor fuzz or a boutique 'vibe clone… anything to take us closer to that tone that haunts our dreams. We spend, play, tweak, play, slide into a lukewarm disappointment, read a few books and mags and web advice pages, then go out and spend some more. That sound is out there, dangling tantalizingly just out of reach, and maybe the next new secret ingredient is finally going to let us nail it.

But let's face the facts: none of us is ever going to sound exactly like Jimi Hendrix, B.B. King, Eric Clapton or George Harrison, so it's deceptive to say, "Here are the rigs these great stars used; play this gear, and you'll sound just like them." I'm sure we have all seen too many books and guitar magazine articles that do exactly that, and it's an appealing line to sell – but one that usually just disappoints. Instead of treading the old 'Sound like Stevie' road, this book contains a selection of rigs that are universally acknowledged as classic pairings, and the real interest – and education – lies in reading about how these rigs work in and of themselves, and how they sound when an 'ordinary guy' plugs in and plays.

This approach strips away all those considerations that cloud any effort to mimic a great artist's sound: recording technique, studio effects, and of course 'secret studio gear swaps', where something is used on record but not acknowledged to the press and the public. *Guitar Rigs: Classic Guitar & Amp Combinations* shows you what these great pieces of gear really do, along with how and why they do it, and is therefore the only book that gives you a window on what these great combinations of guitars and amps might sound like for you.

Naturally, many legendary guitarists have been associated with various pairings discussed here, and many such associations will be discussed in the following chapters. But lots of these rigs are 'classics' in their own right without being specifically or precisely linked to one particular artist's consistent use of that setup. For one thing, many great players changed their gear frequently over the years – or recorded with one rig, while touring with another – but retained their signature sound and style nonetheless. For another, many of the stars' rigs have been modified or adapted in ways we might not be privy to, or they might simply consist of such rarified vintage instruments that we 'ordinary' guitarists never stand a chance of getting our hands on the stuff. Is it worth spending your entire playing life being frustrated, chasing a tone you can never fully achieve because, in fact, no one alive today remembers quite what made that sound in 1969? Probably not.

For that reason, this book takes a real-world view of the classic rigs discussed. Wherever possible it also acknowledges the versions of these guitars, amps and pedals that you are more likely to get your own hands on, rather than simply detailing the precious ideals that will only ever live in our dreams. Along the way, though, *Guitar Rigs: Classic Guitar & Amp Combinations* comes closer than other books to telling you what many stars actually did play, by cutting the bull and concentrating on the equipment – and what goes into making the equipment tick – rather than the legend and the myth.

The classic tones of rock, blues, jazz and country make great places to start from, and can point to examples of certain sounds that might appeal to us as players. It is important, however, to use these as templates and adapt them to get your own sound. Only by exploring all the variables will you learn how to craft a tone that speaks to your voice as a player, and then – with this book's help – you'll have an entire arsenal of sonic information at your fingertips. Your fingertips; not Jimi's, or Eric's, or Stevie's. We can go to extreme lengths to construct a rig that's exactly like that used by our favorite guitarist of all time, but we are never, ever going to sound just like him. It makes sense, therefore, to use this knowledge of the building blocks of many great rigs to works towards sounding like *yourself*. In the end, that is going to impress a lot more people, and probably make you a happier, better player, too.

TONE PRIMER: THE 'SOUND CHAIN'

In order to craft and fine-tune any electric guitar sound, you need to start with a comprehensive knowledge of all of the ingredients that go into making up that sound. I'm talking about building an awareness of the Big Picture, and coming to terms with what really affects your tone, and what doesn't. To that end, this chapter comprises a detailed examination of each of the links of what we can best describe as our 'sound chain,' the entire signal chain that begins with your fingers (even your brain, arguably) and ends with the pumping speaker that sends the sound waves to the listeners' ears.

That the sound chain begins at your fingers can sometimes be too easy to forget. But let's pick apart the more mechanical aspects of sound creating and shaping to start with – keeping the fingers in mind throughout – and deal with the human factor as best we can in our own individual ways as players. As we work our way along the chain it quickly becomes apparent how different combinations of wood, metal, wire, magnets, electronics, and even finish compositions contribute to the overall sound we produce as guitarists. Master just a portion of these, and you're already in far better control of your tone than the average player.

THE GUITAR

As most players already know, the broad range of electric guitar types available already throws up near-infinite variation in tone. Breaking this down further to a dozen or so crucial ingredients of the guitar itself might at first seem to only confuse matters more. But it shows you where you can make crucial differences in your own sound-shaping efforts, and where you can save energy (and money) by not dwelling on things that matter very little, if at all.

Picks

Even before we get to the instrument itself, let's give a little thought to one crucial 'external' that is frequently overlooked: the pick, or plectrum. Picks of different sizes, shapes and thicknesses, and which are made of different materials, all exhibit different sounds. Bare fingertips – flesh – makes a different sound still. Since the pick's or fingertip's contact with the string or strings is where it all begins, this is really the first ingredient in the sonic stew.

As a simple rule, thinner, more flexible picks yield a lighter, softer sound, but one that can also be effectively percussive in rhythm playing. The heavier a pick's material, the less it gives when attacking the string, and the more energy it transfers into the string rather than into its own give-and-take (the clearly perceived bending of a thin pick). All of this, naturally, translates to a heavier sound and a more aggressive attack. Go at a set of heavy strings with a thin gauge pick and you'll just end up with a choked sound and a grooved, gnarled pick. Hit them with a heavy or extra-heavy gauge plectrum and you can really start moving some steel. Old tortoise-shell picks are the epitome of this: the rigid material has negligible give, and yields a firm attack with sparkling high harmonics. Being made from an endangered material, they aren't available any more, but if you come across an old one give it a try; the difference will probably startle you. Many man-made alternatives offer similar performance, but few are quite the same as the real thing.

The shape of the attacking edge or corner of a pick also greatly affects the resultant sound. A triangular or pointed tip digs into the string sharply, inducing sparkling highs and good harmonic content thanks to its narrow but firm point of contact. A rounded edge blurs the attack slightly, yielding a warmer, 'rounder' sound. Plenty of good guitarists understand this well – or, sometimes, just come to it intuitively – and make very conscious selections of both pick type and shape to suit their desired sound. While a firm, pointed pick will suit the precise, attacking style of one player, another might prefer a softer, thinner piece of plastic for its squashier, slightly compressed playing feel, and of course either – or anything in between – is a valid choice.

In contrast to all of these, the bare thumb or fingertips yield a slightly muted, thick, warm sound, but one that can vary greatly depending upon technique. Many fingerstyle players are also capable of producing sudden bright, attacking riffs by snapping or plucking the strings heavily (sometimes difficult to achieve while holding a pick), and adding a little fingernail tip to the brew will brighten things up, too.

It's often difficult to know what type and gauge of pick contributed to the sound of any particular 'classic rig,' unless the player in question offered up the info in a reliable interview, and tended to stick with the same pick consistently. We more often know at least whether a great player routinely used thumb and fingers, a flat pick, or a thumb pick, and even these are starting points for significantly different tones.

Strings

Many elements of guitar construction come into play simultaneously in affecting the sound of each note produced, but it's best to start where the note is generated: the string. I'll put in a little more attention to strings here than to the other stages and components dealt with in this chapter, because strings are one of the totally unpredictable variables on whatever make and model of guitar you might play. While the specific sonic qualities of wood types and pickup designs will be put under the microscope in the following chapters where the guitars that employ them arise, there's no such thing as 'Strat strings' or 'SG strings,' so let's give them a closer look here and now.

Many guitarists think about strings more in relation to feel than to sound, and put little consideration into elements of their strings' make-up other than seeking a thickness – or gauge – that feels good to their fingertips and is easy to bend and fret. Some sacrifice a little finger strain for a heavier gauge that offers a punchier tone, or simply in an effort to achieve a firmer, less 'rubbery' action, but still don't give much thought to the tonal properties of the strings themselves. The metal that strings are made from, and the quality of their overall manufacture, are both going to have a major effect on how they vibrate, and therefore how they sound. Most players will be aware of these differences at some level, whether or not they know where the tonal variations are coming from, or why they are occurring.

We're talking purely about strings for use on the electric guitar; the variations of phosphor bronze and copper content and so forth in acoustic strings introduce an equally wide range of variables in that realm, but even with guitars that derive their detectable volume from some form of small, medium or large amplifier, the steel of the strings comprises the first mechanical variable in the sound chain.

In the rock'n'roll and classic rock eras of the 1950s and 1960s, pure nickel wrapped lower E, A, D and (in earlier cases) G strings were used, with plain steel B and E strings (and G string, if an unwrapped third was used). A pure nickel wire wrapped around a plain steel core gave the wound strings of this day a warm, full, rich tonality and generally longer life, although nickel's lower magnetism also meant a slightly lower output from the pickups. The high cost of nickel led to a widescale change to nickel-plated steel windings around 1970, with a resultant tone that was brighter and somewhat thinner, if perhaps punchier, and usually saw a reduced life span in the wound strings, too. The significantly reduced nickel content in nickel-plated strings means a greater magnetic reaction between strings and pickups, and therefore a slightly higher output; it's worth noting that they also wear out frets a little quicker than softer pure-nickel wrapped strings. Other compositions introduced over the years, such as 'stainless steel' and 'chromed' strings offer further proportional increases in overall brightness of tone compared with nickel-plated and, certainly, pure-nickel strings.

Pure nickel string types were virtually unavailable for many years after their initial disappearance, but the demand from fans of vintage rock tones has helped to bring back a few makes in recent years, and they have won many converts. The German company Pyramid is probably the best-respected brand devoted to manufacturing pure-nickel strings today, and even some big-name string makers like D'Addario have brought back nickel sets.

All of the above-mentioned string types do indeed sound slightly different but, if you have never played the type before (or haven't for many years), you will probably notice the differences most when switching from nickel-plated or stainless steel to a set of pure nickels.

They certainly resonate differently – with more depth and richness, many would argue – and their relative softness compared to the others can even make them feel a little easier to fret. These strings might prove a simple means of warming up an over-bright single-coil guitar; on the other hand, an overly dark instrument with humbuckers and dense body wood might be crying out for the added brightness of nickel-plated or chrome strings. Experiment with a few types that are different from your usual brand and style, and see what results.

String gauge does certainly affect guitar tone as well – and affects far more than mere 'bendability' – but this works in conjunction with other factors such as scale length and tuning (in other words, tension), action or string height, and playing technique, namely the lightness or heaviness of your touch and pick attack. All things being equal, heavier strings do offer a greater signal to the pickup, but that's not to say they are universally 'a good thing.' It takes more energy to get heavy strings moving, so they need to be hit relatively harder with pick or fingertip; lighter strings will vibrate to a similar intensity with a lighter touch, but can be overwhelmed and vibrate off-pitch in the early part of their attack when hit too hard.

The repercussions of what we could call 'the legend of Stevie Ray Vaughan' have sent hundreds, maybe thousands, of players diving for heavier string gauges in search of his heavy, driven, stinging tone. For some, the switch might have worked. Others just wore out their wrists, picks and fingertips in the effort, and were probably closer to achieve a heavier, more dynamic attack with their own playing style applied to .009s or .010s than by slaving away against a set of .011s, .012s or .013s. Facing the facts and returning to a lighter string gauge doesn't make you less of a man, or woman; it just means you have better learned which strings suit your playing style. And pity the poor SRV fan who bought his new .012s but had never been told that Stevie tuned down to E flat…

Which brings up another important point about string tension and resonance. Most players know that installing strings of the next gauge heavier increases the stiffness in the playing feel, but many don't know that dropping from standard tuning by a half-step per gauge virtually equals out the change in tension (within reason, as you approach the extremes). In other words, experiment with a set of .011s if you're curious about what it might do for your sound and touch, but try dropping down to E flat if the strings feel too stiff and unforgiving. This exercise also quickly proves to many that simply increasing string gauge doesn't magically introduce a heavy, powerful blues tone. Some player's techniques just don't get a heavier set moving in an optimal manner, resulting in a dull, constipated-feeling sound that lacks shimmer, bounce and compression; adjustments made elsewhere, while sticking with your habitual .009s or .010s (or maybe trying a better brand of the same gauge), might be a quicker route to the desired result.

Scale Length
The points mentioned in the above paragraphs regarding string tension, string gauge and detuning all relate equally to the differences that variables in scale length can have on your

sound, and on the playing feel of your chosen guitar. Given the same tuning and string gauge, guitars of different scale lengths resonate differently, and therefore possess somewhat different harmonic contents and core tonalities. They also feel different to play in ways that are largely allied with the differences in playing, say, a set of .009s and a set of .010s, the lighter/shorter being a little easier to fret and bend, but heavier/longer being somewhat firmer, less likely to vibrate off pitch when hit hard, and possibly more precise when hit with some playing styles.

The most common scale lengths for electric guitar are generally known by the makes and models that most famously employ them. Fender Telecasters and Stratocasters are made to a 25½" scale (that is, the distance between bridge saddle and nut), while Gibson SGs, Les Pauls, ES-335s and many others – though not all – are made to a 24⅝" scale (the Gibson scale length is often quoted as being 24¾" but in fact it is a little shorter than that, and every bit makes a difference). Some Fenders, such as Mustangs and Jaguars, are made to a 24" length, although the Jazzmaster is 25½" like the Strat and Tele, while many so-called ¾ or 'student' models from various makers are shorter still, often 22" or 22½". Some others, including low-enders Danelectro/Silvertone and high-enders Paul Reed Smith, have used a 25" scale length, which has a feel and tonality all its own.

Gibson's and Fender's most popular models are – to generalize – widely known for their respective 'warmth' and 'brightness,' a lot of which gets attributed to woods and pickups. But scale length plays its part, too. To put it as simply as possible, shortening the vibrating portion of a string (known as its 'speaking length') from 25½" to 24⅝" squeezes its harmonic points closer together, with the result that high harmonics sparkle and shimmer just that little bit less. On the other hand, this also offers something of a warming of tone by reducing the harshness that a plethora of high harmonics can sometimes introduce. With this in mind, Fender players seeking a little more of a Gibson feel and tonality (just a little, mind you) can try detuning a half-step or dropping down a string gauge. The reverse doesn't work quite the same – that is, stepping up by a gauge or tuning up by a half-step on a 24⅝" Gibson to achieve a Fender feel and sound – because the scale length is still determining the placement of the harmonic nodes along the lengths of the strings, and with shorter scales these can get pretty cramped.

Of course plenty of players select a guitar without much consideration of scale length, they just go with one that feels and sounds right. And there's nothing wrong with that. But knowing how the length of the strings, along with the strings themselves, influences a guitar's voice – before the signal even reaches wood, pickups, wires, amps – can help you better frame your own sonic desires, and potentially avoid many frustrated hours trying to correct or doctor a sound that can't be helped because it has already fallen at the first hurdle.

In his lecture to the 1995 convention of the Guild Of American Luthiers, guitar maker Ralph Novak said that, of all components that affect a guitar's tone, "scale length comes first because the harmonic content of the final tone produced by the instrument begins with the string. Factors such as structure and materials can only act as 'filters' to tone; they can't add anything, they only modify input. Therefore, if the harmonic structure is not present in the string tone, it won't exist in the final tone." Top luthiers understand this point intuitively. It is impossible to overemphasize the significance of scale length. It all starts with the string: its composition, tension, length, condition, how you hit it, what you hit it with, and so forth.

Bridge, Saddles and Nut

Okay, we have begun with a vibrating string; so the next significant links in the sound chain are clearly going to be the points at which that string are anchored: the bridge saddles at one end, and the nut at the other. Beyond these, the tailpiece and tuner posts respectively make secondary anchor points, but we'll deal with these below. Also, from here on out we don't need quite the detail on different specific types because that will be addressed when we encounter the guitars that carry these parts. For now, let's mainly make ourselves aware of the existence of the numerous variables.

Every note you play is going to vibrate along a length of string anchored at your guitar's bridge or bridge saddle, while any open note you play is going to emanate from a string that's also anchored at the nut (forget 'zero fret' designs for now, like many Gretsch and Höfner designs). If either of these anchor points is unsound, it will inhibit the string's full vibration. If either is positioned wrongly, it will affect the string's ability to vibrate in true pitch. But the clarity and purity and quality of the note isn't affected only by flaws in these anchor points; their design and composition are of major importance, too.

The solidity and completeness of the bridge's coupling with the wooden top of the guitar has a major effect on tone. A bridge – or saddles set into a bridge – that has a loose, partial, 'soft' or otherwise unstable or incomplete coupling with the guitar's top is going to yield a sound that's relatively thinner and less sustaining than the sound from one that is solidly joined. Any undesired movement in an anchor point will dissipate the string's vibrational energy into its own vibration – a vibration which has no sonic usefulness (unless it's a piezo pickup in itself, though similar principles apply, and loose and rattling piezos aren't much help either). Loose anchor points mean deadened strings that don't vibrate as cleanly and as long as they should. They also fail to transfer this vibrational energy efficiently into the wood of the guitar's body and neck, thereby further inhibiting the instrument's resonance and choking its tone. None of which, as you can see by now, is likely to be desirable in itself, aside from any annoying and unwanted noises the rattling might produce.

Which is not to say all bridges should be solid steel bolted directly to a lump of wood, and different designs do have their advantages for certain sounds and styles of playing, and consequently their fans. All of these considerations lead us naturally to the subject of vibrato bridges/tailpieces, which inherently employ moving and indirect coupling with the guitar body, and certainly less-than-solid anchor points by their very design. On one hand, many players are indeed aware that vibratos offer tonal compromises, but they are willing to make the sacrifice in order to have the versatility of the vibrato effect at their fingertips. On the other hand, the sonic characteristics of certain vibrato designs have become tonally desirable in themselves (put any sound on enough hit records and it's going to become desirable, whether you can consider it tonally 'pure' or not by objective, universal standards). Regardless, the designers of vibrato bridges and tailpieces – the thoughtful, intelligent ones anyway – go to great lengths to adhere to the same principles of solidity and bridge-to-body coupling that make for good tonality in a non-moving bridge, while accepting that they've got to make the thing wobble and bounce to do its job.

You can try out the effect of bridge design – and more to the point, the different degrees of string-to-body energy transfer offered by different string-bridge-body couplings – simply by comparing the sounds of an unplugged solidbody electric and an acoustic. Strum a full chord with the same strength on each guitar and listen not to the volume, but to the sustain and resonance of the strings themselves as they continue to vibrate and fade through the full length of the natural sustain of each instrument. To make sure you're listening to string vibration and body resonance alone, rather than projected volume, press one ear to the side of the guitar's upper bout as you strum (if you want to make it an even fairer fight, put an earplug or some tissue into your other ear).

An open G on my Froggy Bottom Model H-12 sustained for a full 20 seconds. It's a beautifully made little flat-top with a spruce top and rosewood back and sides (all solid woods), is extremely resonant, and sounds absolutely gorgeous. Next, I tried the same chord strummed with approximately the same attack on my '57 Fender Telecaster – a classic, sure, but not a guitar designed with the same consideration of tonewoods and resonance as a handmade acoustic. Believe it or not, the Tele sustained for a full 26 seconds, before I finally damped the strings with my palm just to make sure it wasn't some machinery hum coming up through the ground that I was hearing. I tried it several times and had difficulty stopping myself from damping the strings in the end, mainly out of disbelief that the thing was still vibrating, however slightly. I think the final, absolute tail-off of the sustain into silence usually fell at around 27 or nearly 28 seconds. Sheesh.

There are fewer moving parts in the Froggy's saddle and bridge, which is coupled very soundly to the top of the guitar, as compared with the Telecaster's three-saddle bridge which comprises threaded bars that rest on small grub screws that in turn sit on a partially suspended steel plate; but the difference is all in transference of string energy. Acoustic guitars are designed very intentionally to transfer their strings' vibrational energy efficiently into the thin top of the guitar, which in turn vibrates to produce the bulk of the acoustic sound and volume we hear. A flat-top acoustic is not designed along principles of pure sustained string vibration alone, and it would be pointless to do so. Even the top of a medium-bodied flat-top like this one takes a fair amount of energy to get moving, and while that energy is moving the top, it's also draining from the strings. In comparison, the Tele's steel bridge and solid swamp ash body soak up a lot less energy (though enough that we can hear the resonance of it through the wood with our ear pressed tightly to it), and allow the strings to keep vibrating for longer. Sure, there are many other factors at work here, but the exercise goes some way toward illustrating the effect of the efficiency of the coupling of different anchor points on the guitar, and how significantly they can alter the instrument's sound and performance. Incidentally, I later strummed the same open G on a steel-bodied National Delphi single-cone resonator guitar; acoustically, this is easily the loudest of the three – and I've got heavy .013-gauge strings on it, too – yet it only sustained for about 15 seconds. A lot of energy goes into moving that biscuit-bridge and spun-aluminum resonator cone, and pumping out all that volume.

The composition of the anchor points will also play a part in the guitar's sound. Steel, brass, aluminum, wood, nylon or plastic bridges and saddles will all sound slightly different, thanks to their own resonant qualities and their differing abilities to transfer vibrational every from the strings to other parts of the guitar. Likewise, bone, brass, plastic or other nuts will all sound slightly different on open strings. Whenever a guitar part plays a role in transferring or restraining string vibration, its design, solidity, density and material composition will be of significance in the guitar's overall sound. And they do so in at least three ways: they don't soak up and transfer energy, and therefore the strings themselves retain more of it and vibrate longer; they do soak up the energy but don't transfer it efficiently, so the energy dies with the saddle and/or nut; or they both absorb and pass along the energy, so a resonance is imparted to the guitar's body and neck woods. Of course none of this is black and white, and usually a guitar is doing a little of all three.

Tuners and Tailpiece

Although the speaking length of the string sits between bridge and nut, the solidity and design of the anchor points beyond these do play some part in the virtue of the string's vibration. These are factors that will be noticed more when wrong than when right: a buzzing or resonating trapeze tailpiece, for example, or a tuner post that rattles because its gear bushings are worn and not sitting tightly together. Either case could cause both an unwanted buzz or rattle and a detrimental effect on tone, either through the part's failure to anchor the string end securely, or through the amplified noise that blends in with the guitar's natural tone when it hits a set of tubes or transistors.

Tonally and functionally, most players would observe far more variables in tailpieces than in tuners. That is to say, while there are many different types and makes of tuners, most look and function roughly the same from the string's point of view, whereas tailpiece designs vary as widely as do bridge designs. There's another consideration regarding tuners as used with some types of guitars, and one of sonic importance beyond the mere efficiency of the tuning gear to tighten or loosen the string and allow you to tune it to pitch. Certainly with acoustic-electric or semi-acoustic guitars, the overall lightness of the instrument contributes to its resonance, and overly heavy fittings at either end are just likely to deaden the tone.

Let's look to a far greater authority than myself for confirmation of this, master archtop builder Robert Benedetto. "If we keep in mind that a lighter instrument produces a more responsive sound," writes Benedetto in his chapter on 'Archtop Guitars' in *Guitar: A Complete*

Guide For The Player (Thunder Bay Press), "then it is relatively easy to understand that a smaller Schaller mini tuning machine with ebony buttons will certainly have an advantage over the massive and considerably heavier Grover Imperial tuners that appeared on many high-end vintage guitars." Related to this, Benedetto also points to smaller headstocks as another means of reducing weight at the neck end. A heavy set of Grovers or other large, weighty tuners might arguably have a less noticeable detrimental effect on a solidbody electric, but many players have come to appreciate the frequent correlation between light guitars and resonant, toneful instruments. In any case, it's a factor worth keeping in mind.

The tailpiece, if the guitar has one, is likely to affect tone and performance in a wider range of ways. I have already noted that it needs to be sound and vibration free – and if it's a moveable or trapeze type it certainly needs to avoid bouncing up and down to create an unintentional vibrato – but, crucially, it should ideally anchor the ball-end of the strings at a point that creates the optimum break-angle over the bridge as well. Some bridges, such as the stop-tail type on a Les Paul Jr or Special or similar, act as their own 'tailpiece' so this isn't a consideration, and certainly Fender Strats and Teles are a law unto themselves, given their through-body or through-trem-block stringing. All others, however, need to take the strings down from the back side of the bridge saddles at an angle that allows the most toneful vibration to occur in string, saddle and body.

This angle varies somewhat with guitar type; in many cases, however, too sharp an angle can choke the tone a little, while too flat an angle can lighten and thin it out considerably, even give the strings a 'loose' feel at the bridge and some buzzing, by not allowing an efficient energy transfer from string to bridge to body (note, however, that string *tension* between bridge and nut always remains the same for strings of the same gauge tuned to pitch). Many solidbodies with long string lengths behind the bridge stretching to cumbersome or awkward-to-set tailpieces, or vibratos, are prone to this: Fender Jaguars and Jazzmasters can be notorious victims of poor tension over the bridge, as can some Gibsons with vibrola tailpieces, and many guitars fitted with Bigsby single-roller vibratos. As with so many components of the sound chain, so much is a matter of employing a well-designed part made with the optimum materials, and using it correctly.

At the other end of the guitar, either the back-angle of the headstock or the angle at which the strings break downward from nut slots to tuner posts – or the placement and height of string guides or string trees – similarly affects the transference of vibrational energy from the strings into the nut. Some classic makers have changed the pitch of their headstocks over the years, and players often note this as yet another determining factor in defining 'vintage' instruments, or at least those which are most desirable tonally.

Frets

You may rarely or never think of them as such, but your guitar's frets form another of its anchor points, and play an equal role with the bridge in determining the speaking length of the string during its vibration while played. Press a string to the fingerboard, and the steel fret in front of it now surpasses the nut in determining the end of the string length, and plays a part in transmitting some of the vibrational energy into the fingerboard, neck, and body of the guitar. Most guitarists put far more thought into the feel of their frets than into any contribution they make to the overall tone of the instrument, or indeed the whole rig. The fact is, a guitar's frets contribute simultaneously to its sound and playing feel, and their size, shape, condition and composition all play a part in both factors.

Many players believe that wide, low frets help relay more neck resonance into the sound, but the point is much debated and difficult to prove ("Quick, now refret that guitar with jumbos before I forget what the high-thin wire sounded like!"). I know plenty of first-class luthiers who swear that fret size has no effect on a guitar's sound, while countless tone-hungry players have refretted their Stratocasters with wider Gibson-style fret wire to make them "sound big and fat like SRV's Strat." Rory Gallagher also fitted his famous battered 1961 Strat with wide frets, and there's no denying the man had a big tone, but the choice might have been as much to facilitate note bending as anything else.

There's no doubt that wider frets are easier to bend, but they do offer a less precise end-point to the string, and therefore can be responsible for somewhat 'blurrier' pitching and imprecise intonation. High, narrow frets, though, offer precise chording and accurate noting.

Little is said about the composition of fret wire, but whatever its shape most sources used in the manufacture of modern electric guitars contain about 18 per cent nickel-silver (also known as 'German silver'), which in fact contains no silver but is an alloy of copper and nickel. The result is actually quite a soft steel, as can be seen by the rapid fret wear experienced whenever strings made of harder steel are pressed against them for a period of time. Much harder stainless steel frets do exist, and are used most notably on Parker guitars, but a harder fret is also naturally harder to fit, file and dress, so manufacturers have their own reasons for not turning to them en masse.

Neck & Fingerboard

Not part of the sound chain? Don't fool yourself; the string's vibrational energy passes from fret or nut right into fingerboard and then neck, making it yet another link in the chain. Any musical vibrations in the neck naturally resonate into the body, and contribute to the tonality of that part of the guitar, which few players would deny.

As with all of the components discussed so far that come into contact with strings and/or fingers, and are therefore subject to the wearing effects of friction, the fingerboard needs to be considered from the standpoints of both tone and durability. Add to this the fact that the shape and condition of the fingerboard also contributes enormously to a guitar's playing feel, and that gives us three major angles from which to approach any discussion of this long, thin slice of wood. As for the neck, any quality neck's composition is usually more a factor in feel and tone than durability.

A fingerboard's hardness is obviously going to be what determines its resistance to wear, but this factor also plays a part in whatever it may contribute to the guitar's tonality, just as different body woods' hardness, weight and densities are contributing factors in their inherent sounds. Of the three most common fingerboard woods in use both today and on vintage electrics, ebony is the hardest, maple the second hardest, and rosewood the softest. Of course even woods of the same type can vary widely, as will be discussed in more detail below under 'Body Woods.'

As far as any tonal considerations go, it's probably best to think of neck and fingerboard in conjunction. And while the neck and fingerboard woods don't influence a guitar's overall tone as much as its body wood, they can add their own special flavor to the sauce, heard in nuances detectable by many sharp-eared players. The classic '1950s Fender' neck of solid maple with integral maple fingerboard adds tightness and definition to both the low and high end of a guitar's frequency response, bringing notes into sharp focus. The maple neck/rosewood fingerboard combination introduces some roundness and smoothness which is often perceived as a louder bottom end, with extra sizzle in the highs. A mahogany neck with rosewood fingerboard is characteristically full and warm, with a well-balanced frequency response, while the same neck with an ebony fingerboard – often the upmarket option – adds some note definition and clarity.

Other types of wood than these are used for both neck and fingerboard, but they have usually been chosen as more affordable – or more readily available – alternatives to the classic selections, and fall roughly into the same bands of characteristics as the more expensive 'ideals.' Nato often stands in for mahogany, basswood for alder, and so forth.

The neck joint – that is, the way in which it is fixed to the body – is another point worth examining. It stands to reason that guitars that are made with the neck and body bolted or screwed together, glued together, or carved from the same piece of wood (as in a 'through body' neck) will have varying tonal characteristics, and we'll get into the differences in detail when we examine specific classic rigs in further chapters. The type of neck joint also lends further to the feel of the instrument when played in the upper fret positions, and this is as much a factor as strength or tonality for many players.

Body

The design of the body and the materials used in its construction together play an enormous part in determining a guitar's voice. Different types such as archtop acoustic-electrics, semi-acoustics, and solidbody electrics obviously vary widely, but even within the realm of the latter the specific shape, constructional techniques and woods used are integral to the instrument's tonal characteristics. Whether the body is constructed from a slab all of one type of wood, whether it is made of glued laminates, is thick or thin, has a carved or flat top and so on are all going to contribute to either sound or feel, or both. Adding routed 'sound chambers' to an otherwise solid body will introduce different resonant characteristics, and clearly broadening the 'air content' from there to include semi-acoustic designs (with fully acoustic 'wings' bound by a solid center block) or an entirely acoustic body alters the tone in stages from that of a solid slab.

Following chapters will talk in more detail about the tonal characteristics of specific designs and models, but it is worth getting the concept of this major variable lodged firmly in your brain right now. It's little secret that the wood or woods a body is made from plays an enormous part in shaping its character and, as discussed above regarding necks, each different type of wood resonates and rings with a different tonality.

As a rough guideline, swamp ash is perceived to have solid lows and sparkling highs, with open, breathy mids; alder produces a thicker midrange, with firm lows and enough high-end articulation to cut through; mahogany exhibits a dense, warm voice, blending gutsy lows and powerful mids; basswood yields a well-balanced frequency range with full mids; and maple offers a snappy, bright, articulate response. The 'classic combination' found in multi-wood solidbodies – a mahogany body with a maple top or 'cap,' the latter often carved into an arch – offers meaty, powerful mids with sharp definition and a musical, balanced response in both high and low frequencies. Of course even woods of the same type can vary widely, depending on the overall quality of the supply, as determined by factors such as the source's geographical location, the speed of the tree's growth, the way in which the wood was cut and dried, its age, and so forth.

Still not convinced that the body (and for that matter, neck) woods make much difference in a guitar's sound? Such an argument seemed most rife in the late 1970s and early 1980s, when the 'hotrod pickup' industry was booming, every experienced player was suddenly aware of what he could achieve by fitting a set of high-output pickups to his guitar, and many started mistakenly looking to the pickup itself as the home of tone and the heartbeat of the entire instrument. I can't count how many times I heard the argument, "Hell, you might as well just bolt a good set of pickups to a plank of wood and save all the money and hassle" – or words to that effect.

Okay, try it: buy yourself a $140,000 late 1950s Les Paul 'burst, remove its hallowed PAF humbucking pickups, and mount them in a plank of wood on which you have also installed a bridge and tuners. Now strum.

You're not likely to do this (and if you do, I know a couple guitar-playing doctors ready and waiting to sign your commitment papers), but you can already guess the tonal results, I'm sure. Even trying the exercise with a far lesser instrument quickly shows you what a vast difference body and neck design and wood content can make.

Many guitar stores will display a range of more affordable electrics of different designs, but carrying similar humbucking or single coil pickups (Epiphone Les Pauls and SGs, for example). The sonic differences between 'budget' guitars are sometimes less pronounced, but even a quick A/B comparison of a few of these should help to convince you that the difference is in more than just the pickups.

Finishes

Even the finish with which you cover a guitar's body, or don't, can have an effect on the instrument's sound. While players were coming around to appreciating the detrimental tonal and chiropractic effects of some of those lead-heavy Fenders in the 1970s, many were also struck by the revelation that the thick-skin polyurethane finishes of the day were impeding their instruments' tone. Most vintage electric guitars, and many quality reissues and handmade types, carry relatively thin nitrocellulose (lacquer) finishes. These are prone to premature wear and sometimes color-fading, so many makers brought in acrylic types at one time or another to introduce a harder-wearing (and in some cases easier to apply) finish that should keep a guitar shinier and looking newer for longer. The older nitro finishes 'breathe' more than the acrylic jobs, however, and don't seal the wood as entirely, and therefore constrain the bodies own vibration somewhat less. Many players will also tell you they simply prefer the 'woody' feel of a thin lacquer finish to the 'plastic' feel of heavy coats of acrylic. It might seem a fine point, but it's a point nonetheless.

Pickups

Up to this point we have sketched for ourselves an entire acoustic instrument. It might be a solidbody, but without means of transmitting a signal for amplification the sound chain has come to an end, and any sound we get from it will only be acoustic in nature, however quiet that sound is. It's important for tone-conscious guitarists to put some thought into this matter, though; strummed unplugged most solidbodies are extremely quiet – but they *do* make a sound, and that's the crucial point. The many variables described in the parts so far that make up this guitar all contribute to the timbre and quality of that acoustic sound, and however soft it is, make no mistake that there are indeed vast differences in acoustic timbre and quality. Together they play a big part in forming that guitar's voice before the pickups have even been figured into the equation.

It's even easier to hear how electric guitars with partially or totally hollow bodies add an acoustic element to the electric brew, but even with your bolt-on maple neck and solid slab of swamp ash, it's there too, believe me. Play any solidbody or semi long enough and you will soon get used to its acoustic voice, and you will be able to hear that as an element of its overall sound when you plug it in and fire up the rest of our sound chain.

Recall the piece of wrong thinking mentioned earlier, that defines an electric guitar as nothing more than a plank of wood with a couple of pickups mounted on it. The Fender Broadcaster (which became the Telecaster) was described that way by its detractors when it hit the scene in 1950, and critics slung the same insults at Gibson's Les Paul when it came to the market in 1952. They are certainly very different-sounding guitars, and that is thanks primarily to two elements: body design, and pickup design (the differing scale lengths certainly play a part, but to keep things simple let's argue that that is integral to body design). Sure, we know damn well that our favorite electrics are more than logs with transducers, but once you get the wood and strings ringing, those transducers – the pickups – do matter, a hell of a lot. This is where all that vibrational energy from the strings, enhanced by the resonance of the body, affects a change in the magnetic field of the pickups and is thereby converted to an electrical signal. We are passing into another world.

Most players are well aware of the basic sonic differences between different types of pickups – humbuckers verses single coils, for example – and we'll define the characteristics of these in more detail when we cover the guitars that carry them. Aficionados realize, however, that the variables run far deeper than 'two coils vs one.' They will point to enormous differences in tone and power even between the same types of pickups from the same manufacturer as they evolved over the years, even if these look much the same to the inexperienced eye. The windings of Fender's Broadcaster/Telecaster's single-coil bridge pickup, for example, changed to a different gauge wire from its original in the early 1950s (from 43 gauge to 42 gauge), and also became progressively weaker from the 1950s to the end of the 1960s, as did the Stratocaster's pickups. Gibson's humbucking pickups, introduced in the late 1950s, were significantly different by the late 1960s, Gretsch and Guild pickups changed frequently, and the units on many modern makers' guitars even seem to evolve rapidly.

Wire type and gauge, magnet size and composition (whether alnico or ceramic), the width or narrowness of the windings in the pickup coil, and even the mere positioning of the magnet will all play a part in determining power, frequency range, and overall tonality. More powerful pickups will drive an amp harder and send it into distortion quicker, introducing another tone-changing factor, and different pickups will react slightly differently with effects plugged between guitar and amp, thanks again to varying powers and frequency responses. Alnico magnets were used exclusively in the early days, with the transition away from them in the mid 1960s and particularly after around 1970, when the cobalt contained in their construction became extremely expensive. Pickups made with such magnets (as well as speakers, see below) have always been considered a little sweeter and more musical than those using ceramic magnets, to which some players attribute a hard edge and a certain lack of roundness of tone.

Alnico is usually quoted as being an alloy of aluminum, nickel and cobalt – and those elements do make up its name – but it also contains other materials, and usually more iron than all of these combined, a fact less often discussed in vintage gear-related articles (thanks to its lack of romance, I guess). Different alnico alloys are numbered according to their composition, and therefore their ascending strength, with II through V being the most common for pickup and speaker magnets. The average composition of alnico (with the percentage of each element in parentheses) is roughly: aluminum (10), nickel (18), cobalt (12), copper (6), iron (54), but some types also contain a little titanium and even traces of niobium. In tonal terms, alnico II is a little sweeter and softer than the others (thanks to a slightly weaker magnetic field), alnico V is more full-frequencied and a little punchier, while alnico IV is considered muscular with clear highs but a little less aggression than V. The differences are subtle – and as ever, other variables in the manufacturing process usually mean that no two vintage pickups of even the same type sound exactly the same – but many players and makers in the know do express definite preferences for, say, alnico II vs alnico V, or what have you.

Ceramic magnets make it easier to create hot, punchy pickups, and these certainly have their fans, too. Most high-gain heavy rock replacement pickups will carry ceramic magnets, and players who use them don't often pause to regret their lack of a certain subtle smoothness while driving their 150W Mesa/Boogie Triple Rectifier stacks through the roof. Then again, many do still prefer vintage type humbuckers with alnico magnets to push their rigs for even heavy rock and metal sounds.

However you slice it, the pickups on your guitar do matter a hell of a lot. Crucially, this is our first electronic link in the sound chain, and the first departure from mechanical acoustical factors… which in most cases we won't return to until the signal hits the speaker. In short, the pickups are a big, big variable. So, even if your guitar was just a plank of wood, that plank would sound very different each time you mounted a different type of pickup on it.

Switches and Potentiometers

The perceived jobs of an electric guitar's switches and potentiometers (volume and tone knobs) are to select which pickup is active, and determine its output level and its tone. But because they are conductive components carrying a signal, and in some cases possessing electrical resistance, they have the potential to affect the actual sound that passes through them.

A guitar's switches shouldn't impart any noticeable sonic artifacts unless there's something wrong with them, but the volume and tone controls can alter the tone in a couple of ways even beyond those their names imply. When used as a volume control for guitar, a potentiometer's resistance has a bearing on the treble content of the signal that it passes along. Fender has traditionally used 250k ohm potentiometers for its guitars, which carried bright, sparkly single coils. An increase in resistance to 500k or 1000k (1M) means an increase in high frequencies – which might only make a Fender sound harsh and spikey, but is just the ticket for getting a little extra sparkle out of darker, heavier-sounding Gibson guitars. Unbuckle a Gibson's control plate, therefore, and you'll find a collection of 500k pots, and most makers using humbucking pickups or darker types of single coils follow suit.

Unless rigged to avoid the effect (see below), these volume pots also reduce the signal's treble content when wound down even slightly. Some players prefer to modify their guitars to retain a full proportion of high frequencies at all volume settings, while others find this a quicker and subtler means of achieving a little treble cut than the tone control when their sound needs just a little deharshification.

The capacitor attached to the tone control or controls makes a difference, too. Passive tone controls on electric guitars are very simple 'treble bleed' networks that pass off a portion of the signal's high-frequency content to ground, and the value of the capacitor attached to the potentiometer determines how much treble is bled away, or 'rolled off.' The lower the value of the capacitor, the less highs the tone control taps off from the signal as it is turned down. For example, the tone controls on a Gibson with humbuckers usually run through .02μF capacitors, but if you changed those for .01μF caps – halving their value – the knobs would muddy the tone a little less when turned down (Strats traditionally carry .047μF caps). Capacitors and even resistors sometimes come into play with volume controls, too, mainly as a means of lessening the treble loss when the control is turned down.

Another type of treble bleed network takes the form of a small .001μF cap connected between first lug and wiper on a volume pot, but this time it bleeds some high frequencies from the original signal through to the reduced signal when the pot is turned down, rather than tapping it off to ground and away for good, to avoid the common loss of treble experienced as you turn down the volume. The .001μF cap is found as a modification on some guitars, but was original equipment on post-1967 Fender Telecasters, and helped to preserve the famous Tele twang even at lower volume settings. A resistor of between 100k and 300k is sometimes used parallel with this cap to reduce the 'thinning' effect that a capacitor by itself can have, by retaining more of the low end as well.

Jack

Hello signal, bye-bye guitar. The main variable here is whether the thing's hot contact is kept clean or not, which can make a surprising difference in your sound, even when everything otherwise appears to be functioning.

BETWEEN GUITAR AND AMP

Connecting Cables

A player who is hip to the tip knows better than to take his or her connecting cables (cords or leads) for granted. These are frequently the longest link in the sound chain, and all too often the weakest, in terms of function and efficiency. In an ideal world, an audio connector transfers a signal totally unchanged from the output of the stage before it (say a guitar) to the input of the stage at its end (effects or amp); it introduces nothing, it takes nothing away. In the real world, however, the average cable of any significant length fails at both jobs: it adds some resistance that loads our hard-suffering pickups, adds capacitance, adds noise, and thereby saps some of our guitar's treble content, and sometimes signal level.

There are many cables available today from manufacturers who go a long way toward minimizing this coaxial connector's effect on the signal passed through it. Whatever its quality, however, the degree to which any passive cable adds impedance, capacitance, microphony (handling noise) and sometimes radio interference is really down to its length. These artifacts become noticeable especially with cables of lengths of about 20′ or more, and increase dramatically with extra-long lead lengths. If you're playing at home or on a small stage and running straight to your amp with a 15′–20′ cable, you're probably not going to suffer too badly.

Any gigging guitarist who also uses a few pedals, however, is likely to have a 15′–20′ cable before the pedals, a few in between, and at least a 15′–20′ cable carrying on to the amp. If all pedals are bypassed in the 'true bypass' style, where the complete effect circuit is switched out, you can basically add up those cables and any connecting jumpers between the pedals, plus a few feet of wire inside the pedals themselves, and prepare to live with the high-frequency loss induced by 40′ or 50′ of wire. If a pedal early in the chain is one that keeps a buffer switched in even when bypassed, to drop your source impedance to a low level for everything past it (and preferably a high-quality buffer that alters your tone little or not at all), the tone should revert to the short-cable-straight-to-amp scenario.

Keep in mind that this book's intention isn't to pass judgment on different setups, or to say "this is good, that is bad," but to outline the variables thrown up by a wide range of rigs, and compare their sound and performance. But how often do you hear cables mentioned in any discussion of 'classic rigs'? It's important to keep that long run of cable between guitar and amp in mind. By its very nature, it should be one of the most obvious links in the sound chain, but is all too often ignored.

Also, be aware that many classic sounds rely on the effect of a little high-frequency loss from long or poor cables. In the old days, those coiled leads that were so often seen suspended in midair between a strutting guitar hero and his Marshall double stack were far from audiophile-quality connectors, but often the high-end loss they induced was just enough to make a treble-soaked Strat into a crackly-bright Marshall 100-watter a warm, crunchy, toneful combination and not merely an ice pick to the eardrum. As with many other links in the chain, there are some 'flaws' we get used to – thanks mainly to their contribution to many great sounds, or their presence in the midst of stunning playing – and, weak links though they may be, they become another part of the classic setup.

PEDALS

Effects pedals are such an enormous variable that it probably suffices to point out this fact and move along. But a few specifics won't go amiss.

It's plainly obvious that this link in the chain alters our sound more severely than any before; it's in the very names and natures of the devices: distortion, tremolo, echo, chorus, phaser, whatever. Aside from the self-declared sonic adulteration of the effect, its circuit can also introduce forms of 'conditioning' that further affect how the signal is handled by subsequent stages in the chain. Modulation, distortion, delay, phasing, tone filtering (wah-wahs and their brethren) – and digital vs analog variants of each – all react differently with effects of other types that follow, and with amplifiers. To give one simple example, a chain that runs guitar-phaser-overdrive-amp will sound quite different than a chain that runs guitar-overdrive-phaser-amp. The individual links are the same, but they can't be reversed indiscriminately without sonic consequences. You might prefer the results one way or the other, and which one works for you isn't the point. It's the awareness of the differences that matters. Also, aside from the sound effect they introduce themselves, the changes in level and frequency response of the signal that reaches the amplifier after a pedal is switched in are also going to alter the way that amp performs its duties; they might change the headroom and onset of distortion, alter the amp's own frequency response, and so forth. It all adds up, and every change introduces further changes down the line.

Beyond this, as mentioned briefly above, even pedals that are switched out can alter the sound that passes through them, or affect how well the signal makes the onward journey to the amplifier. A pedal with no true bypass and no quality buffer/line-driver stage – as is the case with many vintage pedals, and wah-wahs notoriously – can load down the guitar's pickups with all or part of the effect's circuit, even when that circuit is 'off.' A pedal with true bypass (often called 'hard-wired' bypass, though in truth it isn't hard-wired because it is switchable) can pretend it's not there when switched out, although some internal wiring between switching and jacks can introduce nominal impedance and capacitance. A pedal with a quality buffer stage can also lend a helping hand when it's switched out, by putting the signal into a condition that is better able to pass the rest of the distance with minimal level or tonal losses.

The digital vs analog question is another that is far too involved to deal with adequately here, but the issue deserves a nod at least. Put your signal into a digital effects circuit that is set to a heavy (wet) depth/mix level – and switched on, of course – and that signal will be subjected to analog-digital then digital-analog conversion and, however good the resultant sound, will come out the back end of the unit only an approximation of its original self. Early units that functioned at as low as 8 bits did unspeakable damage to the signal that entered them; the later standard of 16 bits (CD standard) still hacked off a considerable portion of the sonic picture, and even 24-bit units, by definition, still must leave behind a sizable slice of your sound. However you look at it, that digital conversion is taking away portions of the original analog sound that can never be restored. But of course keeping a low or middle mix/depth level feeds a portion of the original analog signal around the effects circuit to preserve some of the natural dynamics and full frequency range of your guitar's true sound.

AMPLIFIER

Many players see an amplifier as a single, self-contained unit. The sound goes in, it gets louder, it comes out. As with the guitar, however, any amp contains a number of individual stages within it, each of which becomes its own link in the sound chain. Even the most basic 'vintage' style tube amp – leaving out any onboard effects, which obviously change the sound in their own ways – contains three major stages worth investigating, each of which has a number of elements contributing to its performance, with the further contribution of an arguable fourth link in the form of the power rectification and filtering stage. Thanks to the fluidity and linearity of most tube amp circuits, it is easy to visualize the amp as a series of links in itself, once you lift the lid on the black box. (For ease of discussion I am going to use tube amps as our reference here, as these are the types most associated with the classic rigs that are the subject of this book.)

Preamp Stage

The first thing your signal hits after disappearing through that ¼″ jack-plug hole in the amp's control panel is, in most cases, a single 68k grid-stopper resistor put in place to stop oscillation, then it's a straight, short trip to the input of the first tube stage in the preamp. In actual fact, the preamp is generally considered to contain everything between the input and the phase inverter (explained below), which can include this first gain stage, any tone controls, sometimes a further gain-makeup stage following the tone stack, and perhaps a few other elements. To break it down, however, let's consider the first true point of amplification, known as the first gain stage.

As the name implies, the preamp – any preamp, for the most part – is merely a small amplifier designed for the task of bringing an audio signal up to a level which the power amp can handle, and therefore boost to an even greater level ready to be converted to audible airwaves pumped by a speaker. The simple version is that a guitar amplifier's preamp contains a gain stage that boosts the signal (usually one half of a dual-triode tube, most commonly a 12AX7), a coupling capacitor that helps to determine the frequencies that are desirable – and not – to pass along to the next stage, and a volume control (actually a variable resistor) to let the player determine how much level to pass along. Other capacitors and resistors take the jobs of conditioning the power supply and biasing the tube (that is, setting its operating level), but that's the gist of it, and many preamp stages are just as simple as that.

Even the preamp of the great tweed Fender Bassman 5F6A of the late 1950s, considered by many to be the greatest rock'n'roll and blues amp of all time, contains precisely those ingredients and no more (as considered separate from the tone stage that follows it); the signal passes through a 68k resistor, one tube gain stage, a .02μF capacitor, and a 1M volume control. Bye-bye preamp, nice knowing you. But as ever, the beauty is in the details. Each of the same elements of a different make and/or composition will introduce subtle sonic changes – a metal film resistor versus a carbon comp, a polyester versus a polystyrene verses a paper-in-oil capacitor, a GE tube versus a Mullard, a 12AX7 versus a 12AY7, and so forth. Incidentally, the preamp stage up to this same point in the Normal channel of a Vox AC50/4 from the mid 1960s – as used by The Beatles for a time – carries exactly the same elements, aside from an ECC82 (12AU7) tube in place of the Bassman's 12AY7, but it's a very different sounding amp, for sure. Beyond type and composition, change the value of the coupling cap, or of any of the resistors and the capacitors that feed the tube its voltage, and the sound changes further.

Tone-Shaping Stage

The topologies of tone-shaping stages – known by amp techs as 'tone stacks' because of their conventionally 'stacked-up' appearance on many schematic diagrams – vary far more than those of first gain stages in tube guitar amp preamps. Many early amps, smaller ones especially, had no tone controls at all (the tweed Fender Champ, for one). The signal went straight out of the Volume control and on to the output stage via a second coupling capacitor, and this lack of any tone control certainly affects their inherent tonality. Others, such as many smaller Voxes and Marshalls, tweed Fender Deluxes and its siblings, and many smaller contemporary boutique amps, have just a single Tone control, while everything from the Bassman mentioned above to bigger Marshalls to most modern channel-switchers have a three-part bass, middle, treble tone stack.

Factors like the number of controls, the way they are configured, and the value of the capacitors they employ for frequency shelving will clearly affect the signal passing through them in different ways. More controls don't add more tone, they merely provide more fine-tuning over what's there. In truth, more controls usually deplete tone slightly – or deplete level, in any case – and require further gain stages to make up the loss. In any event, in the case of passive tone stacks (as the majority are) adding a Middle control to what was previously a two-tone-control amp doesn't give the amp more midrange, it just gives you more precise governance over how much of that midrange stays in the signal. The two-control amp governs its midrange content by the relative settings of the Bass, Treble and Volume controls. And as with the preamp, the makeup of any components in this tone stack also plays a part in shaping the voice of this link in the chain.

Beyond that, even the placement of the tone controls significantly affects how they perform. If the potentiometers follow the cathode of the first tube gain stage (known as a 'cathode follower' tone stack), the amp will most likely feel and sound a little different than one in which they are placed between the anode of the first tube stage and the grid of the second. Many guitarists say the former gives a very dynamic, touch-sensitive playing feel, while the latter contributes to precise, solid response (a tweed Bassman verses a blackface Twin Reverb, for example, these being amps that contain the different types of tone stacks, although each has a Treble, Bass and Middle control). Rather than merely shaping the amp's tonal response, many types of tone controls also help determine how hot the signal is that's passed along to the output stage – the tweed Deluxe is a prime example – and thereby act in effect as a secondary level/distortion control. Tone in every sense.

Once the signal has cleared the tone stack, many amps pass it straight along to the output stage – often through a single coupling capacitor – although some send it first through further gain make-up stages, or reverb and/or tremolo in the case of amps with these effects onboard.

Output Stage

A tube amp's output stage begins at the phase inverter (PI, or 'driver') tube, which has the job of splitting the signal into two signals 180 degrees out of phase with each other to feed the output tubes. It ends at the other side of a transformer that converts these tubes' output into a signal that will power a speaker. Each of these sub-stages in the output section – PI, output tubes, output transformer – has a major impact on the voice of the amplifier, and the components that connect them play their part, too.

Different PI topologies have different sounds in themselves. Firstly, the signal passes through this tube, so its type, quality and configuration will obviously have some effect – however subtle. Secondly, some types of PI circuit impart a little of their own distortion on the sound when pushed hard. Thirdly, different PIs 'drive' the output tubes in different ways – some inspiring good headroom, some leading to an earlier onset of distortion – so they very much play a part in how the output tubes themselves will sound. Players rave about vintage Fender tweed amps of the 1950s, but relatively few are aware that Leo and co went through at least three different evolutions of phase inverter designs in that decade alone, all with very different sonic and distortion properties, before arriving at the version that has become the most-emulated PI topology of all time for large, high-output guitar amplifiers. From the PI, the signal passes to the output tubes via a further pair of coupling caps, sometimes in series with resistors (or a quartet of resistors, in two parallel strands, in the case of an amp with four output tubes).

For guitarists who have owned the same amp over many years and had to re-tube it every 12 or 24 months or so following periods of rigorous gigging, it'll come as no surprise to hear that the output tubes are one of the most influential single links in the entire sound chain. Weak, badly mismatched, or wrongly biased output tubes can seriously impede an amp's sound; even operational but poor quality tubes can choke its tone immensely. Beyond mere functionality, however, different types – and even different makes of the same type – of tube have varying sonic signatures that many sharp-eared players can detect, and use to their advantage. Factors like the DC voltage level that the tubes run on and the way in which they are biased also greatly affect their tone and performance, not usually in a 'more is better' fashion, but in a 'matter of taste' manner that throws up further variables. If variety is the spice of life, the output tubes alone offer a sizzling jalapeño to the tone connoisseur.

The signal runs straight from the output pin of the power tubes to the input of the output transformer (OT), which is called the 'primary.' The OT that you can see hanging from the underside of many an amp chassis (they are usually the smaller of two, or the middle-sized of three) plays a part that would outwardly seem purely functional, in that it transform a high-impedance current from the tubes to a low-impedance current that will drive a speaker. But as the entire product of our sound chain up to now passes through it – with only one link in the chain to follow – you can already guess that it is likely to have a major impact on the resultant sound.

The OT's efficiency or lack thereof, its physical size, the ratio at which it converts the current, and many other factors, all affect how it will sound. The way it converts your signal into one capable of pumping a speaker – and therefore, becoming sound waves again – is enormously significant. Roughly speaking, bigger transformers (relatively speaking, given the same output tubes) offer more headroom and better bass response, or simply put out a more accurate reproduction of the signal the tubes send them. On the other hand, some vintage types exhibit juicier distortion, while more efficient moderns designs offer impressive clarity and definition. OTs can be designed to roll off low frequencies that might overload speakers, or to exhibit other frequency-related characteristics. As with virtually every component we have analyzed so far, the choice isn't usually a matter of bad, good, better, best, but more of being aware that different OTs contribute to different sounds. And sometimes contribute a lot.

Other factors and what we could call 'side chains' are often involved in the performance of an amp's output stage and its circuitry generally, but one we call the 'negative feedback loop' often has the most sonic significance. In simple terms, this loop taps a portion of the output at the OT's secondary and feeds it back in negative to, usually, the input point of the output stage. The result is some suppression of resonant peaks and extremes in the frequency response, and what we hear as a tighter, firmer operation with more headroom, but a harsher onset of distortion when it finally comes. Removing the loop (or never installing one in the first place) yields an amp with a more raw, aggressive voice, usually with a pronounced midrange response and a smoother onset of distortion, but with less headroom and a looser feel overall. Either has its uses, depending upon your sonic goals, and numerous classics have been made to either formula.

Power Stage

A tube amp's power stage is not in the signal chain itself, but it provides the fuel that keeps the engine burning, and the amount of fuel it provides and the speed at which it can cough it up at times of high demand greatly affects the feel and, to some extent, sound of the amp. This stage consists of the power (or mains) transformer, the rectifier, and the filtering stages that clean and condition the current that the tubes feed on.

The power transformer (PT) really is a purely functional device, but as with everything quality obviously counts, especially considering its role in handling high voltages. The PT takes the power from your domestic wall socket, around 120VAC in the USA and 240VAC in the UK, for example – and steps it up to the higher voltage required by the amplification duties of the tubes, while splitting off lesser voltages to run the tubes' AC-powered heaters (filaments) and that of the tube rectifier, if there is one. This latter component, the rectifier, is where we begin to encounter variables that the player will really notice.

The rectifier converts the stepped-up AC voltages supplied by the PT into even higher DC voltages required by the tubes' plates (anodes). Solid state rectifiers, usually made up of twin strands of silicon diodes in series, supply this voltage very quickly on demand, with very little lag between 0VAC and, for example, the full requirement of 450VDC in a big Fender or Marshall. Think fuel injection, with a quick acceleration equating to a tight, firm, detailed attack and playing feel for the guitarist. Tube rectifiers take a little longer to ramp up to full voltage when a note is hit hard and the demand comes from the tubes, and this results in a dip and swell in the amp's output response, referred to as 'sag.' It's a compression-like sensation that lends a softer edge and tactile feel to some tube amps – making them suitable, for example, to certain blues and classic rock styles, but perhaps less suitable to firm, heavy contemporary rock and metal or ultra-tight, clean work.

Beyond the rectifier, the DC voltages are also subject to the filtering of electrolytic capacitors and sometimes a choke (a small transformer with a single input and output), which serves to remove 'ripple' in the current that would end up as unwanted noise and overtones, and the degree of filtering also affects the amp's sound and performance. Lightly filtered amps tend to be a little grittier and sometimes rawer, but often with a softer, looser bass response, while heavily filtered amps usually exhibit a little more definition, clarity and solidity.

SPEAKER & SPEAKER CABINET

We are finally on our way back out of the kingdom of the electrical current. For the first time since that vibrational energy molested our guitar pickups' magnetic field, the signal chain is about to be converted back to vibrational energy and sound. In a very rough sense, a speaker works something like a pickup in reverse; it receives an electrical signal, and translates it to electromagnetic impulses that drive a paper cone, which in turn pumps out sound waves into the air. In so doing, its type, quality and construction also have an enormous effect on our final tone.

Speakers vary enormously, obviously in size and power-handling abilities, but also in resonant character, construction of cone and magnet, efficiency (loudness relative to power input), and so on. A lightly-built, low-powered speaker can contribute quite a large amount of its own distortion when hit with an amp that is driven hard, while a firm, high-powered speaker stands up to the blow and yields a sound more representative of what it's hearing from the output transformer. The latter might still be distorted, but mostly because it is broadcasting tube distortion from the amp; the former is a hairy, juicy brew of both tube distortion and speaker distortion (ie, the flap, ripple and excessive vibrations of a cone and speaker assembly being driven past its operational limits).

Beyond power handling and distortion characteristics, different speaker makes and types also exhibit an enormously varied range of voices and tones of their own. Magnet composition plays a big part in this, with alnico-magnet speakers (the 'vintage' type) characteristically sounding sweet and musical, and ceramic-magnet units having a harder, punchier edge. Changing to a different type of speaker can instantly alter your sound about as much as, say, swapping to a different type of pickup on your guitar. Often it's a different sort of sonic change, but just as severe in degree as that of the pickup swap. Also, players who rave about the sounds of classic amps are often very surprised to learn the extent to which the standard speaker choice of each make and model influences the overall sound of that amp. This final link in the signal chain offers another enormous variable, and it's one worth getting a handle on.

In combination with the speakers themselves, the cabinet into which they are mounted contributes enormously to an amplifier's overall tone. The size and construction of the cabinet influence resonance, low-end content, projection and even frequency content; closed-back cabinets sound different than open-backed, solid pine sounds different from plywood, and chipboard sounds different from both. So, in effect, even after the sound waves have hit the air again you could say there is yet another link in the chain with an influence on what eventually enters our ears, that being the ways in which the internal space of a speaker cabinet helps to shape the sound waves that finally emerge from it. I'm not even going to start metnioning the effects of room acoustics…

So that's our Big Picture, and any tone-conscious guitarist needs too keep as much of it in mind as he's got the cranial storage space to deal with. Ignore the Big Picture, and you find yourself fiddling with the Treble and Presence controls of your high-gain preamp for hours trying to dial out an annoying high-end harmonic that you don't realize is actually coming from a G-string that has too flat a break-angle over the nut of your Telecaster, or you spend hundreds of dollars on effects and EQs that never prove satisfactory because the gut-rumbling low-end you are seeking to generate has already been lost by a bass-sucking overdrive that comes first in your chain.

Having seen how many links this chain can consist of, it's also important to understand that each piece doesn't not get an equal vote, and some links in the chain influence the overall sound far more than others. Change to a different type and rating of speaker, for example, and I bet you you'll notice the sonic shift far more than, say, going from swamp ash bodied to alder bodied Strat, all else being equal. Pickup changes are likewise dramatic, as can be simple swaps of preamp tubes or output tube makes and types. And think of the difference that putting on a fresh set of strings can make, not to mention a set of a different composition. On the other hand, many players might not appreciate the difference in swapping from a PAF humbucker with alnico IV magnets to one with alnico V magnets, but to some it might be a crucial improvement. All stages are not created equal, but they do all play a part in the overall delivery of your tone.

To some extent there is an element of the Zen notion of 'everything is everything' in the sound chain, in that occurrences early in the chain will have an effect on the sound and performance of everything that follows.

But some links possess greater degrees of everything than others, if you will… Or maybe it is better aligned with chaos theory: just as a butterfly beating its wings in Hawaii might trigger a hurricane off the coast of South Carolina, perhaps the way your maple fingerboard resonates sharply with a second harmonic in your guitar's upper register tips the gale from your Marshall cab's Greenback speakers into sweet, hovering feedback. And when feedback occurs, hey, everything really is everything once again: the output triggers the input, and each end of the chain is having a direct impact on the other, with all stages between chipping in to make their mark on the sound.

Now it's time to take matters further by looking at a selection of the classic rigs used for electric guitar over the past half a century or more, and finally applying some model names and designs to the myriad links in the sound chain that we have outlined in this chapter.

Electric pioneer Alvino Rey plays a Gibson archtop-acoustic with add-on DeArmond pickup.

SETUP 1
EARLY JAZZ COMBO

The era of the 'electric-Spanish guitar set' really begins in the mid to late 1930s. Various makers had been experimenting with electric guitar designs for a few years already – notably Rickenbacker, ViviTone, and Kay/Stromberg-Voisinet – but the concept really stormed onto the scene in 1936 with the introduction of Gibson's first electric guitar, the ES-150, and thanks primarily to the playing of jazzman Charlie Christian. History tells us that Eddie Durham, a guitarist with the Kansas City Six, was the first to record electric guitar solos. Durham purportedly turned Christian on to the new instrument, and the young guitarist picked one up and flew with it, becoming far and away the most influential and best-remembered early electric player.

Before a simple and reliable means of amplifying his instrument arrived, the guitarist was confined to the back corner of the rhythm section of swing and dance bands of the 1920s and 1930s, hacking away with the beat and just occasionally stepping forward toward the vocal mike for a plaintive, muted solo that he hoped someone could hear. Christian essentially paved the way for the guitarist as a soloist in the jazz band context. For the first time his ES-150 and accompanying Gibson amp allowed him to execute adventurous single-note breaks that were previously the sole territory of the horn players. Guitarists like Durham, Alvino Rey, Tony Mottola, and Mary Osborne either followed or paralleled Christian in the electric revolution, and the guitar has never looked back.

Eddie Durham, a guitarist with the Kansas City Six, was the first to record electric guitar solos

It's also notable that a direct line can be heard from Christian's playing to that of many early rock'n'rollers of 12-15 years later. Listen especially to elements like the sliding, riff-style lines and rhythmic phrasing of his solo from 'Air Mail Special' for example (plenty of rockabilly players are still sounding like that today). In the hands of a Charlie Christian, the bold new instrument seemed a sonic miracle; the guitarist's time had finally come.

The first 'electric-Spanish' guitars, as they were generally known, were somewhat woofy in tone, didn't offer a lot of sustain, and were of course susceptible to howling feedback – but man, what a revelation. Spend some time listening to Christian's playing and it's clear that he wasn't simply using the ES-150 and accompanying EH-150 amp as a means of making an acoustic guitar louder, but was the first to thoroughly appreciate the significant sonic differences of the electric guitar/amp pairing. The guitar itself has a plummy, thick tone, but recorded examples of it from the late 1930s and early 1940s also exhibit a bright, cutting edge thanks partially at least to Christian's own playing style, which employed heavy and precise downstrokes and a very thick, triangular pick.

Archtop Advances

It's hard to say exactly why the acoustic archtop was the first format of guitar other than the slab-style lap steel to widely adopt the magnetic pickup, except to note Gibson's coup in introducing the first broadly accepted electro Spanish models, coupled with the fact that archtops were the company's forte. Many other makers were already copying Gibson's success in the acoustic arena, and would naturally follow them to electrification. Orville Gibson invented the archtop in the 1890s, and the form reached its zenith in many collector's eyes with the Lloyd Loar-designed L-5 of 1922. These were elaborate efforts, to say the least, made with painstakingly hand-carved solid spruce tops, backs that were at first of solid birch but later book-matched maple, sturdy maple necks with ebony fingerboards, and two radical new advances

Caption (right hand page, main pic): This electric combo from the 1930s makes an archaic pair today, but back in their time this ES-150 guitar and EH-150 amplifier were nothing short of a revolution in sound. With their help, guitarists stepped out of the rhythm section and into the spotlight.

De Armond
MICROPHONES FOR STRINGED INSTRUMENTS

...UNDISTORTED POWER VOLUME!

ROWE *Industries* 1702 WAYNE ST.
TOLEDO 9, OHIO

Add-on pickups became a hot item as previously unplugged guitarists got amped up. This adjustable DeArmond is a jazz classic.

in guitar design: innovative adjustable truss-rods, and two-piece adjustable bridges. The guitar-making industry stood up and took note in a big way, and the L-5 was rapidly the object of every player's dreams. There were improvements and refinements of the archtop acoustic yet to come, but at the height of the jazz age, this was the baby. For an acoustic guitar, it had pretty good volume, too, but get it up on a big bandstand with a horn section, and...

The first electrified models followed the designs of the existing acoustic archtops in most makers' catalogs, usually augmented with slightly modified lap-steel pickups bolted on to them in one way or another. In terms of construction, this meant the carved solid spruce top mentioned above, often joined by a carved or flat solid maple or mahogany back joined to solid sides, and other features long intended for optimum acoustic performance. Major makers like Gibson and Epiphone quickly understood that the very act of amplifying a guitar meant that it didn't need to meet the requirements for acoustic tone; also, the early electric instruments were seen more as workingmen's tools than as artistes' prized instruments – a fringe market at best – and they were made to be more utilitarian from the start.

Nevertheless, even the lowliest of the debut models from the top makers were still laboriously hand-carved, solid-wood guitars – which inevitably wasted a big portion of their acoustic potential as soon as that heavy magnetic pickup was bolted to a hole hacked into the top and the whole thing was run through an extremely low-fi amp.

Thanks to Charlie Christian, the clear choice of guitar for our 'Early Jazz' rig is the Gibson ES-150. At its introduction, the 16 ¼"-wide non-cutaway guitar had an X-braced top of solid spruce with carved arch, a flat maple back, mahogany neck and bound rosewood fingerboard, narrow f-holes, two-piece adjustable ebony bridge, and no decoration to speak of. The most notable feature in both look and performance was its single neck-position 'blade' pickup, forever after known as a 'Charlie Christian pickup,' and controls for volume and tone. The unit was designed by Gibson employee Walter Fuller, and looks from a distance like a fairly conventional single-polepiece pickup, but the blade seen through the black housing actually connects to a large magnet suspended under the top of the guitar, held in place by three adjustable screws visible under the strings.

When compared to similarly constructed Gibsons with P-90 or humbucking pickups, models with Christian pickups exhibit a powerful, round voice, with quite a thick but musical center to it. The pure-nickel flatwound strings of the day would have contributed their own warm, yet slightly sizzling and percussive element to the brew. The unit also appeared on the upmarket ES-250 that followed (Christian also played natural and sunburst versions of this model before his death in 1942), and evolved slightly between its introduction in 1936 and its disappearance in 1940, going from single blade, to single blade with a notch under the B-string, to three separate flat polepieces under the treble strings, to six separate flat pieces. The 17"-wide ES-250 carried the latter version, along with upgrades such as a carved maple back and more deluxe trim.

Compared to other Gibson pickups the Charlie Christian unit is rarely encountered today (although, rather oddly, it was available by custom order from the mid 1950s to 1960s, and popped up on the ES-175DCC of the late 1970s), so another early single-coil unit might make a more appropriate 'tonal standard' for our 'Early Jazz Combo' sound. The pickup that appeared on the ES-125 of 1940-42, with six individual polepieces running through a coil/bobbin arrangement, or the ubiquitous P-90 that evolved from it by 1946 – when Gibson resumed production after the war – might make more broadly representative reference points.

The P-90 remains in production today, although with some changes in materials and manufacturing techniques over the years. It's a gritty, thick, hot-sounding single coil – significantly hotter, for example, than standard Fender single coils – with a pronounced and punchy midrange emphasis. Mounted in the neck position of a hollow-bodied archtop (with either a pressed ply or solid spruce top) it yields a warm, percussive, and occasionally slightly honking tonality but with decent balance and an appealing frequency response overall. A 16 ¼″ non-cutaway early 1950s Gibson ES-125, a model which can be surprisingly affordable on the vintage market, is one of the quickest routes to approximating the feel and sound of Gibson's very first electric, but is already quite a ways from a late 1930s ES-150 in many details, foremost of which are its pressed laminated top, rosewood bridge, and of course the vastly different pickup.

Electrics Go Upmarket

Gibson took the electric even further upmarket with the ES-300, introduced in 1940 and available in two-pickup versions by 1948 (P-90s by then). At a body width of 17″, it was a larger guitar than the original ES-150, although that model was stepped up to 17″ upon its reintroduction in 1946, while the ES-125 – a mere 14 ½″ in the early 1940s – grew to 16 ¼″. Aside from the size and a slight difference in materials, the ES-300 was a fancier guitar altogether, with triple-bound front and back, crown peghead inlays, double parallelogram fingerboard inlays, a deluxe tailpiece and more. Overall, all three of the larger prewar models were pretty well-made and good sounding guitars, even if their playability feels a little cumbersome by modern standards. At the time, other large makers like Epiphone and Gretsch quickly followed suit, and turned out roughly similar models to chase Gibson's success.

After the war, however, the ES-150, ES-300 and even more deluxe ES-350 that returned to the market were very different guitars, and major changes followed in other makers' models, too.

Other makers offered rival electric sets, but Gibson was quick to grab a foothold in the burgeoning new market, as a growing artists roster confirmed.

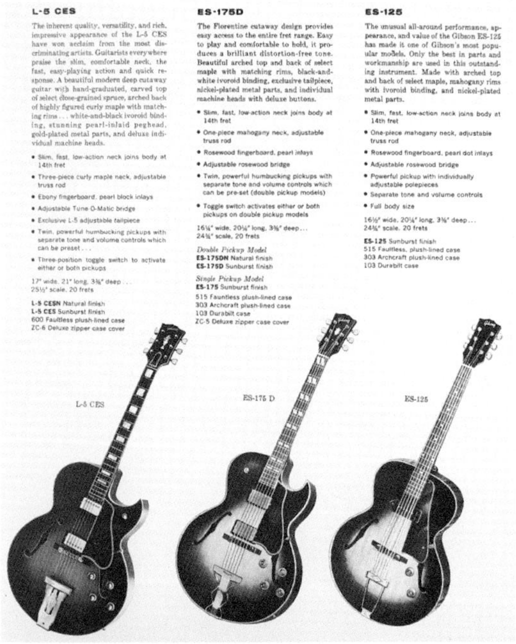
L-5 CES
The inherent quality, versatility, and rich, impressive appearance of the L-5 CES have won acclaim from the most discriminating artists. Guitarists everywhere praise the slim, comfortable neck, the fast, easy-playing action and quick response. A beautiful modern deep cutaway guitar with hand-graduated, carved top of select close-grained spruce, arched back of highly figured curly maple with matching rims . . . white-and-black ivoroid binding, stunning pearl-inlaid peghead, gold-plated metal parts, and deluxe individual machine heads.
• Slim, fast, low-action neck joins body at 14th fret
• Three-piece curly maple neck, adjustable truss rod
• Ebony fingerboard, pearl block inlays
• Adjustable Tune-O-Matic bridge
• Exclusive L-5 adjustable tailpiece
• Twin, powerful humbucking pickups with separate tone and volume controls which can be preset . . .
• Three-position toggle switch to activate either or both pickups
17" wide, 21" long, 3⅜" deep . . . 25½" scale, 20 frets
L-5 CESN Natural finish
L-5 CES Sunburst finish
600 Faultless plush-lined case
ZC-6 Deluxe zipper case cover
ES-175D
The Florentine cutaway design provides easy access to the entire fret range. Easy to play and comfortable to hold, it produces a brilliant distortion-free tone. Beautiful arched top and back of select maple with matching rims, black-and-white ivoroid binding, exclusive tailpiece, nickel-plated metal parts, and individual machine heads with deluxe buttons.
• Slim, fast, low-action neck joins body at 14th fret
• One-piece mahogany neck, adjustable truss rod
• Rosewood fingerboard, pearl inlays
• Adjustable rosewood bridge
• Twin, powerful humbucking pickups with separate tone and volume controls which can be pre-set (double pickup models)
• Toggle switch activates either or both pickups on double pickup models
16¼" wide, 20¼" long, 3⅜" deep . . . 24¾" scale, 20 frets
Double Pickup Model
ES-175DN Natural finish
ES-175D Sunburst finish
Single Pickup Model
ES-175 Sunburst finish
515 Faultless plush-lined case
303 Archcraft plush-lined case
103 Durabilt case
ZC-5 Deluxe zipper case cover
ES-125
The unusual all-around performance, appearance, and value of the Gibson ES-125 has made it one of Gibson's most popular models. Only the best in parts and workmanship are used in this outstanding instrument. Made with arched top and back of select maple, mahogany rims with ivoroid binding, and nickel-plated metal parts.
• Slim, fast, low-action neck joins body at 14th fret
• One-piece mahogany neck, adjustable truss rod
• Rosewood fingerboard, pearl dot inlays
• Adjustable rosewood bridge
• Powerful pickup with individually adjustable polepieces
• Separate tone and volume controls
• Full body size
16½" wide, 20¼" long, 3⅜" deep . . . 24¾" scale, 20 frets
ES-125 Sunburst finish
515 Faultless, plush-lined case
303 Archcraft plush-lined case
103 Durabilt case
L-5 CES
ES-175 D
ES-125

By the late 1950s, Gibson's archtop electrics had achieved forms that remain classics today. The PAF-equipped L5CES and ES-175 above are still lusted-after by jazz guitarists of the 21st century, although downmarket the non-cutaway ES-125 has fallen by the wayside.

When production ramped up again in 1946, Gibson had fully evolved the notion that the electric guitar was a very different beast from its acoustic predecessor, and that pressed laminated arched tops would do just as well in the case of guitars that were primarily heard as electrified instruments. Recognized jazzers – who could afford them, and appreciated the difference – often aspired to instruments that were still totally handmade, with solid carved-spruce tops and floating pickups designed to impede their acoustic resonance as little as possible: Gibson Super 400s, Epiphone Emperors, Gretsch Synchromatics, D'Angelico New Yorkers and the like. Accordingly, Gibson now made the ES-125, ES-150, ES-300, the cutaway ES-350, and soon the ES-175 and ES-5 (both also cutaways) with laminated tops joined to laminated maple backs and sides. Many became hugely popular with working pros nonetheless.

A neck-position P-90 works well, when reined in, for jazz tones, and great for blues when pumped full-throttle, giving a raw, hot, driving and feedback-inducing sound. Gibsons with two P-90s have always been prone to an output imbalance, with the neck pickup frequently much stronger than the bridge pickup. This is due to the stronger string vibrations and broader, deeper tonality sampled at that position, which is toward the middle harmonic of the string's length. The bright, twangy rock'n'roll sounds that later came from guitars much like these often relied on the bridge pickup in the later two-pickup variants, with players like Scotty Moore (a Super 400CES), Chuck Berry (an ES-350), and Carl Perkins (and ES-5 Switchmaster). Others sought out even more brightness still, in the likes of Gretsch 6120s and Fender Telecasters (more of which in the following chapter).

The amplifiers that the early electric jazzers were plugging into were pretty nifty devices in themselves, with no shortage of raw, warm tube tone. But the notion of amplified electric guitar was in its infancy, and the links in the chain didn't join up to the most toneful possible results just yet. Pickups weren't yet optimized for their applications, guitars were boomy and feedback prone, and the amps – while embodying some of the best technology and components available in the day – were underpowered, inefficient, just generally a little touchy, and couldn't easily handle the abundant low end these guitars dished up. Still, what a combination.

In the late 1930s, 1940s, and often even in the 1950s guitarists would buy their gear as a 'set' or 'combo' – a guitar and amp together from the same manufacturer, although in many cases the amp was a rebadged model manufactured by an offsite contract house. Charlie Christian is understood to have used a 'matching' Gibson EH-150 amplifier with his ES-150 guitar, and an EH-185 with his later pair of ES-250s. Either way, between guitar and amp there are few signal-chain variables to discuss, other than the rather low-grade cord – usually included in the price of the guitar.

These early amps were a fun blend of art-deco furniture and early tube radio technology

These early amps were often a fun blend of art-deco furniture and early tube radio technology, and you could argue that this 'electric suitcase' would evolve far further by the late 1940s and early 1950s than would the hollow-bodied versions of its pickup-toting partners. Which is not to say that the manufacturers of the late 1930s weren't trying to produce good amplifiers – but making a 'Spanish' guitar louder was already novelty enough, and most any circuit that did so with acceptable frequency reproduction and no excessive noise or distortion was considered a success.

Gibson's EH-150 amplifier had arrived a little before the ES-150 as partner to the EH-150 lap steel (these were Gibson's true 'first electrics,' and the amp retained the set's 'Electric Hawaiian' designation). The amp originally carried a 10″ and later a 12″ speaker that was powered by a truly archaic circuit design, and now-obsolete tubes such as 6F5 and 6C5 triodes and 6N7 pentodes in the preamp, and 6N6s, or sometimes 6V6s, in the output. Even when the later design of the EH-150 had evolved to 6L6 output tubes (which would become the most common tube for big US-made amps from the 1950s until today), with 6SQ7s in the preamp, they were still only capable of a maximum output of probably about 15W-20W. The 6L6 wouldn't become the bold, efficient and loud tube that we know it as today until the early 1950s, and aside from that, amplifier designs just weren't ready to make the most of their output sections yet anyway.

Still, 15W or so sounded pretty darn loud next to an acoustic-only rhythm guitarist comping to beat the band (but failing miserably), and this measly rating was enough to let loose the guitar player as soloist on most bandstands of the day, amid the average swing ensemble (and of course the horns usually reined themselves in a little when the guitar solo rolled around). Tonally speaking, when played short of flat-out, the low-gain preamp tube types and relatively low-powered output varieties of the day contributed to a fairly clean, rounded sound with some emphasis in the mids and lower mids, and a muted high-end response. Of course lows weren't brick-busting either – but these players didn't have to get a mosh pit jumping – and the entire sound was prone to some squash and softening, with especially loose bass, when pushed hard.

On top of all this, other elements of these amps' design weren't helping matters much. Speakers were generally both inefficient and incapable of handling much power (on the odd chance that they ever got the opportunity, and the cabinets certainly weren't designed with much thought to resonance and projection. Portability was clearly a major design factor, and even in the 'larger' amps of the day a single 12″ speaker was squeezed into the minimum space that would hold it and a chassis plus transformers and tubes. Many were designed as what are commonly referred to as 'suitcase amps,' with hinged and removable front and back sections, each carrying either speaker or amp guts, although sometimes the back was merely a protective cover. Early versions of the EH-150 followed the latter format, although Gibson did go some way toward attempting to broaden the amp's projection by offering an 'Echo Speaker' output – really just an extension speaker jack. Well, put it far enough away from you in an empty dance hall and, sure, it would echo.

Even players who stuck with their beloved prewar ES-150s and ES-300s

well into the late 1940s and early 1950s generally upgraded their amplifiers as better designs arrived, or were forced to as the rigors of the road took their toll on quickly obsolete 1930s electronics. Consequently, other than on the early recordings of the likes of Charlie Christian and Eddie Durham and their contemporaries, these first-wave Gibson amps won't have been heard by many players alive today. Recordings made even ten or 12 years after the fledgeling 'Early Jazz Combos' arrived would mostly have been done on much improved Gibsons or new Fender amps, which really were a world apart from an EH-150 of 1936.

Bangin' Out The Blues

Naturally the early electric blues players were doing their thing on rigs much like those used by these first electric jazzers. Often, in fact – since the hard-suffering blues man generally had even less spending cash than the working jazz man (quite an accomplishment in itself) – those who were still struggling with their careers in the late 1940s and early 1950s would likely be picking up secondhand rigs cast off by jazz players who had bought them new in the late 1930s and early 1940s.

I have already mentioned T-Bone Walker's use of a prewar Gibson ES-250 guitar, and he is one of the best examples of the transition from jazz to blues in both sound and playing style. Early photos of a young B.B. King show him playing a downscale Gibson archtop acoustic with retrofitted DeArmond pickup, plugged into an early Gibson amplifier, and a few years later he had evolved to a P-90 equipped ES-125 and a late 1940s TV-front Fender Pro Amp. A young Muddy Waters similarly played a 1940s Harmony archtop with added DeArmond. Whatever the combination, and aside from the obvious differences in musical styles, the blues may have existed before or at least alongside jazz, and its electrified sound evolved from the sound of jazz gear, but it was differentiated mainly by a looser, more aggressive attack, and by playing through an amp that was cranked up for a hotter, grittier, dirtier overall sound.

Despite the evolution of the gear, the differentiation remains the same today, although the 'blues sound' then and today would be quite different. As already discussed, these old hollowbody guitars packed a pretty high output (although somewhat less so with a retrofit DeArmond than with a Charlie Christian pickup or a P-90), and when driven hard the early Gibson amps tended toward the soft, smooth and squashy. The guitars weren't big on sustain, but

Scotty Moore backs up Elvis on a Gibson Super 400 plugged into a Ray Butts EchoSonic amp – a jazz classic meets a rock'n'roll revolution.

the right feedback techniques could improve that when desired; overall, however, it was a raw and edgy riff-based music, with middly vocal tones and plenty of bite. Gibson amps were designed to take the high gain of the company's pickups and remain clean (although this didn't always work at full volume), but when Gibson players stepped over to Fender amps of the late 1940s and early 1950s, the sound evolved further, the result being a hotter, brighter, punchier tonality with a little more cut.

The other notable style of the era was western swing, or country, and this makes up the third main genre of early electric guitar playing. Of course the same limited range of gear was available to jazz, blues and western players of the day, so the variables were relatively few, and came mainly from the players themselves, and how high they cranked the volume control. While the first recognized country artists of the early 1930s – the singing cowboys and honky tonkers – remained mainly acoustic acts for some time, guitarists playing the western swing derivative took up electric guitars almost from their introduction, for the same reason that the jazzers did: they wanted to be heard. The best example of this is found in the music of Bob Wills and the Texas Playboys, which featured Eldon Shamblin, Tiny Moore, Jimmy Wyble, and occasionally Junior Barnard on guitar – all of whom had gone predominantly electric by the early 1940s (although Wyble only appeared on the scene around 1945).

The Road To Rock'n'Roll

Even before the electric Spanish guitars became widely acceptable to players, many country and western swing bands had incorporated lap-steel guitar players – a sound readily identifiable in their seemingly ill-matched but oddly inseparable blend of 'hillbilly' and Hawaiian stylings – so they were already hip to the whole concept of amplification. With the Texas Playboys, Wills had formed a swing-band sized orchestra that usually consisted of about 16 players just like many larger dance-hall jazz bands, and the inclusion of horns, drums and heavy orchestration meant the electric guitar must have been a godsend for the belabored Shamblin. He is seen in numerous photographs playing an upmarket Gibson archtop, with an early Gibson amp placed next to him. The style called for the clean, precise lines of jazz, too, and Shamblin's own single-note solo lines were often not a mile away from those of Charlie Christian or Eddie Lang, so the gear was used to much the same effect.

Western Swing bands like Wills's and others that toured the country were generally much showier, more flamboyant outfits than the usually more subdued jazz swing orchestras, and adventurous playing certainly ran to the guitarists, too. More so than jazz players, country and western swing players were soon experimenting with something closer to distortion, and stylistically were one of the main precursors of rock'n'roll, alongside the bluesers of the day. The wild, adventurous Junior Barnard in particular is documented as having exhibited some exciting pre-rock'n'roll techniques, including string bending, aggressive rhythmic single-note and double-stop riffing, and so on.

Whether it was jazz, country, or blues, the cat was out of the bag for sure. These were early days, certainly, but they gave birth to some radical new sounds. For the newly electrified guitarist – who no doubt felt freed from some especially muting, restricting sonic chains – it was all onward and upward.

Nothing oozes pure rock'n'roll like Eddie Cochran and a Gretsch 6120.

What a cultural, artistic and technological explosion the 1950s was. Sure, we had unchecked nuclear testing, a Cold War just starting to gather momentum, unforgivable squandering of natural resources… But the era gave us rock'n'roll, so all is forgiven. Well, okay, a musical phenomenon can't make up for horrendous wastage and a hefty dose of social injustice, but in posterity's eyes it seems to go a surprisingly long way. (Be honest: think 1954 and what comes to mind first? H-bomb testing at Bikini Atoll, or Elvis, Bill Black and Scotty Moore tucked away in Sun Studios banging out 'That's Alright Mama'?)

Look at the other side of the coin of that jumbled decade: black meets white, country meets city, polite popular suit'n'tie dance music meets rollicking roadhouse rebellion – bam! How could it not happen? Add to that the significant advances in electric guitar designs, major improvements in amplification (finally allowing drummers in guitar combos to whack that snare to their hearts' content), an emboldened adrenaline-fired teenage populace with more social freedom than ever before seen in the western world. Rock'n'roll. An utter inevitability.

Gretsch started off jazz, segued through country, and ended up rock'n'roll – which included embracing a range of stylings that verged on the shocking for the 1950s.

Rockin' From Archtops To Solids

The swift confluence of sounds that gave birth to the music of the time is thoroughly documented. It is less often pointed out that the wilder, out-of-left-field rhythmic riffing styles developing in near-equal measures in country, blues and jazz were all being played on very similar equipment, and it's fascinating to consider the rapid evolution of both playing styles and rigs in the short space of the preceding decade.

It would have seemed to players of the late 1940s that electric guitars had already come a long way from the first widely available 'electric-Spanish' guitar, the Gibson ES-150 of 1936, but the variety of gear available was still extremely limited. Players of any note were mostly toting acoustic archtop electrics from Gibson, Epiphone – and eventually Gretsch or Guild – usually partnered by amps from the same maker. Even by the late 1940s, however, and into the early 1950s (but still well before the 'plank' style guitars was fully accepted), players were benefiting from an electronics revolution in the making, in the form of the Fender amplifier. Other amps still vied for space on the bandstand, but even before his solidbody guitar hit the scene in 1950 – and for the first few years after, while it remained to many players more a laughing stock than a viable professional option – Leo Fender's tube-powered creations were rapidly becoming the touring musician's electronic suitcase of choice. Many combinations of gear helped to give birth to the rock'n'roll sound, but a hollowbody archtop electric plugged into a big Fender tweed amp would be the most heard of the bunch.

Although he died ten years before the music was given a name, much of Charlie Christian's driving, catchy single-note riffing clearly prefigured rock'n'roll stylings, and even the playing of Eddie Durham and others carried elements that would surface in the new music waiting to be born in the 1950s. Country players like Junior Barnard of Bob Wills and the Texas Playboys, Bob McNett with Hank Williams and the Drifting Cowboys, Merle Travis, and 'boogie' artists Arthur Smith and The Delmore Brothers were all cutting loose with string bends, rapid runs and gutsy double-stop riffing that all might have been called 'rock'n'roll' if the term had been applied then. Meanwhile, blues artists like T-Bone Walker, Muddy Waters, John Lee Hooker and Lightnin' Hopkins added sexy and addictively rhythmic elements to the playing, while R&B acts such as Jackie Brenston paved the way with massive crossover hits like 'Rocket 88' (actually recorded with Ike Turner and His Rhythm Kings as backing band, with Willie Kizert laying down what is widely considered the first known recording of distorted guitar).

By the mid 1950s rock'n'roll was busting out all over as an established genre with its own accepted name and so many notable proponents of the guitar style that they're almost too numerous to credit here. Chuck Berry, Scotty Moore with Elvis Presley, Danny Cedrone with Bill Haley and His Comets, Cliff Gallup with Gene Vincent and His Blue Caps, Bo Diddley, Carl Perkins, Paul Burlison with Johnny Burnette and the Rock 'N Roll Trio, Eddie Cochran, Duane Eddy… All vied for the title of 'king of rock'n'roll guitar' within the space of just a few short years.

Each of these players started doing his thing on hollowbody archtop electrics, and many would graduate to solidbodies toward the end of the decade, but a few played what was arguably the rock'n'roll guitar of the day, an instrument born of the era itself: a Gretsch. The classic models of the era were the semi-solid Duo-Jet, launched in 1953 and played by Bo Diddley and the incomparable Cliff Gallup, and the fully hollowbody 6120, launched in 1955 and played by Eddie Cochran and Duane Eddy. Both are archetypal rock'n'roll guitars, but the latter is probably a better instrument to focus on as part of our 'classic rig' for this chapter, given its enduring status in the genre and its continuing dominance as *the* rockabilly guitar.

The Fred Gretsch Manufacturing Company was founded in New York City primarily as a drum and banjo maker in 1883, by German immigrant Friedrich Gretsch, who had arrived in the city 11 years earlier. In 1916, under the supervision of the late founder's eldest son, another Fred, the company moved across the bridge to a new factory in Brooklyn, and that location became this historic musical instrument

However mediocre Gretsch's acoustics were, its electrics were a top brand by the end of the 1950s

manufacturer's most famous address. The first Gretsch guitars appeared in the 1930s, and for a time rivaled the big-bodied archtop jazzers of Gibson and Epiphone, although they never had the same reputation for build quality as these esteemed makers.

Come the 1950s, Gretsch jumped on the electric wave and quite wisely put its resources into promoting these newfangled tools to the jazz, country, and eventually rock'n'roll markets. The brand eventually fizzled and all but died in the eyes of jazzers, but the next two markets took off like wildfire by the mid 1950s. However mediocre the company's acoustics always were, its electrics were one of the top brands to bag by the end of the 1950s.

After much consultation with the man himself and plenty of prototyping in 1954 (the guitar in our main photo appears to have been one example), Gretsch launched the 6120 model as the 'Chet Atkins Hollow Body' in 1955, alongside the Atkins Solid Body, a semi-solid design that was outwardly similar to the Duo-Jet guitars. Both arrived with hokey cowboy trim, which Atkins despised, although this vanished from the

Hollow Body over the next couple of years, while at the same time the Solid Body vanished altogether. Atkins was no rock'n'roller himself, but he appeared on countless session dates for pop and rock hits of the era, and was a rising star as a solo artist, with a string of hit pop-country instrumentals behind him. Gretsch had originally aimed to capitalize on Atkins's popularity in the country & western market – hence the wild-west regalia – but the company probably could have taken an across-the-board marketing approach right from the start, and the model quickly became Gretsch's most popular guitar. Even from the beginning, when you looked past the G-brand and cow-and-cactus inlays, the 6120 was pure rock'n'roll. The Chet Atkins endorsement quickly made this instrument a hot must-have for a budding generation of guitar stars, but I like to think it would have attained its classic status with or without the Nashville whiz-kid.

The lure of the 6120 comes as no surprise to anyone who has ever viewed the beast in the 'flesh' (well, the pressed plywood, at least). It is undeniably one of the all-time coolest and most distinctive-looking rockers' tools – yet it also produces a more polarized love-hate reaction from players than almost any other guitar ever built. For looks, this guitar is the object of many a rock'n'roller's dreams, and for 'that'

Taming the beast and reaping the ultimate in rock'n'roll rewards can be a mighty challenge

sound, there's nothing else quite like it. But a high proportion of those who pick one up – pick up any Gretsch for that matter – find they just can't get on with it as a practical instrument. And therein, perhaps, lies part of the charm: taming the beast, and reaping the ultimate in rock'n'roll-toned rewards, can be a mighty challenge at times. Do so, and you can spend the rest of your career with one of the sweetest looking stage props in existence slung around your neck. But many players facing the notoriously unstable setups, quirky electronics, howling feedback and myriad tonal compromises of a Gretsch hollowbody electric choose to put the guitar down and move on to another brand.

A Fickle Format

The 6120 changed enough over the years to warrant quite a few entirely new model designations, yet in its various guises the guitar remained a cornerstone throughout the company's heyday. Cowpoke cosmetics aside, the proper 6120 Chet Atkins Hollow Body production models of 1955 appeared as 16"-wide guitars carrying arched tops of pressed laminated maple, with a single rounded cutaway in a fully-hollow 2 7/8"-deep body. Back and sides were also of laminated maple, joined to a maple neck with bound rosewood fingerboard. The model carries a 24 3/4" scale length for a playing feel that is in some ways on par with the Gibson standard, although Gretsch neck profiles are generally quite different from those of their Michigan-made rivals of the day; in fact the two makes have a very different feel overall.

Gretsch electronics have always been quirky. Simpler than many that would follow, the first 6120s were born with a pair of the DeArmond-made pickups that other models had been wearing since 1949 – but commonly known by this time as 'Gretsch Dynasonic' pickups – which were wired to a traditional three-way pickup selector switch, individual and master volume controls, and a master tone control. Their appearance fools plenty of players not familiar with them, but these DeArmonds are single coil pickups; the secondary row of six smaller screws that looks like extra pole pieces for a nonexistent second coil are actually height-adjustment screws for the fatter, magnetic slug pole pieces. The pickups have a bright, slightly brittle sound, with plenty of high and mid kick to it. Of course the nickel-wrap flatwound strings

This pre-production 1954 Gretsch 6120 Chet Atkins Hollow Body and matching 6160 Electromatic Twin amp make a stunning pair. A rare find in each other's company after more than 50 years. Note that the rear view of this amp (main photo) is almost as elegant – and perhaps more interesting – than the front view (inset photo).

in use in the 1950s would warm this package up a little, but the combination would still offer plenty of sparkle, snap and twang.

Compared to other fine archtops of the day, Gretsch hollowbody electrics were never especially resonant instruments in the acoustic sense, but their dullness contributed to a certain punch and twang that could really be advantageous to the rock'n'roll sound. Also, while many other non-vibrato Gretsches came with intonation-adjustable Melita bridges – innovative components for their day – Atkins's insistence that his namesake carry a Bigsby vibrato meant that the 6120 came with the indifferent and tonally inferior molded metal compensated 'rocker' bridge that has been standard equipment with Bigsby units for many years. This in itself was another tone deadener, but further boosted that percussive, muted twangy sound that became huge stuff on instrumental records and rock riffs of the era. The Bigsby, in any case, is an essential element of the rock'n'roller's arsenal, and gave added movement and dimension to the sound

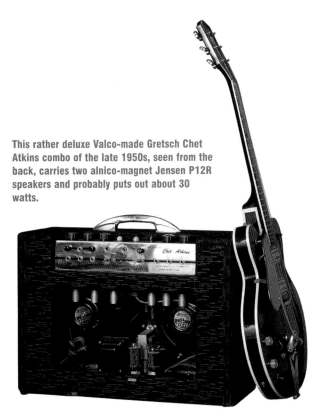

This rather deluxe Valco-made Gretsch Chet Atkins combo of the late 1950s, seen from the back, carries two alnico-magnet Jensen P12R speakers and probably puts out about 30 watts.

when there were very few, if any, electronic effects to help guitarists struggling to make their way to the front of the stage.

The Bigsby only offers about a semitone of bend in either direction, maybe a little more with a high spring, but has decent stability when set up right and has a cushiony, playable, controllable feel that many players really get into. Grab some other vibrato pieces' arms and give them a heated waggle and you can send your sound into seasickening dips and leaps, and end up sound altogether just a little too 'carnival' to do your style any good. A Bigsby allows a pretty liberal attack on the arm without ever coughing up very extreme results, and that makes it a good vibrato to grab for in the heat of a searing solo or moody rhythm passage that calls for just a little emotive wiggle, and not a real key-changing plummet.

Chet Atkins models originally came with fixed-arm units, and soon evolved to the free-swinging arm that remains the standard today. For modern players, the old fixed-arm tailpieces look archaic, and suggest they would constantly get in the way of your playing style; but sit down with one for a while – for instance the beautiful example in our main photo for this chapter – and your pick-hand style soon adapts. If you plan on using that Bigsby a fair deal, having it locked right in place there proves a real boon. Regardless of the bridge with which it is is paired (and many of the guitar-makers' own efforts definitely improve upon Bigsby's own oddly primitive looking 'rocker' job), the vibrato tailpiece itself definitely softens and loosens a guitar's resonance and resultant sound slightly, but for players who like to indulge in this effective waggler it is often a fair tradeoff. The detrimental sonic dampening will be noticed most when a Bigsby is retrofitted to a guitar with good, solid end-point anchoring that has been played for some time and has become familiar to the owner; on others, like these classic Gretsch hollowbodies, it seems like a Bigsby was meant to be there. And hell, those guitars don't resonate worth spit anyway, so who cares, right? Grab that arm and give it a sensual dip and a jiggle, and all tonal shortcomings are quickly forgiven.

Many players feel the model reached its zenith in 1958 when a considerably rejigged Chet Atkins 6120 Hollow Body hit the stage. The body was no longer G-branded and neck trim included the subtler and more classy horseshoe headstock inlay and 'neo-classic' (also 'half-moon' or 'thumbnail') position markers on a bound ebony fingerboard. The compensated molded bridge was replaced with a sturdy notched bar bridge of $\frac{1}{2}''$ in diameter. More significantly, though, it had picked up Gretsch's new Filter'Tron humbucking pickups and a three-position tone switch beside the pickup selector on the upper bout as a replacement for the master tone control.

The latter hinted at more Gretsch wiring tomfoolery to come, but the pickups were a real revolution. Named for their ability to 'FILTER elecTRONic hum,' the Filter'Trons had been developed by amplifier designer Ray Butts at Chet Atkins's urging, and are considered by some to be an invention to equal Gibson's famous PAF humbucker, the development of which they appear to have paralleled, by pure coincidence. Atkins disliked the sound of the original DeArmonds on the guitar, and also claimed that the large magnetic polepieces dampened the strings' resonance and even pulled the low strings slightly out of tune. This magnetic pull can indeed impede the low-end response on some 6120s where strings and polepieces are set too close together, but it's also another element in the twang factor. The new pickups were a shade warmer than their predecessors – although still pretty bright for humbuckers – and were a little rawer and

Onstage, hollowbody electric guitar players were experiencing more and more howling feedback

grittier, too. Alongside Atkins himself, rockabilly revivalist Brian Setzer has always favored the late 1950s 6120 with Filter'Trons, but Eddie Cochran and Duane Eddy's use of 6120s from 1955-1957 is enough to make that version our rock'n'roll guitar of choice. This was the model with the raw twang and cut that really set the whole sound in motion. (Note that Eddie Cochran replaced his neck DeArmond with a dog-ear Gibson P-90, so his 'rhythm' pickup or two-pickup sounds is going to be different still.)

There are plenty of places you can hear the sound of these early 6120s. Any of Eddie Cochran's recordings exhibit the sound, and his big hits 'Summertime Blues' and 'C'mon Everybody' are as good a place as any to go for that raw and rumbling Gretsch rock'n'roll tone. Duane Eddy's bass note-heavy twang on the 1958 breakthrough single 'Rebel Rouser' makes another fine example of what these DeArmond-loaded hollowbodies can do, as does his 1959 follow-up 'Peter Gunn Theme.'

Chet Dumps The Chet
Obviously much of Chet Atkins' own playing from the mid 1950s was done on his new signature model, but it seems the late guitar legend was never entirely satisfied with his Gretsches, and the design and features of his preferred models continued to evolve. In addition to preferring his 6120s with the Filter'Tron pickups, Atkins had largely moved over to the third of his signature models by the late 1950s, the upscale Country Gentleman. Along with the new humbucking pickups, the Gent had a wider but thinner body (17″ and 2″ respectively), was built with superior woods and, most noticeable of all, carried the new 'fake' f-holes that would appear on many other Gretsch guitars in the future. Louder onstage playing situations meant that hollowbody electric players were experiencing more and more of the howling feedback that had plagued any musician who dared to turn up the volume since the dawn of such rigs in the 1930s.

With consultation from Atkins, Gretsch closed off the f-holes in the Country Gentleman (and a few

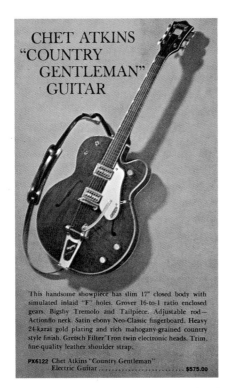

CHET ATKINS "COUNTRY GENTLEMAN" GUITAR

This handsome showpiece has slim 17" closed body with simulated inlaid "F" holes. Grover 16-to-1 ratio enclosed gears. Bigsby Tremolo and Tailpiece. Adjustable rod—Actionflo neck. Satin ebony Neo-Classic fingerboard. Heavy 24-karat gold plating and rich mahogany-grained country style finish. Gretsch Filter'Tron twin electronic heads. Trim, fine-quality leather shoulder strap.

PX6122 Chet Atkins "Country Gentleman"
Electric Guitar $575.00

The Country Gentleman, complete with painted-on f-holes, represented Chet Atkins's personal upgrade of his own signature model.

earlier custom or prototype models), then stopped carving them altogether – merely continuing the visual element with painted-on f-holes – in a bid to prevent a loud amp from getting the guitar's top vibrating and triggering the feedback cycle. The new design helped some, as did a pair of strengthening posts placed inside the Gent's body to add further rigidity to the top, but Atkins would eventually move on to semi-solid guitars that were a far cry from his original signature model.

To hear the 6120 with Filter'Tron humbuckers, check out any of Brian Setzer's work, from the early Stray Cats hits through to the recent 'new swing' CDs recorded with The Brian Setzer Orchestra. It's a slightly hotter, more full-frequency sound, with a raw, gritty energy and plenty of bite and twang.

Recorded examples of semi-solid Gretsches from the 1950s show us how many of the same ingredients work in a non-hollowbody format. Bo Diddley's records of the day, generally recorded on a red Jet Fire Bird with non-vibrato tailpiece, display an aggressive, percussive tonality that clearly carries more meat behind it than many of the recordings made with the Chet Atkins Hollow Body models. Cliff Gallup's fiery, jazz-inflected riffs with Gene Vincent and his Blue Caps display the Duo Jet's potential as a soloist's tool – impressively tight, defined noting paired with a muscular, slightly dirty tonality being the notable characteristics. And flash forward to the late-1970s recordings of California punk-rockers X, featuring guitarist Billy Zoom playing a mid-1950s Silver Jet with DeArmond pickups, for an example of these guitars' potential as power-chord rockers. Despite their solid appearance (no doubt inspired by the Gibson Les Paul and Fender Telecaster that appeared shortly before them), the Duo Jet and its colored siblings had mahogany bodies with numerous large routes and channels carved into them, capped with a pressed arched top. As such, they still don't possess quite the woody sustain of a Les Paul, but have more of a solidbody's midrange punch than the Gretsch hollowbody models that paralleled them.

Models that evolved from the roots of the Hollow Body through the 1960s inspired further waves of success for Gretsch. Although the first 'quality' guitar George Harrison owned with The Beatles was a 1957 Gretsch Duo Jet, bought in 1961, it was a pair of double-cutaway 6122 Country Gentleman models acquired in 1963 prior to the band's groundbreaking US tour of 1964 – and a Tennessean acquired during the tour itself – that really sparked the next Gretsch frenzy among young players. The Byrds sparked further Gretsch fever in the 1960s, as did Crosby, Stills, Nash & Young's use of flamboyant White Falcons in the early 1970s… but this begins to take us a good ways away from our seminal rock'n'roll sound.

Our amp choice for this rock'n'roll rig is a tricky one. Even though his name is on our guitar, we're not trying to emulate Chet Atkins's sound as such, which has always been far too pristine country-clean in nature to suit genuine rock'n'roll. Throughout the mid 1950s, however, Atkins did do much of his recording through an EchoSonic amplifier with built-in tape echo, as also used by Scotty Moore and Carl Perkins to create far more fundamentally rockabilly tones. But this is such a rare amp – built in limited numbers by Ray Butts to custom orders mainly from name musicians – that it's just not a widely representative choice for our rig. No end of budding rock'n'rollers would have plugged their Chet guitar into a matching Chet amp; Eddie Cochran played through, apparently, a Fender Bassman and a number of others; Duane Eddy used a Magnatone amp and a DeArmond tremolo unit; Buddy Holly used, at

different times, a Magnatone and a Fender Bassman; Cliff Gallup played through a Standel amp while his Blue Caps replacement Johnny Meeks used a Fender; Danny Cedrone plugged his hollowbody Gibson into a Gretsch amp with Bill Haley and his Comets... And so it goes. Many of the same amp makes come up a number of times, but there's not enough consistency to form a single, obvious choice for our rig in this chapter.

So let's look to a range of rigs that plenty of rock'n'rollers no doubt played, and which any retro rockabilly stylist of today would undeniably label as classics, rather than trying to achieve the almost impossible job of pinning this down to a single amplifier. And, since we have a 1954 Gretsch 6120 Chet Atkins guitar slung rebelliously around our necks on its matching tooled-leather cowboy belt strap, let's stick it into a matching 6160 Electromatic Twin amplifier first off to form our headline rock'n'roll rig.

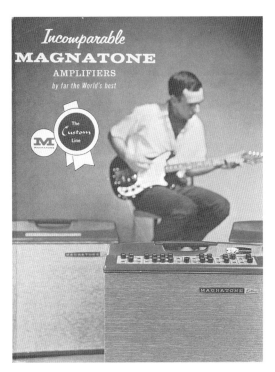

Magnatone retains little street cred today, but the make was respected for some good-sounding amps in the early days of rock'n'roll. As for the guitars...

Amps A-Go-Go

Back in the early days of electric guitars, if you were marketing either a lap steel or electro-Spanish model, you really had to have an amplifier to sell with it. Many guitar-makers had been newly dragged into the electric game, however, and few had their own amplifier manufactory as well. The rule of the day went, 'if you can't build it, buy it in and re-badge it.' Gretsch was one such company, and from the early 1950s it received its amps from Valco, one of the largest OEM suppliers of amps – and electric guitars – in the country. Valco's Gretsch amps are in fact probably among the company's best looking and best known, but the Chicago manufacturer also supplied for Supro, Oahu, Airline, Danelectro, National and many others. And while they were never a high-end make, they usually sounded very good and were mostly sturdy and reliable, and many examples survive to this day in playable condition under the guises of a range of different brands.

Despite the slightly 'under the counter' nature of this major manufacturer, Valco has a long and colorful history in the musical instrument industry. Seminal resonator guitar manufacturer Louis Dopyera transplanted his National Dobro company from California to Chicago in the mid 1930s, changing its name to Valco early in the following decade to represent the first initials of the three owners at that time (Victor Smith, Al Frost, Louis Dopyera = VAL + co for company). By the mid 1940s the company was cashing in on the Hawaiian guitar craze and supplying sets and individual units to the broad range of brands already mentioned, along with many smaller names that have since fallen by the wayside. In the late 1960s Valco was bought up by the enormous Kay company, but both were out of business by the end of the decade.

Valco amps are often slightly quirky, and usually fairly basic (they tend to lag well behind Fender designs of comparable years, for example). But, cranked toward max, most of the 1950s models really get you quickly to that archetypal rock'n'roll sound: raw, slightly compressed, snappy and edgy, and definitely anything but hi-fi. Dressed in Gretsch clothing they look great, too. As such, they underwent about half a dozen changes in styling and covering between the early 1950s and the late 1960s, the coolest of which are arguably the offset, asymmetrical, wraparound-grille models of the late 1950s, such as the various Electromatic amps. The example from this chapter's main photo, which is also played on the CD, precedes these designs, but is still an extremely sweet partner for the 6120 guitar of the same year (in fact this pair have spent their lives together, a rare thing for a 50-year-old guitar and amp set).

Internally, the 6160 displays elements of design that leading amp makers like Gibson and Fender were already leaving behind by 1954, along with certain similarities. One thing that stands out about so many of these earlier Gretsch amplifiers – or any of the Valco-supplied makes, for that matter – is that they are even closer to the generic tube amplification circuits in the handbooks and application manuals of the day than the products of the Big G and Big F, to mention the most obvious. While these makers' amps were still pretty simple stuff, they were state of the art for guitar at that time, and were adapted from basic circuits to be suitable for the specific use of that instrument. A lot of the early Valco products, on the other hand, look more like the spiritual siblings of the portable gramophone players and radios and other tube-powered consumer electronics of the day. This one carries two channels (Bright and Normal) with Volume and Tone for each plus a tremolo section, a pair of 6V6s in the output, two metal 6SC7 preamp tubes, a 5Y3 tube rectifier, and a pair of elliptical 6″x10″ speakers with light alnico magnets. The amp chassis is mounted vertically across one side of the back of the cabinet, which itself is on the flimsy side, though sturdy enough for its mere 22 lb weight.

At most, the thing probably puts out 12W-15W on a sunny day in a stiff tail wind, and no self-respecting guitar amp manufacturer would be caught using oval speakers for much longer… but you know what? The thing actually sounds damn good when used as intended, especially with the 1954 Chet Atkins Hollowbody injected. It's got a great, cutting edge of growl and sizzle, isn't the least bit woofy or boomy (well, just a little woofy on low-down runs with a neck pickup selected), and feels extremely playable and dynamic, too. No great frequency spectrum here, nor much gut-thumping punch or clean headroom, but it suits rootsy or rockin'-twangy styles to a tee, and makes a great recording amp even today. Crank it up and it digs in

Echo was the hot new sound of rock'n'roll, and the Maestro Echoplex quickly became – and remains – king of the tape-loop heap.

beautifully, keep it reined back and it's snappy and bright, but still gives you that tinkle of breakup when you pick hard, and retains an easy though not overemphasized compression that makes it a smooth, intuitive amp to play.

Plugged into a wide-panel tweed Fender Super Amp of the same year, with two 10″ Jensens and a pair of 6L6s – still cathode-biased at the time, though fixed bias in another year – our 6120 would have a lot more volume and frequency range to play with, though still only about 28W maximum output, and a pretty quick onset of distortion when pushed even towards halfway on the dial. Such amps were offering more clean headroom, which was still the main goal of the day, but also far more growl and distortion when walloped up to anywhere between 7 and 12 on the Volume. These 5D4 Supers still carried just two Volumes and a shared Tone control and, much like the Deluxes of then and later, you could push the latter to feed a hotter signal to the output stages and get an even earlier distortion along with your treble lift. These still appear pretty basic amps by today's standards, and not very loud ones either, but they would have offered the mid-1950s rock'n'roller a more muscular performance all around.

A later, narrow-panel Fender Bassman – which will be examined in depth in the next chapter – would offer even greater quantities of the same in a couple of years, with far more punch and clean headroom in particular, and more overall volume, too. But its predecessor of 1954 was still a 1x15″ design with about 35W on tap; a little louder than the Super, sure, and with a slightly plummier tonality, but likely to go pretty woofy and farty when cranked toward max – though in a potentially very cool way. A great rough'n'ready blues amp, it has to be said, but not what most rockers of the mid 1950s would be looking for past halfway or so on the Volume.

EchoSonic Sensations

Gibson was already offering some well-made larger amps that could punch out the Gretsch's hollowbody/DeArmonds pairing with a certain tight, clean sparkle, reaching pretty good volumes for the day. These were designed to handle the P90 pickups of the company's own guitars, which were hotter and fatter than the DeArmonds, and therefore were many pros' choice for loud, clean work from a range of guitar models. The best of the really great performing models from the likes of Magnatone and Standel were still a couple of years away, but these would become additional serious options for players wanting to be heard as this new hormone-fueled teenaged music found its way onto bigger and bigger stages. While rock'n'roll guitar style didn't stay as ultra-clean as jazz for long, it wasn't blues-dirty either. So few 1950s guitar stars would have cranked any of these up towards maximum filth, other than maybe the occasional leather-clad rebel rocker looking to strut for his big solo, or to finally blow that big-lunged sax player to the back of the stage (he'd end up there eventually).

The other great way to get noticed, and one which all seminal rock'n'rollers applied at some stage in the 1950s, was to add a little slap to your tickle. Following on from Scotty Moore and Carl Perkins and others' use of Ray Butts's EchoSonic amp with built-in tape echo, the external tube-powered tape echo unit became a must for adding a bouncing, atmospheric thickness to your guitar sound. A range of makes eventually surfaced, but the Echoplex was among the most popular, and best sounding.

Butts's amp really was a revolution in sound, but relatively few were ever made, and far more guitarists wanted that slap-back echo sound than there were amps available to do it. A company called Market Electronics in Cleveland, Ohio, copied the tape echo section of the EchoSonic amp in the late 1950s and offered it as the Echoplex (Butts was eventually paid a nominal sum for the use of his design, but this doesn't seem to have brought in the kind of dollars he might have earned had he patented the invention). A few years later the design was taken up by Harris-Teller of Chicago, and these were the units marketed by Gibson's sibling company, Maestro. These changed a little cosmetically through the years, and some features came and went, but the classic models carried controls for Echo Repeats, Balance, Volume, Echo Delay and Recording Level, and also featured Sound On Sound,

And Now! the "ANNIVERSARY STEREO" Guitar

All the "features of the future" of the famous "Anniversary" model now combined with true stereophonic sound!

- **SPLIT HI-LO'TRON HEADS**
  Separate head for bass and treble. No electric hum – just pure sound.
- **INDEPENDENT BASS AND TREBLE VOLUME CONTROLS**
  Gives complete and separate volume control over bass and treble sides.
- **SEPARATE BASS AND TREBLE TONE COLOR SWITCHES**
  Controls bass and treble heads separately with three-way switches for natural unshaded head tones. Deep mellow tone or brilliant high in any combination.
- **3-WAY CLOSING SWITCH**
  Controls single amp performance; double amp performance (full sound through two amps); Stereophonic biaural sound distinctiveness (bass and treble through separate amps).
- **SEPARATE GRETSCH BASS AND TREBLE AMPS**
  Plug individually into two different sides of dual Jack Box.
- **DUAL GUITAR CORD**
  Plugs directly into guitar from Dual Jack Box.

Distinctive "Anniversary" styling and richness of tone. 16″ cut-away body. Neo-Classic fingerboard. Gretsch adjustable rod-Actionflo neck. All metal parts chrome plated. Black leather should strap.

PX6119 "Anniversary Stereo" guitar, shaded finish $350.00
PX6112 "Anniversary Stereo" guitar, 2-tone green $350.00

letting you add to your own echo. They were capable of some slightly longer delays, too – though still on the shorter side of 'medium delay' by today's standards – the likes of which guitarists like Chet Atkins and Les Paul sometimes played with for atmospherics. For the true rockabilly sound, however, tapping a short-delay head for that bouncy slap-back effect was the only way to go.

Still a classic today, and highly desirable for a range of playing styles, the Maestro Echoplex has an overall tonality outside the delay timing itself that is warm, rich, and full-bodied; not quite hi-fi, given the technology (and the gradual degradation of a constantly looping analog tape), and prone to introducing some noise to the sound, but a real plum of an effect. Even with the echo turned entirely out of the Balance, depending upon Volume adjustment the unit can pleasantly thicken and warm up a signal, and its dimension and soundstage are elements that many players would claim have never been equaled by solid-state analog delay pedals or advanced digital delays. While the Echoplex ruled supreme in the United States, British and European musicians were grooving to units from Meazzi, Binson, Watkins and others, and for a few years at the end of the 1950s and the start of the 1960s, that driving, slightly retro-spacey echo sound was the hippest thing happening to juice up the sound of the guitar instrumentalist.

Reverb actually hit a couple years after the slap-back echo, and while it has become another essential element in some rockabilly styles (and was often used early on as a sort of pseudo-slap-back itself), it was never quite as much at the heart of the seminal rock'n'roll sound that is the main focus of this chapter. Still, it was often a part of the brew, and another of the relatively few very effective ways that early electric players had of adding interest to their sound. For all things sproingy, though, let's hold fire until we visit 'Surf's Up!' a few chapters from now.

Vintage originals of most of the pieces of gear discussed here are pretty hard to come by, and expensive when you find them. Early-issue Gretsch 6120 guitars are becoming extremely collectable, especially those in the unusually fine condition and very early livery or our example here; the Filter'Tron-loaded models of later in the 1950s are nearly as prized, and almost as high-priced. What is kind

Danelectro arrived in the 1950s as an affordable brand for the up-and-coming rock'n'roller. The company offered some creative guitar and amp designs, which proliferated under the Silvertone name with the giant Sears & Roebuck catalog company.

of cool, though, is that you can sometimes bag an early Gretsch amp for really quite reasonable money – far less than you can their Fender contemporaries, at least – and similar sounding (if not looking) Valco models will usually fetch even less. The reissue market helps to balance out availability for those of us living in the real world, although even Gretsch's more period-precise 6120s are expensive guitars off the shelf.

As for the Gretsch amplifiers, no such thing as a reissue of any sort there, but as mentioned, a range of B-list but still very hot sounding 1950s tube amps can still be had for less cash than a new channel-switching combo. Boutique amp-makers like Victoria and Clark cover the tweed Fender-style range beautifully, and while their products aren't cheap, they are extremely accurate repros of the originals, both in looks and sound, and are more likely to hold up to the rigors of heavy gigging than your precious 1956 Super or Pro. For real rockabilly thrills, though, there's nothing quite like plugging in an original rig that would have seen its share of Saturday night hops back in the day, and just letting those 1950s vibes rock and roll.

Blues supremo Buddy Guy squeezes a bend out of his maple-neck Stratocaster.

SETUP 3
RHYTHM & BLUES

Our rig for Chapter 3 is a strong contender for the title of 'All-Time Most Beloved Rock Rig,' and is accordingly one of the most versatile, toneful and desirable pairings known to the electric guitarist. Teaming the pre-CBS Fender Stratocaster and the late 1950s tweed Fender Bassman amplifier has been a dream for most every guitarist at least once in their playing career, and more stars have used this combination of gear – or something extremely similar – to make memorable music than perhaps any other coupling of guitar and amp.

Strictly speaking, in name at least this rig was born chronologically before the rock'n'roll pairing of Gretsch 6120 and amp of our previous setup, but it is more appropriate to list it after that pair. This is not only because the archetypal version of the Bassman is an amp of the late 1950s, but because the sound of the Stratocaster – and indeed the amp too – didn't really begin to fulfill their potential until the R&B and blues players, and more way-out rock'n'rollers that evolved, started to crank up and dig in. The Strat was invented for country swingers, and the Bassman for the electric bass players, but the pair were never at their best in a 'clean-clean' setting.

Of course Fender's Telecaster arrived first, in 1950 (originally as the Broadcaster), but its 'Classic Rig' status became more assured in a future pairing that would forever seal its immortality as the country-rock staple – a rig that will be dealt with in a later chapter. That said, Leo Fender's early target market was the Country & Western and Western Swing scene that was big in the clubs of California and the SW in the late 1940s and early 1950s, along with a few adventurous pop-jazz musicians. His company had cultivated these players with the lap-steel guitar and amp sets that were its early stock in trade, then won over many hollowbody electric guitarists with the Broad/Telecaster in the early 1950s, and was well placed to stun the pickers with the release of the Stratocaster in 1954 – at the time of its introduction, far and away the most revolutionary production-model electric guitar ever seen.

Leo Fender wasn't a musician himself, but as an engineer he had a great knack for translating the desires of musicians into inventions that would advance the sound and playability of the solidbody electric guitar, as well as that of the amps they were plugged into. Country star Bill Carson, for one, an avid Tele player for a couple years after that model's introduction, suggested numerous ways in which Fender could upgrade its flagship solidbody, but the Stratocaster that eventually arrived was far, far more than a deluxe Telecaster.

The debut Stratocaster's maple neck and ash body woods might have been the same as the Tele's, and the two guitars were certainly screwed together in the same fashion, but from there they departed entirely. Not only was Fender seeking to upgrade its two-pickup single-cut model, but the twin goals of wresting the spotlight back from Gibson's Les Paul range of solidbodies, introduced in 1952, and overshadowing the Bigsby vibrato set up design objectives to create the most versatile electric guitar available. It's fair to say the Strat achieved these goals and more: the model introduced the most-played and most-copied electric guitar design of all time.

Its radical, hotrod shape aside, if the Stratocaster had been outfitted with Telecaster pickups and hardware it would have sounded and performed much like its older brother. But three major points of design development significantly altered the instrument's feel, sound and playability.

Firstly and very simply, deep, rounded contours in the body where it met the player's ribcage and pick-hand forearm made it a much more comfortable guitar to play than either a Telecaster or a Gibson Les Paul, both of which were sharply square-edged and slab-like. For this reason, the Strat tucks right into the gut of the player holding it, and this intimate embrace inspires a oneness with the guitar that many

Bass amp be damned – this 1959 Fender Bassman is one of the finest blues, country or rock'n'roll amplifiers of all time. The gorgeous 1964 Stratocaster adapts equally well to any style you care to wrangle out of it. Together, they're a pair made in tone heaven.

Fender Bassman

players loved right from the start. Secondly, the Strat's electronics ushered in a whole new world of possibilities. Ostensibly much like the single-coils on the Tele, the new pickups developed specifically for the Stratocaster were noticeably brighter, with sharper highs and an ability to cut through a muddy bandstand mix without inducing too much amp distortion at popular settings of the day. They were also somewhat less powerful than a Tele's pickups. The three-position selector switch they were connected to offered a broad range of voices – including in-between settings that many players would soon discover – and the single master Volume and dual Tone controls (for neck and middle pickups) further enhanced this versatility.

Wobbles, Bends And Divebombs

Thirdly, and perhaps most significantly of all, the Strat's fully-adjustable self-contained tremolo bridge/tailpiece was like nothing ever seen before. It allowed a lot more down-bend than a Bigsby or any other production vibrato of the day, plus reasonable tuning stability when set up correctly. Aside from its

Tremolo action? You bet your sweet tail block.

bendability, the design's independent pressed-steel bridge saddles offered even more intonation fine-adjustment of individual string heights and lengths than the much-praised Gibson tune-o-matic bridge that would arrive that same year. The unit was a revelation and revolution all rolled into one, and plenty of players recognized this from the start. The Strat vibrato – now taken for granted – ushered in a whole new range of playing styles, enabling harder-twanging country in the mid 1950s, sproingy, heavily-vibratoed surf instrumentals in the early 1960s, Hendrix's wild divebombing and air-raid effects in the late 1960s, and even further levels of virtuosity from the likes of Jeff Beck and Eddie Van Halen in years to come.

Even when the vibrato arm is ignored by the player or removed altogether, this tailpiece's complex design fundamentally changes the guitar's core tonality. Routing the strings' ball-ends through the tailpiece's steel inertia block taps off a portion of their vibrational energy away from the body's own acoustic resonance and into the block and the anchor springs attached to its bottom. The contraption designed and built by Fender and his colleagues is an extremely clever piece of engineering. Looking at the rig on paper, you'd expect a light, thin sound from the Strat, but the inertia block very nicely makes up for the bridge's angled, indirect and relatively loose coupling with the wood of the guitar's body, so there's still plenty of weight in the Strat's tone when you hit it hard, with impressive sustain. But the whole bridge-block-and-springs arrangement lends a, well, springy, slightly spongy, compressed feel to the attack of a standard Strat, and contributes a certain sizzle to its tone, and this in itself perhaps defines it as the archetypal blues solidbody versus the snap, sharpness and immediacy of the more solidly-anchored Tele, the archetypal country solidbody.

The chromed steel-plate bridge plate of the original Strat vibrato assembly and its individual nickel-plated pressed-steel saddles add to a tonality of ringing brightness with a core of warmth and solid lows, especially when coupled with the breathy, slightly scooped tonality of an ash body and the snap and

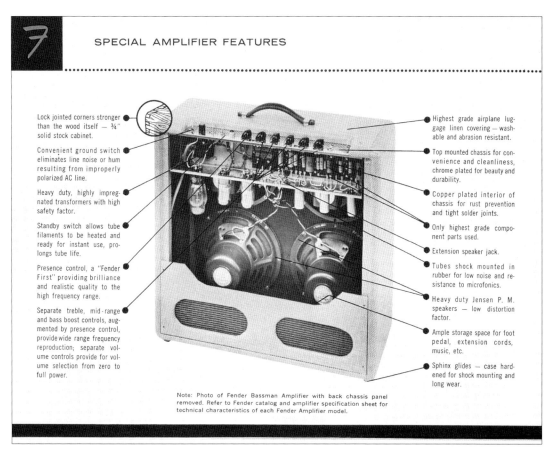

7 SPECIAL AMPLIFIER FEATURES

Lock jointed corners stronger than the wood itself — ¾" solid stock cabinet.

Convenient ground switch eliminates line noise or hum resulting from improperly polarized AC line.

Heavy duty, highly impregnated transformers with high safety factor.

Standby switch allows tube filaments to be heated and ready for instant use, prolongs tube life.

Presence control, a "Fender First" providing brilliance and realistic quality to the high frequency range.

Separate treble, mid-range and bass boost controls, augmented by presence control, provide wide range frequency reproduction; separate volume controls provide for volume selection from zero to full power.

Highest grade airplane luggage linen covering — washable and abrasion resistant.

Top mounted chassis for convenience and cleanliness, chrome plated for beauty and durability.

Copper plated interior of chassis for rust prevention and tight solder joints.

Only highest grade component parts used.

Extension speaker jack.

Tubes shock mounted in rubber for low noise and resistance to microfonics.

Heavy duty Jensen P. M. speakers — low distortion factor.

Ample storage space for foot pedal, extension cords, music, etc.

Sphinx glides — case hardened for shock mounting and long wear.

Note: Photo of Fender Bassman Amplifier with back chassis panel removed. Refer to Fender catalog and amplifier specification sheet for technical characteristics of each Fender Amplifier model.

Bassman ads of the day emphasized the amplifier's quality construction and advanced features, to an extent not often seen at the time.

sparkle of a maple neck. Strats with alder bodies, as used on most non-blonde examples from 1956 to 1972, exhibit more oomph in the mids. Adding a rosewood fingerboard to the brew (as used exclusively from mid-1959 to 1967) enhances the roundness of the upper frequencies, while adding a little sizzle to the highs. The ash body/rosewood fingerboard variation has evolved as perhaps the ultimate blues combination of the instrument. Stevie Ray Vaughan, who can be given more credit for the blues boom of the 1980s and 1990s and beyond than any other player, generally preferred Stratocasters with rosewood fingerboards.

Plenty of other great blues artists, however, like Buddy Guy, Otis Rush, Eric Clapton, Eric Johnson, and SRV's brother Jimmie Vaughan are best known for playing Strats with maple fingerboards, and you certainly can't fault them with 'substandard blues tone' or anything. As ever, there's no saying one is a

For its new Stratocaster, Fender sought to design a pickup with bright, sweet characteristics

better blues instrument than the other – and of course many, many other variables come into play to influence your overall sound; it's merely worth being aware of the potential sonic differences. Plenty of players and collectors alike also gush over the early 'slab' rosewood fingerboards used on Strat and Tele necks between 1959 and around August 1962, reasoning that the thicker piece of wood is preferable to the thinner curved laminate of rosewood used afterward. Tonally, while every change in wood type and thickness will indeed have some effect, we're just talking about changing the fingerboard's rosewood content by a few mils, so any significant difference heard when comparing, for example, a 1961 Strat and a 1963 is just as likely to be the result of pickup windings, body wood densities, setup, and so forth.

I touched on the subject of pickups earlier, and of course they are a major factor in the Stratocaster's signature sound. For its new Stratocaster, Fender sought to design a pickup with bright, sweet characteristics. The resultant tall, narrow coil wound around six individual, staggered-height alnico V magnet polepieces achieved just that. The narrow magnetic 'window' of this tall, thin coil picks up plenty of shimmering high harmonics, while the alnico magnets contribute a sweetness and musicality that helps all this brightness to keep from getting too harsh. The earlier Strat pickups were wound with 42 gauge wire to an average number of turns in the lower to mid 8,000s. This resulted in an average DC resistance of around 6k ohms – giving a reasonable amount of punch and power for a unit of the type, but nothing close to what you'd call a 'high gain' pickup. Again, the goal was clarity and treble content – though with a firm, full low-end – which were consistent tonal criteria of the day. (Interestingly, Telecaster pickups of the day – wound on a larger coil former – were wound to an average 9,200 turns, yielding a DC resistance of around 7.5k ohms. This and other factors contributed to making the Tele units hotter but very cutting pickups, as will be discussed in detail in 'Setup 9.')

Early Fender pickups are spoken of as 'hand wound,' but in fact they were wound on a machine, with a Fender worker feeding the wire onto the bobbin (Would you like to crank a handle 8,000 times to genuinely 'hand wind' a single pickup? It wouldn't make for very efficient manufacture, even by 1950s standards.) When more complete automation arrived in the early 1960s, the average number of turns became more consistent, and also decreased – to around 7,800 or so, with the DC resistance dropping proportionally. This means a slightly brighter pickup, but one with a little less output as well. There's a certain magic attributed to finding the occasional odd pickup that was overwound at the factory and, therefore, is more powerful; but I've played both Strats and Teles whose pickups came in at the lower end of the readings typical of their era, but which had extremely sweet, musical voices and were simply great sounding guitars overall. The pickups on Stevie Ray Vaughan's No1 Strat are often written about as being among the hotter units of the time, and I've heard the same said of many of the pickups on Buddy Guy's older Strats, but plenty of players achieve great blues and rock sounds by running average or even weak Stratocaster pickups into cranked tube amps. The result is plenty of definition and shimmer, yet a lot of bite and muscle from the amp (a booster or overdrive pedal often aids things here). Yes, a Strat's winding/resistance/strength will definitely affect its tonality, but it's not always a matter of better or worse, only different. As ever, the entire sound chain – and a player's style and sonic goals – has to be taken into consideration.

The staggered polepieces – ie, magnets of different heights – found in Stratocaster pickups from 1954 to 1974 are often talked about, and were used as a means of balancing the unequal magnetic output of the different wound and unwound strings which, early on especially, were usually of a fairly heavy gauge, with a wound G-string. From 1954 to 1956 the D-string magnet was the tallest of the set, but from 1956 onward Fender changed the staggering by raising the height of the G-string magnet to make it closest to the strings. On this subject, the closer a magnet is set to its string, of course the more string vibration it detects, and the louder its output. Beyond a point, however, the magnet's own pull on the string begins to impede that vibration, resulting both in a general choking of tone and some false harmonics, or 'ghost notes,' on lower wound strings in particular. Strat pickups are especially prone to this, since the polepieces that extend above the bobbins toward the strings are themselves magnets and are exerting their own strongly focused magnetic field. The neck pickups are most likely of all to cause such problems, since they are placed at a point where the string is further from the solid anchor of the bridge. Within reason, dropping a too-close pickup down further into the body can actually increase output slightly, but lowering it even to the point where output starts to fall can often improve overall tonality by allowing the string to vibrate freely. But note that raising the strings to achieve this, rather than simply lowering the magnets, also achieves the added bonus of letting the strings vibrate more freely from the tone-dampener of fret-buzz, so the two factors often work in conjunction.

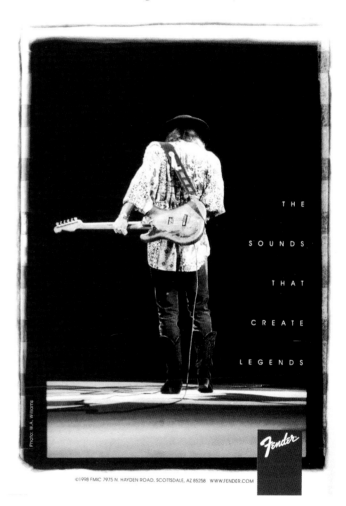

A pair of legends: Stevie Ray Vaughan and the archetypal battered Strat.

Fender's Stratocaster wasn't the first guitar to carry three pickups – Gibson's hollowbody archtop ES-5 is probably the most prominent to have arrived well before it in 1949 – but it made great use of their positioning. And the fact that the pickups themselves were narrower than those of most other manufacturers meant that even cramming three of them between bridge and neck didn't interfere with the player's pick or fingerstyle technique too badly. Examine the efforts of many guitar and amp makers of the 1950s and 1960s and you quickly realize that the attainment of more treble was one overriding goal; consider all the presence controls, bright switches, and treble boosters that were so popular – and which are far less needed today in light of the overwhelming, even spiky brightness most modern amps are capable of achieving. The Stratocaster's pickups succeeded beautifully in this quest for highs, and the bridge pickup in particular did so in spades. The pickup was angled to capture the full sparkle of the higher strings, while enabling the low strings still to produce a full, firm bass (this can thin out considerably when a pickup is placed very close to the bridge saddles of the low E and A strings in particular).

The Stratocaster's control layout also reflects the bridge pickup's role as the treble blaster of the trio. Fender couldn't conceive of players ever wanting to reduce the brilliant highs that this pickup produces, so it was never given a Tone control like the middle and neck pickups (all three share a master volume control). Many modern players find their Strats' bridge pickups too bright, if anything, hence its frequent replacement with an overwound or high-output replacement, and rewiring one Tone control to govern this pickup is a relatively popular mod today. But in the mid-1950s it was just the thing for getting bright, sparkling highs out of the overtly dull, muddy amps available (think back to our jazz rig), and thus helping to cut through the soup of a swampy mix. Even today, get up on stage with a full band cooking, and that bridge position becomes a more tempting option for soloing than maybe it is in your basement studio or bedroom jams.

For many players of later eras, a Strat's real magic often lies in its neck pickup. This unit is well positioned to capture the 'would-be' 24th fret harmonic (its front edge is almost precisely where a 24th fret would be, if a Strat had more than its original 21), so its output is brilliant, shimmering and harmonically rich, but full and ballsy thanks to the strings' wide vibrational travel at that point. For plummy, toothsome tones, this is where a lot of the action is happening, for blues players in particular. And the standard Fender scale-length of 25 ½″ helps to accentuate the harmonic richness that this pickup conveys. The middle pickup also does its job well; its tone is probably less characterful than that of either of the others, but on a good Strat this selection is full, punchy and aggressive, yet with plenty of twang and brightness. Throughout the late 1970s and much of the 1980s, players participating in the high-gain revolution often swapped out their Strat pickups for hot replacements, or single-coil-sized or even full-sized humbuckers, in order to drive those Mesa/Boogies or master-volume Fenders and Marshalls that were all the rage. As guitarists started to appreciate the true beauty of many vintage, non-master-volume tube amps again, many also took another listen to the standard-issue pickups on pre-CBS Fender Strats and Teles, and quickly realized what an amazing job these designers had done in the first place. The Stratocaster's three original-style pickups achieve their goals beautifully, and remain titans of tone to this day.

'True fidelity bass reproduction...' Well, an ad-man can dream.

A few other details of Strat design warrant a mention, most of them up at the headstock end. The light but efficient Kluson tuners are great at maintaining neck/body balance without impeding resonance, and have the added bonus of slotted posts into which you can tuck sharp string ends, which also provide a good anchor for tuning stability. The now famous six-in-line headstock, which evolved from the Telecaster's, is not merely a striking visual element, but puts the strings in a straight line to the tuners, rather than splaying them out at sideways angles from nut to tuning post as many three-a-side headstocks do. Also, the headstock and fingerboard faces being parallel – but the former on a slightly lower plain to the latter – means there is just enough break angle down from the nut to create the required downward pressure for good string anchoring in the slot (with the help of a string retainer on the high B and E strings), but not so much as to encourage strings to snag in the slots and create tuning nightmares, as is sometimes experienced with headstocks designed with severe back angles. This is especially important on a guitar that carries a vibrato unit that is truly meant to be used.

Beyond issues of sound and stability, the Stratocaster's playing feel suits many players beautifully, too.

The very first Strats had relatively full, round neck profiles, but were still pretty comfortable and fast when compared to other real club-necks of the time. Each of the neck's evolutions through V-shaped, ultra-slim, and back to slightly fuller profiles has earned plenty of rabid fans, and each and every one of these is usually a very playable, natural-feeling neck when compared to much of the competition. Fender's standard pre-1983 fingerboard radius of 7″ doesn't make any of its instruments the most bend-friendly available, and coupled with the thin, slightly high frets, any extreme bend efforts are prone to choking-out on this noticeably convex playing surface. Still, plenty of players have learned to get around the problem – or just live with it – and the precise noting of this fret and fingerboard combination, coupled with the neck's overall rounded, smooth-in-the-hand feel, is often considered a justifiable tradeoff.

Tone Will Not Break Up Or Distort...

Now, from the vintage pleasures of a glorious guitar to the aural excitement of one of the greatest amplifier designs of all time. Full-grown guitarists are known to flop to the ground and convulse in gurgling spasms of lustful froth at the mere mention of the phrase 'tweed Bassman,' and anyone who has played one in good condition

The Bassman was already becoming the guitar amp of choice for lead players of the mid 1950s

knows exactly why. From snappy, biting clean sounds at lower volume settings to plummy, full-throated overdrive when whacked up to 12, with plenty of chewy crunch in between, a Bassman maybe can't absolutely do it all, but it can do most of it. Sure, there are other amps in the sea, but this 40W 4x10″ combo from the late 1950s has inspired more desirous dreams, and more imitators, than any other, and it all happened largely by accident.

As with so many other great pieces of gear, there was and is more than one version of the model, and as we see elsewhere, the true classic of the breed isn't even the first version issued. When guitarists say 'Bassman,' they invariably mean the narrow-panel 4x10″ version of the beast, and ideally the 5F6A circuit from around 1958 onward, with four inputs for two channels and Middle and Presence controls.

Fender introduced the model in 1952 as partner to the Precision Bass, which was initially the far more sensational newcomer. The amp first fell to earth as a tweed-covered 1x15″ combo in a 'TV-front' cabinet with a semi-closed, ported back and a pair of 6L6 tubes in the output section (this cab type earned its name because the dimensions of the grille cloth visible over the speaker baffle closely resembled the dark screen of a TV set of the day). The amp carried just Volume and Tone controls, and Fender promotional literature of the day promised that the "tone will not break up or distort, even at extremely loud volume..." Yeah, right.

The classic small bass combo, you would think, but at the time the format couldn't quite cut it. As much as we have associated the 15″ speaker with bass reproduction over the years, the fact is that the big drivers just weren't hacking it, being particularly prone to flapping out on the low E string, and receiving harsh treatment all round from the extreme cone travel demanded by the fundamental notes of the electric bass. To rectify this, in 1955 Leo and friends made the first of a number of formative changes that brought the design ever nearer to twang Valhalla, by expanding the tone stack, introducing a Presence control, and changing to a more durable 4x10″ layout with Special Design Jensen P10R speakers. At this point the design begins the journey that leaves it looking so ill-named today. Undoubtedly the most powerful amp of its era for low-end reproduction (although a feeble 'pro bass combo' for high-volume use by today's standards), the Bassman was already becoming the guitar amp of choice for lead players of the mid 1950s seeking its unbeatable combination of power, grit and tone.

A year later, with the 5F6 circuit design, a Middle control joined the Bass and Treble, and the inputs were upped to four, with a high and low sensitivity jack on each of the Bright and Normal channels. By about 1958 the design reached its final evolution as the 5F6A, dropped an 'ultrasonic oscillation-dampening' resistor between the power tubes and the bias circuit and connected the negative feedback loop to the amp's phase inverter, slightly altering the way in which the Presence control operated and, in the process, making this the most desirable Bassman ever built. The fact that this ultimate version of the amp was only produced for about three years, until its withdrawal part way through 1960 for the new front-mounted control panel Tolex designs, only serves to increase its rarity.

As Fender continued to tweak the Bassman circuitry in a quest for more clean power and higher headroom before distortion, guitarists realized more and more that it was precisely the warmth, grit and soft breakup provided by this 'inefficiency' that made the amp sound so good. Throughout the early 1960s, Fender made essential changes in the preamp circuit, changed from tube to diode (solid state) rectification, changed noticeably from 4x10″ combo to 2x15″ 'piggy back' head and cab arrangements, and eventually lost both the Middle and Presence controls. The results brought the company closer to a genuine bass amp as we know it today, and yielded an amp that's still great for guitar, too, as many players aptly prove (Brian Setzer, for one, runs his Gretsch 6120 through a pair of blonde early 1960s Bassman piggy-back amps). But all of this encroaching cleanness further highlighted how wonderful the dirtier tweed models sounded.

The Bassman magic didn't fall into place by chance; a wealth of ingredients inside the 5F6A circuit design makes this a gorgeous guitar amp in so many ways. If you look at the development of Fender amps even over the company's first 14 years, from 1946 to 1960, you can see that some feverish R&D work went into constantly improving the designs, not just through trial and error but

Feverish R&D work went into constantly improving Fender's amp designs

through sound science and a firm grasp of tube electronics. The preamps on the big amps went through a good half-dozen or so evolutions in the tweed years alone, and the first gain and tone stages of the Bassman of 1958-60 were highly advanced creatures for their day. Preamp distortion was never a goal of amp makers in the 1950s and 1960s, and the Bassman's 12AY7 – in the way it was used – did an excellent job of passing a clean, round, full-frequency signal along to the further amplification stages.

The positioning of the three-knob cathode-follower tone stack (something that would change in the Tolex amps) helps to make this an especially touch-sensitive guitar amplifier that adheres to a player's pick or finger dynamics more than later brown and blackface Fenders. This passive EQ section is also effective as a tone shaper, while the Presence control – tapped from a negative feedback loop run around the amp's class AB output section – enables players to retain a bright edge and cut in the tone without excessive harshness. Tube rectification adds a further degree of touch and tactile 'squash' to the Bassman's playability when the amp is driven hard, yet three other ingredients – a quality choke, a hefty output transformer, and the aforementioned negative feedback loop – serve to keep this slightly compressed feeling amp firm in the lows, snappy in the mids, and crackling in the highs. A choke is a filtering coil that looks much like a small transformer, which helps to negate DC hum when placed in series with the power supply feeding the tubes; smaller or cheaper amps rarely carried them, so it was an upscale feature of the time. Fender output transformers of the late 1950s were the product of extensive research and testing, and built to rigorous standards which Leo and his team supplied to the Triad company, while most other amp-makers were using off-the-shelf supplies. The heavy-duty, large-core interleaved OTs of the Bassman were among the finest ever employed in a guitar amplifier to that day, and translated more of the amp's full 40W into clean output power – and with a bolder low end – than almost any player would have heard before. Finally, that negative feedback loop helped to keep the output section from running away with itself, quelled oscillation at high volumes, and smoothed out the frequency response.

Beauty In The Details

An extremely advanced 'long-tailed pair' style phase inverter did a great job of passing the preamp's signal along to the output section without adding any major distortion or inefficiencies of its own, and once this signal arrived at the 5881 power tubes (a 6L6 type) it was treated to the sweetest ride of the entire trip. These tubes are driven with high enough voltage to yield good power and decent headroom up to a

The piggy-back Tolex Bassman is a great amp, but a world away from the tweed design.

point, but not so much as to render the sound brittle and sterile. Keep the volume down to 4 or 5 with a Strat, and the amp is crisp and bouncy; crank it past halfway or right up to max, and it growls and sings. A weighty and extremely well-built output transformer translates plenty of oomph and a solid bottom end to the alnico-magnet speakers, which themselves – in this configuration of four – pump a full, round, multidimensional tone out into the air. Even the box in which all this is housed contributes to the amp's sonic signature; the solid pine cabinet adds a slightly soft, appealingly blurred edge to the tone, while the 'floating baffle' – so called because it is secured only at the top and bottom panels – pumps and vibrates with the speakers themselves at higher volumes, and further enhances the resonance of the entire package. The open-backed design plays its part, too, by providing a room-filling sense of 'surround-sound' projection, with tinkling, bell-like highs. Considering all this, as a unit unto itself the 5F6A Bassman makes an excellent study in the importance of the Big Picture, its many components and design features adding up to so much more than the mere sum of their parts.

The four 10″ alnico-magnet P10R Jensen speakers are themselves a big part of the equation. While the reissue P10Rs are rated at 25W power handling, various literature records the originals as rated at 15W, 12W, and as little as 9W – a severely lightweight driver indeed. Individually, a P10R can barely take the full whack of an old 10-watter without fuzzing and farting out, but in fours they handle the Bassman's blast admirably. There is plenty of bark and snarl from their ridged, seamed pulp paper cone, and a sweet musicality contributed by the small alnico magnet, for an overall tonality that is plummy, rich, slightly gritty and just a bit boxy, but smooth and really growly when cranked hard. (Almost any description you find of these speakers includes the adjective 'bell-like,' whatever that means. I'd call their high-end response more edgy and razory, though in a good way, than shimmering and crystalline.)

Even the configuration of four lightweight speakers rather than one heavy-duty driver makes a difference in the amp's sound. Multiple drivers, even of the same type, offer a very slight mismatch of response that yields some slight phase cancelations at certain listening positions, and in the right context this can offer a pleasant smoothing of the tone. Also, the parallel wiring of the Bassman's speakers – four 8 ohm units wired individually to the OT's secondary for a 2-ohm load – offers a little more self-damping, for a smoother sonic result than that of many series-wired speaker cabs (although in truth Fender probably chose the configuration to save players from losing output – and risking OT damage – when one of the speakers blew, as would happen with a series-wired configuration.)

There are many places you can turn to hear classic recorded examples of the Bassman, and often with a pre-CBS Stratocaster played through it. Many, many classic electric bluesmen and many great rock'n'rollers of the 1950s and 1960s played through a narrow-panel Bassman at one time or another, although many have more recently gotten 'that sound' from boutique copies or reissues, with originals growing extremely expensive or just too risky to take on the road.

Buddy Guy's early recordings are an example of what this 'classic rig' sounds like when pushed to extremes. Guy habitually winds all of his Bassman's controls up towards max, other than the Bass tone control, which is kept low, and hits it with the full power of his aggressive, stinging Strat attack, with characteristic broad bends and quirky, emotive vibrato. Most of his early recordings display this, and his more recent recordings maintain much of the same characteristics, although the gear now usually consists of a newer Fender signature model Stratocaster and a repro 5F6A-style tweed amp from Victoria Amp Company. For a cleaner, brighter dose of Strat-meets-Bassman, check out Jimmie Vaughan's Texas boogie-blues on the first album from The Fabulous Thunderbirds (often referred to as 'Girls Go Wild'), on which he puts an original late 1950s Bassman to great use. For another early example of the pairing, check out Otis Rush's track 'I Can't Quit You.' And for a notion of what a vintage Telecaster sounds like through the same amp, you can revisit most of Bruce Springsteen's early work. The Boss has played a vintage Bassman since the 1970s; to hear him cranking one up, check out much of his lead work on *Darkness On The Edge Of Town*, where the main riffs to 'Adam Raised A Cain' and the stinging solo on 'Candy's Room' are archetypal cranked-big-tweed.

Hitting It Harder

Plugging a humbucker-loaded guitar such as a Gibson Les Paul or ES-335 with PAFs into a tweed Bassman yields even more ferocious results, and plenty of players have used these or similar combinations to great effect. The fat, hot sound of a humbucker drives a Bassman to even quicker distortion, so there's less headroom from the start but a swifter onset of serious grind. And the Les Paul into Bassman-on-12 combo will do a roaring, classic rock sound that might even have you thinking 'Bluesbreaker' if you're not in view of the rig producing the maelstrom (although in truth those four 10″ Jensens in an open-backed cab do sound very different from two 12″ Celestions).

Fender started including its dual low and high-gain inputs partly out of an awareness that players of other popular, more powerful makes of guitars – again, mainly Gibsons – might end up as Fender amp customers and, with loud-clean tones being the design objective of the day, would need an instant means of avoiding distortion. Since the Bassman's sweetest clean-with-bite and overdrive tones come from pushing the output tubes hard rather than merely overloading the preamp, many players of LPs and ES-335s and similar have learned the sweet trick of plugging into their tweed amp's Input 2, and then

Few players need to be reminded of the Stratocaster's impact on electric guitar

pumping up the Volume a little higher to pass along a more full-frequencied preamp signal to those 6L6s. Drive that hard enough, and the whole shebang will distort eventually, but it will do so with more body and dynamics than an over-hot input will allow.

On the other hand, many other players have discovered that they like to get things cooking right from the first gain stage, and substituting a hotter 12AX7 for the original-spec 12AY7 is one easy way to get there. They are direct replacements in the operational sense, but the former's gain factor of around 100 floors the 12AY7's gain factor of about 40 to 45, and the hotter preamp tube will get even single coils sounding thick and grindy by the 4 or 5 mark.

Plenty of other players have learned that if they want that sweet, cranked tweed Fender sound at lower volumes, they need only plug into a smaller tweed Fender. The 5E3 narrow panel Deluxe is the classic choice, and does for the small club or barroom gig what the Bassman does for the dance hall or theater stage concert. This said, however, while the most immediate characters of each amp cranked are outwardly similar, though at different volumes, they are very different amps when you peek beneath the upper back panel.

For starters, the Deluxe's preamp, although another 12AY7-loaded design, is a very different circuit. Its lone Tone knob offers extremely touch-sensitive control over the signal's treble content, but in any position above the halfway mark it begins to pass a much hotter signal on to the phase inverter than do the two- or three-knob tweed tone stacks. The PI itself is of the less efficient 'paraphase' or 'split load' design, and doesn't handle its job as cleanly as the big Bassman's relatively hi-fi PI configuration, and the cathode-biased output stage with no negative feedback likes to run hot and gritty right from pretty low settings on the Volume dial. In short, the Deluxe transmits distortion to the output from many more parts of the circuit, resulting in a juicy, hot, sizzling tone that can be hard to clean up – and is therefore loved by many, many players.

This chapter has run a little longer than the others in this book, but two such archetypal pieces of gear deserve the extra ink and paper. Few players need to be reminded of the Stratocaster's impact on electric guitar, and popular music in general. But not as many realize that the Bassman has been nearly as influential on the course of amplifier design. Aside from being a great amp in itself, the model stood as the inspiration for Jim Marshall and Ken Bran's seminal Marshall JTM45 – which, aside from look, layout, and numerous European component replacements was virtually a direct copy of the 5F6A circuit – and the Bassman has made its presence felt, in design terms, in more tube amps than any other amplifier. They are a match made in tone heaven. It's no surprise they have been paired time and time again.

Fifteen years after The Beatles, Paul Weller of The Jam uses the same rig to make a little more noise.

SETUP 4
BRITISH INVASION

Our rig for this chapter illustrates how a string of variables in the gear can result in greatly different sounds and suit very different playing styles. Artists as diverse as Pete Townshend, Tom Petty and fellow Heartbreakers guitarist Mike Campbell, Paul Weller, Peter Buck and many others have at one time or another played a Rickenbacker through a Vox AC30. But 'that sound' was launched by The Beatles, and their use of the rig has inspired more interest than any of the others who made it equally their own.

In fact you could credit many other players with more consistent, defining use of the Ricky-AC30 sound, because both Beatle guitarists, John Lennon and George Harrison, proved to be enthusiastic gearheads who collected guitars and amps as different models caught their attention – or promised to serve their sonic goals – and changed their instruments pretty frequently over the course of The Beatles' career.

Lennon was fairly faithful, and used his original short-scale 1958 model 325 Rickenbacker with retrofitted Bigsby vibrato from 1960 up until 1964, when a black 325 replaced it to become his main live and studio guitar for a while thereafter. But at various times, in the later years especially, Lennon also played a sonic blue Fender Stratocaster, Gretsch 6120, Epiphone Casino, and of course his faithful acoustics. Harrison was far more fickle, and went from Gretsch Duo Jet to Country Gent to Tennessean to Gibson SG to Epiphone Casino to Les Paul to rosewood Fender Telecaster... But he also played for a time a Rickenbacker 425 and, more famously, a 360/12.

The latter, a 12-string electric (as the model number denotes) became very much 'the sound of The

Where the legend was born.

Beatles' for the majority of the band's mid-1960s period, appearing on early tracks like 'You Can't Do That' and 'I Should Have Known Better,' and again on the vast majority of the songs on *A Hard Day's Night*. The most famous of these is probably the title track itself, with its unmistakable chiming RIcky 12-string intro chord and the distinctive lead break toward the middle of the song. Of course by mid 1964 The Beatles were a big, big band, and since they played comparably big arenas (with still severely underdeveloped PA systems) they had moved up from their 30W AC30s to 50W Vox AC50s and soon even AC100s. Somehow, however, most gearheads would agree that the AC30 still nails 'the sound' – and the AC50 and AC100 are too big and loud for most bands to deal with in the latter age of satisfactory PA rigs. (Sure, plenty of guitarists play equally powerful rigs from other makers, but these bigger Vox piggy-back amps were always efficient loud-clean designs and never great rock amps, so players needing that kind of power usually shop elsewhere.) So Rickenbacker 360/12 and Vox AC30 it is, and few would argue this combo's place in tone heaven.

Despite the many famous players of the brand, Rickenbacker occupies what many guitarists today would probably think of as the 'B-list' of vintage American electric guitars, sitting – along with Gretsch, perhaps – a rung down from the stellar position occupied by Fender and Gibson. In the 1960s, the picture was different; for a time, the brand stared out from about as many music mags, album covers and concert stages as the Big F and the Big G. And Rickenbacker had the history to support this status, too, which included playing a major part in the very birth of the electric guitar.

Like Orville Gibson and C.F. Martin before him, Adolph Rickenbacker started life in 19th century Europe and came to the USA to ply his trade, and eventually to found a legend. By 1918 Rickenbacker had made his way from Basel, Switzerland, to Ohio, to Illinois, and finally to Los Angeles, California, where his tool-and-die manufacturing operation eventually led him into contact with some then more radical strands of the guitar business. For a time, Rickenbacker made both metal bodies and resonator cones for National guitars and, by around 1930, was moving toward getting into the guitar business for himself.

Roots Of Rickenbacker

Around the same time, National employees George Beauchamp and Paul Barth were expanding on the company's acoustic means of amplifying the guitar sound – that is, using an onboard resonator cone – with early experiments with magnetic pickups. The final practical evolution of these early designs, the now-famous 'horseshoe pickup,' found its way onto a maple-bodied prototype built by Beauchamp, Barth and fellow National employee Harry Watson. This 'frying pan' guitar – so called for its small, round body and long handle-like neck – became the first guitar to carry a magnetic pickup. Throughout this time all of these designers had had close associations with Rickenbacker, and after Beauchamp and Barth were fired from National they joined forces with the tool-and-die manufacturer to bring out cast-aluminum frying pan-style lap steels with horseshoe pickups, which by the mid 1930s were taking the Rickenbacker (and sometimes Rickenbacher) name. Although the name on the headstock was in a state of flux through the early 1930s, there's a good case to be made for crediting Rickenbacker with the first commercially available electric guitar, a feat that was consolidated in 1932 by the launch of the hollowbody archtop Electro Spanish, the first electrified production 'Spanish' guitar.

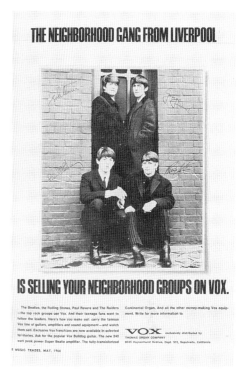

This Vox trade ad appeals to dealers. They wouldn't need prompting for long.

Rickenbacker's more conventionally shaped, but still archaic looking, bakelite lap steel and Spanish electric guitars arrived in the mid 1930s, and designs remained fairly backward looking until after the break in production during World War II, when new owner Francis Hall eventually introduced the new, forward-looking, even modern-styled solidbodied Combo Series guitars of 1954. These still carried that cumbersome horseshoe pickup, but a variety of more conventional-looking single coil pickups arrived in 1956 and 1957, culminating in the familiar, long-running 'toaster-top' pickup that has graced so many Rickenbacker models... and we're now just a hop, skip and a jump from the first Beatle Ricky.

Though they now look like a slab of something left over from the Stone Age, those horseshoe pickups are nevertheless powerful, toneful beasts. Modern players are more likely to encounter them on a sturdy old Ricky lap steel than anywhere else, but they make an interesting alternative for beefy, raw sounds from a conventional solidbody, too, and guitar-maker Rick Turner for one has used a version of the design on many of his interesting instruments. But let's move along to the tones that made history.

By the end of the 1950s Rickenbacker was selling a broad range of guitars – including many hollowbodies and a variety of short and full-scale solidbodies with one, two and three pickups – while a young John Lennon was walking the streets of Hamburg in search of his dream guitar. For Lennon and Harrison, or any young British rock'n'roller of 1960, the term 'quality guitar' was synonymous with 'American guitar;' Lennon found both in the form of a natural-finish 1958 Rickenbacker 325 hanging in a back street Hamburg guitar shop. This would become *the* sound of Beatles rhythm guitar for five years from 1960 to 1965, thanks to this first 325 and a replacement supplied by Rickenbacker in 1964.

The Ricky 325 is an unlikely candidate for the status of highly-desirable vintage guitar. For one thing, unless my recollection fails me, with a 20 ³/₄″ scale-length it is probably the shortest electric to have attained topnotch vintage status. (Often referred to as a 'three-quarter scale' guitar, the 325 isn't quite as short as all that; do the math – it's actually closer to ⁵/₆ scale.) Size aside, its design and features do little to lend itself to the notion of 'a great player' either. Its fingerboard is notoriously narrow and tight-feeling in most players' hands, and its semi-hollow body benefits from being light but is not redolent of any great sustain-bolstering resonance, especially when coupled with the loose jangle of that short scale. But those single coil 'toaster-top' alnico pickups are chimey, bright and percussive, with more bite than most Strat pickups (something closer to a good Telecaster bridge pickup, if anything).

Whatever the specs, John Lennon loved it, and given the string of hit records and seminal sounds that flowed from this little maple wonder, it's hard to fault the 325, despite its inherent drawbacks. If the guitar could talk, it would probably say it loved him too; without the Beatle's endorsement, it surely would have been merely a footnote in electric guitar history.

Tonally, the 325 is bright, bright, bright, with an added helping of chime and jangle, but just a dollop of openness and midrange grit and sizzle, aided somewhat by those hollowed out slabs. Hit it hard with anything but heavy strings, and the looseness of that short scale lets the force send it vibrating out of tune for just the first nanoseconds of the note's attack, which in itself is a defining characteristic of shorter-scale guitars, and this Beatle-bashed gem in particular. Overall, though, that brightness

Brightness was a boon on early Beatles recordings, supplying that hunger for treble that would help the guitar to cut through

was a real boon on early Beatles recordings, supplying that eternal hunger for treble that would help the guitar to cut through – and help a single to get heard on the radio. In Lennon's hands, played mainly through an AC30 or a range of other, larger Voxes by the mid 1960s, the 325 forged one of the most chased guitar tones of all time.

Rather than the through-neck construction of many of the larger Rickenbackers, the 325 had a glued-in 21-fret neck. Its body was made by joining two slabs of maple, routing them extensively from the behind, and covering the air spaces with a thin wooden back. The majority of 325s sent to market had a single f-hole (the large white or gold pickguard covering the entire space where a second would appear), but Lennon's original – one of the first built – had none, nor did its black replacement, as it was built specifically for him by the Ricky factory.

If the 325 is a surprising candidate for legend status, the 360/12 was a true brainstorm, a useful and viable new design from the start, and the Ricky that most players would put forward for the electrics hall of fame if there was room on the walls for only one model per maker. The notion of a 12-string electric is so well-established today that it's difficult to think of the type never existing. In the early 1960s, however, the 12-string was yet the dual domain of prewar bluesers and the burgeoning coffee house folk

This early 1960s Rickenbacker 325 and 1965 Vox AC30 Top Boost are the essential ingredients of John Lennon's rhythm guitar sound in the early days of The Beatles. Similar rigs have supplied an incredibly broad range of tones for countless bands over the past 40 years.

scene, with only a few odd electric efforts surfacing to date. The folk boom was becoming big stuff by 1963, even threatening the survival of the electric's status in certain musical circles (they were great days for acoustic makers, for sure). Rickenbacker owner Francis Hall thought he could see some crossover potential in the format, and sent down instructions for the Ricky designers to see what they could come up with…

Three 12-string prototypes received enthusiastic responses from the musicians who tested them, and the debut model settled into form as the 360/12 toward the end of 1963. A couple months later, in February 1964, The Beatles came to the USA for three concerts and a pair of appearances on the hugely popular Ed Sullivan show. Hall presented a 360/12 to George Harrison to try out, Harrison liked it, and the instruments' success was assured for eternity. By mid-1965 there were three models in the Rickenbacker electric 12-string lineup, the 360, the 370 – with three pickups, but otherwise identical – and the solidbodied 450. But the former, Harrison's choice, was always the most popular.

Birth Of The Jangle

The 360/12's body was another semi-hollow affair, carved and routed from solid slabs of maple like that of the smaller 325, but this time universally given the soundhole at the bass-side (a 'slash' design on most models, and a more traditional f-hole on some export models). Constructionally, however, the 360 differed significantly in that its full 24 ³/₄″ scale neck was made from a maple/mahogany/maple sandwich with extra mahogany wings added at the headstock sides, and the stripy effect of this can clearly be seen in most photographs. Fingerboards came in either maple or rosewood, though the former is often slightly darker-hued than on a Fender, for example, and easily mistaken for another wood on sight.

Where most other 12-strings, whether electric or acoustic, have their lines spoiled visually by an ungainly elongated headstock, the Rickenbackers appear deceptively like an ordinary six-string at first glance, thanks to a clever and elegant piece of design work. The 360/12 and its siblings squeeze six tuners per-side into the usual space of three by placing three in the usual position, and three more at right angles to them, their posts running through slots routed in the headstock much like those in classical or resonator guitar. The Ricky 12's slots are only partial, however, not extending all the way through the wood to daylight at the back; the overall result makes for efficient functionality and beautifully preserves the model's sleek, modern styling.

Electronics on the 360 were mainly of the same type as those on the 325, but with two toaster-top pickups instead of three. While they appear outwardly to be humbuckers, these pickups are actually single coil units, mounted beneath chromed metal covers with parallel black insets at either side. These housings are shock-mounted to the top of the guitar with black rubber grommets at each corner, a means of reducing potential microphony in the transfer of vibrations from the guitar body to the metal cover. With their covers removed, the toaster tops appear like more conventional single coil pickups, constructed of six alnico polepieces – one below each string – around which a wire coil has been formed on a bobbin. A range of different gauges of Formvar-coated wire has been reported over the years, including 42 and 43, but 44 seems to be the most likely of these. Early toaster-tops were wound to as low as 5k ohms resistance, making them bright and clean, while mid-1960s units – like those on Harrison's 360/12 and on the guitars of other notable Ricky players such as Pete Townshend – were hotter, but also more variable, usually reading something in the 7k to 8.5k range, but sometimes upwards of 10k even. The 7k units are already getting hotter than the average Strat of the day, and remember that the tradeoff for higher windings/resistance and a hotter signal is a loss of high-end definition and potential muddiness. (The example recorded on the CD accompanying this book would appear to have been given one of the higher-resistance sets, because these are pretty hot for single coils.)

Rickenbacker followed its toaster-tops in later years with the 'high-gain' single coils, known to many players as 'button-tops' because of the six rounded, black, button-like steel polepieces that protrude from the top. These thread through an overwound coil to a ceramic magnet mounted at the bottom of the structure; the result is a pickup that's hotter than any of the toaster-tops (although some of the reissues – wound surprisingly hot – come close), and without the sweetness or chiming highs. Vintage Ricky fans don't usually favor them, but they do have their uses, and players who mainly want to drive their amps into early breakup can often find them just the ticket.

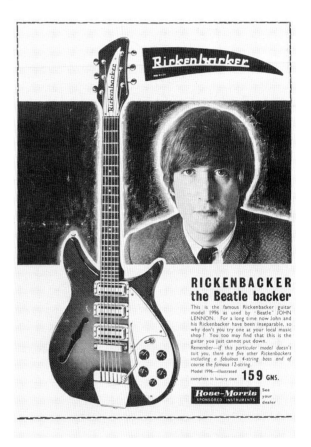

Twelve-string guitars have a very different playing feel to six-strings, and this is one 'conversion factor,' you could say, that Rickenbacker tackled extremely well in order to win over a sector of the electric guitar market. Along with the ungainly elongated headstock, acoustic 12-strings of the day – and today, for that matter – usually carry a wider neck and fingerboard than six-strings, a design feature obviously necessitated by the need to carry six extra strings, however closely spaced these are to the standard set.

Rickenbacker compacted down these dimensions to offer a fingerboard no wider than the average six-string (narrower than some, it happens), so it was no great stretch for the player to get his hand feeling comfortable with the new jangle machine. This can result, however, in a playing surface that feels to some players like a field crammed with narrowly spaced strings, and it often takes some settling in before you are able to finger string to fret with total accuracy, without taking part of a neighboring string along with you. Along the same lines, acoustic fingerstylists familiar with traditional 12-string dimensions might find it difficult to get enough grab down at the picking-hand end of things, with barely enough daylight between string pairs to insert fingertips or fingerpicks. Either way, the Rickenbacker 12-strings definitely have their intended styles and uses, and they suit them well.

Without its links to John Lennon, the 'three-quarter size' 325 might have ended up an also-ran in the Rickenbacker line-up.

Of course these guitars made most of their classic noises with flatwound, pure-nickel wrapped strings. That might sound today like an even odder choice of string for an electric 12-string than it does for a six-string, but I know of plenty of Beatles fans who just couldn't get 'that sound' on their 360/12s until they stumbled on this little piece of magic. Nickel-wrapped flats add further depth and sizzle to the sonic brew that really help to sweeten the overall result, while avoiding the grating harshness of some other string types.

One oddity I haven't yet mentioned is the makeup of the Ricky fingerboard itself, and the rosewood fingerboards in particular. Unlike most makes, Rickenbacker finishes all of its fingerboards with a heavy coat of varnish. This helps to make them long-wearing, but can also make them unfamiliar-feeling to players used to the traditional unvarnished Gibson or Fender rosewood 'boards – or just about any other, for that matter.

Through a Vox AC30, the 360/12 offers a chiming treble assault with just a slightly raw edge to give the sound some grit and bite. The bigger AC50 and AC100 amplifiers that The Beatles were using by the mid 1960s would back even larger doses of the former sonic characteristics, with less of the latter – an overall sound a little closer to that achieved by some US bands, most notably The Byrds, whose Roger McGuinn was often playing his Rickenbacker 12-string through a powerful Fender Showman Amp, or sometimes a large Marshall for British gigs.

If anything, it's arguable that McGuinn's sound is even more archetypal of the Ricky 12-string than a lot of Harrison's work – given its exaggerated chime and jangle – but the Byrds guitarist's sound is in fact a little further removed from the raw article. McGuinn has always been open about the fact that a heavy dose of compression made his 12-string style manageable in the studio, and applying a decent compressor pedal to a

The AC30 was carefully concocted with a firm eye on the needs of the user

360/12 or similar quickly gets you closer to that tone. Such treatment smoothes out the potentially harsh peaks of the instrument, softens the attack slightly, and adds a pleasant sustain that brings plenty of swell and shimmer into the otherwise percussive performance.

For much of his earlier work with The Who, Pete Townshend put similar six-string models through more powerful amps to elicit a bold, pounding rhythm sound – notably via an early 1960s Fender Bassman, a Marshall JTM45 and then 100W model, and finally Hiwatts, by which time his guitar of choice was shifting, too. Into such amps, all with more headroom than the AC30 (barring, arguably, the JTM45... which is probably why Townshend begged Jim Marshall to make him a 100-watter with an 8x12" cab), these toaster-tops fail to offer much breakup, but yield a great crystalline tonal thwack that packs plenty of punch when cranked. Mod British punk-popster Paul Weller brought the rig full circle with The Jam in the late 1970s and early 1980s, running his Rickenbacker 6-strings through Vox AC30 amps; the pairing has been a mainstay of Heartbreakers guitarists Tom Petty and Mike Campbell; and REM's Peter Buck revived the rig again in the early 1980s to make it the archetypal jangle sound of the indie guitar band. All of which takes us a long road from The Beatles, you might think, but Buck's sonic signature is in fact not a mile away from that of George Harrison circa 1964-66.

If the Rickenbacker 360/12 is a guitar legend, the Vox AC30 combo probably has even broader appeal as a vintage tone icon. Both the number of boutique imitations it has inspired and the fervency with which collectors and players alike chase good vintage examples of the original are indications of the status of this classic piece of kit. The AC30 benefits enormously from the same Beatles associations that inspired this chapter in the first place, of course, but has been used far and wide since that time, and for a surprisingly broad range of styles and sounds. A brief listen to the archetypal clean instrumental twang of Hank Marvin and The Shadows, the R&B-tinged pop-rock of The Yardbirds, the searing glam-rock lead work of Brian May with Queen, and the flat-out alt-rock grind of Dave Grohl with the Foofighters quickly defines this 30W tube combo's versatility. And the 45-year-old design has performed plenty of other tricks.

The AC30 is a follow-on model from Vox's original guitar amp of the late 1950s, the AC15, which has the oft-quoted distinction of being 'the first amplifier designed specifically for the guitar.' To make any

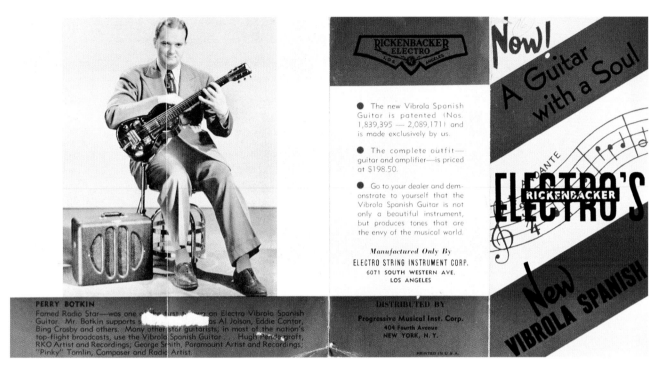

Perry Botkin with an early Rickenbacker Vibrola Spanish electric guitar.

sense to us, this needs some clarification. Of course plenty of amps prior to the Voxes were designed and manufactured specifically for the guitar, but the circuits at their core often came directly from tube manufacturers' application notes and popular design manuals of the time.

In that sense, they were general amplification circuits that were slightly modified by a range of manufacturers for use with guitar. Leo Fender, the Gibson designers, the folks at Valco and Premier and plenty of others would have dipped liberally into this collective circuit pool, and the success or failure of the amps they brought onto the market often relied upon how well they revamped the raw material to suit the needs of the guitarist.

Of course Dick Denney, the electronics wizard who designed the AC15 for Vox owner Tom Jennings, would have worked with many of these circuits himself. With a plethora of good working templates already in existence, no designer is going to start entirely from scratch. It's unlikely, then, that the AC15 can claim originality of its guitar-intended birth from the ground up, but it does carry a lot of features that indicate it was carefully concocted with a firm grip on the needs of the end user.

This amp's cathode biasing and lack of negative feedback give plenty of sparkling, slightly unchained chime to the guitar's upper-mids and highs, thanks to the way they encourage the second harmonics as artifacts of its distortion. This offers a flattering tonality at low and middle volume levels, though often these design elements just aren't suitable in large amps. But of course these elements already existed – in many smaller tweed Fenders, some Gibson's and plenty of others.

Certain things hadn't been seen before, though; the AC15 contained a channel using an EF86 pentode preamp tube, both a higher-gain and somewhat more high-fidelity tube than the 12AY7 and 12AX7 usually used in this position. As used by Denney, the EF86 offered a hot, full-voiced signal to further stages of

Roger McGuinn's playing with The Byrds offers some of the best recorded examples of classic Rickenbacker 12-string jangle.

the amp, which did a good job of passing along the instrument's full frequency range.

In letting the output stage run 'open loop' – that is, free from any negative feedback-derived damping – he offered a rich, touch-sensitive, and therefore very playable performance when slightly pushed with the volume up towards halfway or beyond. Bigger amps generally require some negative feedback at this stage to help prevent them from slipping into runaway oscillation or to generally just keep them from being too howly or uncontrollable at higher volumes. A negative feedback loop suppresses harmonic distortion, which lets you push clean playing to louder levels, and also keeps down the output-stage noise some. In a sub-40W amp, however, refraining from creating such a loop (a simple thing in itself) can yield an amp with an open, aggressive voice that a lot of players love. Non-negative feedback amps can feel more dynamic to the player's attack, and their onset of distortion is smoother (as well as quicker).

Cathode biasing is often found hand-in-hand with a lack of negative feedback not because the two 'go together' by any necessity, but because both elements do cooperate toward similar sonic goals. A designer looking for optimum efficiency and tame, clean performance will employ neither (that is, install a negative feedback loop, and use grid biasing on the output tubes); one aiming for more of a raw, unchained voice when cranked will go the Vox road. Cathode biasing is a more archaic form of biasing in guitar ampsville, and an extremely simple means of setting the tubes' operational levels, too, but not a particularly efficient one. Cathode biasing doesn't allow a set of tubes to reach their maximum output potential in wattage terms, and therefore volume, as does the more advanced 'fixed bias' technique (which is usually in fact a variable bias set via a circuit linked to the grid rather than the cathode of the tube). But the former does induce a certain juicy fatness that sounds great with a lot of bluesy and rootsy-rock'n'roll guitar styles, along with – once again – a smoother and earlier onset of distortion. As they both go part way toward achieving the same results, though via different means, they are often, though not always, used together.

The AC15's tone circuit (and originally that of the AC30) was not unlike the simple treble-bleed Tone controls of so many other amps. But the phase inverter displays some clever new thinking in guitar voicing, in a stage specifically intended to emphasize the midrange frequencies prevalent in the guitar. Add all of these together with the sweet, musical tonality of the two EL84 tubes in its output section, and you have an amp that is extremely flattering to the guitar – especially when used to play the rock'n'roll that was then sweeping the UK and which formed Jennings's main intended market.

Notice that I haven't yet mentioned the term 'class A.' This is a thorny subject, and a very technical one to get to the bottom of, too. Vox's AC15 and AC30 are often pointed to as 'classic examples of pure class A guitar amps.' But without actually putting one up on the test equipment, or going into all the science regarding such an amp's operating class at various drive levels given the output tubes' bias point and operating voltages, it's worth pointing out that an AC15 or AC30 actually shifts between class A and class AB operation depending upon the volume at which it is played and how hard it is pushed. Nominally 'class AB' amplifiers such as Fender's tweed Bassman or blackface Deluxe Reverb or Marshall's JTM45 or Plexi – or any of 'em, for that matter – exhibit similar operational shifts depending on drive levels, but they may do so at different points.

Class Consciousness

Class A performance (or performance of any class) is determined by measuring an amp at maximum output before distortion; run into distortion, or well short of distortion at far less than max output, the amp might be operating at something other than its actual scientifically-measurable class, but this might be where we are playing that amp 99 per cent of the time we plug it in. For this reason class designation is something of a smoke screen for guitarists. Getting over excited about whether an amp is 'class A' or 'class AB' can be misdirecting, and there are better ways to predict if an amp's sound will be to your liking or not than bending over backwards to define supposed class types. As mentioned a few paragraphs ago, a non-negative feedback amp can feel more dynamic to the player's attack, and its onset of distortion is smoother and comes earlier in its output level, and cathode biasing carries similar sonic attributes – both something frequently attributed to class A amps, hence in part, the confusion. The long and short of it is that the Vox AC15 and AC30's legendary tone owes far more to its cathode biasing, lack of a negative feedback circuit, EL84 output tubes, and Celestion-made Vox Bulldog speaker than it does to any rigid adherence to class A operation, trumped up or otherwise.

Players – and marketing departments – today enthuse about the smoother onset of distortion in class A amps, and the sweeter tone of that distortion, thanks to its bounty of second and third harmonics and so forth. All of these may be true, which is to say, true of a good cathode-biased tube amp with no negative feedback in the output section when driven into class A operation. But it's worth remembering that Dick Denney wasn't

The point at which these amps distorted marked the point of the designers' shame and failure

designing an AC15 to be played dirty in 1956, nor Leo Fender his 5E3 tweed Deluxe (also a cathode-biased, no-neg-feedback design, though with 6V6 tubes), and so forth. Amp-makers and most players other than your more rebellious rock'n'rollers and bluesers were still looking for maximum clean volume at a given rating, and the point at which these amps segued into distortion marked the point of the designers' shame and failure. Of course good ears both onstage and at the work bench recognized the significant role 'distortion' in the literal sense played in sweetening and thickening up a tube amp's sound for use with guitar, but this was still a parameter quantified within an overall clean sound; low specs for total harmonic distortion (THD) were still a matter of pride in those days.

As a side note, it is telling that you don't see the term 'class A' bandied about a whole lot in the Vox magazine ads of the early 1960s, nor do you see other makers of the day desperate to jump on the class A bandwagon. Today, however, any amp-maker offering a product with that familiar chimey, harmonically-rich frequency response derived of cathode biasing and a lack of negative feedback sticks a prominent 'class A' badge on their product and all over their advertising. Some of the claims appear truly outrageous when you understand even this little bit about what class A really is, and isn't, but the marketing departments are pretty confident that few consumers are going to put their products to any of the tests required to prove them wrong, and even for a qualified amp tech it's difficult to conclusively prove any such claim an out-and-out lie. Okay, back to the Voxes at hand.

Come 1960 and groups needed more stage volume than the 15W AC15 could provide, so Vox simply doubled the amp's output section to offer the 30W AC30 (actually they usually put out about 18W and 35W respectively, but we'll stick to the nominal figures for now). Not a powerful amp by today's standards, perhaps, but in an open-back cab with two efficient and great sounding Blue Bulldog speakers it was – and is – a powerful package for its size. For the AC30/4, the figure after the '/' denoting the number of inputs (two per-channel), Denney dropped the EF86-powered channel and initially included just a basic Volume plus Tone channel driven by one 12AX7 (ECC83 in Europe), and another with switchable Tremolo and Vibrato; the AC30/6 also had a Bright channel. The EF86 is a pretty cool preamp tube in many ways, powerful and meaty sounding, but the over-fussy design required to employ it, perhaps, and the fact that they were less plentiful than the 12AX7s used everywhere else probably led to its exclusion. Even some examples from great old tube manufacturers like Mullard and GEC can be prone to microphony after heavy use, too, so there are a number of reasons that guitar amp-makers have largely steered clear of it. Note that recent-era boutique makers such as Matchless and Dr Z have employed the EF86 in some designs, and it has occasionally been popular in tube hi-fi circles, although it is used differently in the latter designs, and doesn't take the same vibrational pounding either.

Crank up one of these basic Volume-and-Tone models and there's plenty of chime and a very sweet onset of distortion, along with a certain warmth and 'thickness' that a few AC30 fans have always preferred. Groups of the day wanted even more high-end cut in their guitar sound, however – as we see time and again in the inspiration of designs from the 1960s – so Denney devised the famous active/interactive Top Boost tone circuit. This was available in 1961 as a factory add-on or a couple years later as a factory-original model option, Denny's new creation employed an extra ECC83/12AX7 tube in a highly interactive circuit with Treble and Bass controls that actually boosted these frequencies, rather than merely cutting them as in the passive tone stacks of most amps.

The Top Boost Tops The Line

The Bass, Middle and Treble controls on the standard Fender Bassman or Marshall Plexi, for example, are also interactive tone controls, meaning where you set the Bass affects the available frequency range that the Treble and Middle can play with, and so on. On these and the majority of amps, however, these knobs merely control simple one-capacitor filters that drain off a proportion of the stated frequency range to ground, where it won't trouble your tone as it passes on down the signal chain. A Top Boost tone stage uses very much the same circuit, but its application in the Vox AC30 has the effect of yielding a more 'active' feeling EQ, which can push low and high-frequency levels to greater extremes.. Leave Bass at around 8:00 (as in o'clock) and crank Treble to 3:00, and the tone is thin and emasculated in extremes, a real 'no bass' rather than just a 'low bass' tone, as the Treble robs the other frequencies of the available gain. Set both at 1:00 then wind them slowly down together to around 9:00, and the midrange come pressing forward. Now ease the Bass up from here to just 11:00 or so, leaving Treble alone, and hear the whole thing thicken up as the lower-mids begin to dominate.

It's a powerful tool, but too much so for some players' tastes, and the TB stage usually takes a lot of playing around with to get the hang of. Most who get good results from it use it subtly, and even that subtle boost gives the AC30 added crystalline sparkle and bite, and a kind of hyper sensitivity of EQing that plenty of players love. For that reason, an early fawn-colored AC30 with factory-added Top Boost circuit (its dual controls found mounted on an added plate at the back of the amp in this case) is among the most desirable of all models for collectors, while the vintage 'player's AC30' of choice is the mid-1960s AC30TB model with the Bass and Treble controls added to the main control panel. For years, Vox techs have made a decent sideline out of adding factory-mod style Top Boost stages to the non-TB Voxes of players who acquired them long after the Jennings Musical Industries factory had closed its doors to such work... or anything else.

Not so often discussed is the AC30's Cut control, part of both TB and non-TB models, which is a more unusual variable filter (or treble bleed) that works in line following the phase inverter to reduce harshness in the high end. In effect, this works in the opposite way to a Presence control, although it is derived from a very different circuit, by smoothing out the highs in the signal coming from any or all channels just before it reaches the EL84 output tubes – the higher you turn it, the less treble you are left with. It's a great control for balancing out characteristics of different types of guitars run successively through the amp: taking a little brightness out of a Stratocaster, adding a little sparkle and cut to a thick Les Paul, etc. This is another feature that plenty of modern boutique makers have borrowed from the good old AC30, and you will find Cut controls (as well as Top Boost-derived tone sections) on Matchless DC/30s and TopHat Club and King Royales and others besides.

Add it all up and you've got an amp with impressive versatility in the EQ department, the ability to

In its heyday, Rickenbacker's line-up was broader than many players today might realize.

transmit a broad portion of the flattering and depth-creating harmonic spectrum of the instrument, an extremely sweet onset of distortion, plenty of grind when cranked, and just enough midrange emphasis to add that punch and bite where it really matters, but not so much as to sound nasal or honking. We've already discussed the joys of a Rickenbacker 12- or six-string through the thing; inject a Fender Telecaster and you've got a luscious blend of twang, twinkle and grit, or try a humbucker-loaded Gibson solidbody for a really wailing lead machine. All this, and we haven't even properly assessed the beastie's speaker selection yet.

So many little bits of magic add up to create the sonic splendor that is the Vox AC30, but the Celestion-made, Vox-branded 'Blue Bulldog' speakers are one of the single most influential components in this entire signal chain. Rated at a paltry 15W power handling, they were never going to be a speaker of the arena rock or high gain eras. But singly in an AC15 or paired in an AC30 they are perhaps the sweetest-toned speaker known to man.

The Bite Of The Blue Bulldog

Simply labeled 'G12' at the Celestion factory – for 12″ guitar speaker – these feature the light, ribbed pulp-paper cone, agile 'spider,' paper voice coil former, and efficient and musical alnico magnet that add up to a driver that's both quick to respond and easy to get and keep moving, as well as one beautifully voiced for guitar reproduction. While this combination of design and constructional factors can't take a massive wattage, it makes for extremely impressive efficiency, and at 100 dB (measured at 1W/1m) the 'Blue' has always been among the loudest speakers available designed specifically for guitar amps.

Yes, they have their drawbacks, aside from the low power handling. These include loose lows, not a lot of tight sparkle in the high end, some midrange overemphasis and maybe a little more aggression and growl than some players want in a driver. But in the right format, all of these join in with the G12's many plusses to make a speaker from heaven. A little blurring in the treble when pushed adds a sizzle to the upper frequency spectrum that is really pleasing to the ear, making it less sharp than the bountiful high-KHz assault of a JBL D120F or a Jensen P12N, for example. Most players of amps in which you find this speaker, or would want to install one, aren't looking for a gut-wrenching, moshpit-mashing low-end thump, either, so its absence isn't a major flaw. Similarly, their fast attack, aggression and growl when walloped hard are more delights than drawbacks in the amps that feature them. For all of these reasons, the Blue Bulldog – in or out of its Vox – has become a much valued and proportionally expensive vintage unit in itself, and highly sought-after by tone hounds. Due to both desirability factors and survival rates, individual speakers aren't a lot easier to find than good vintage AC30s themselves (many of which will have recones or replacements anyway), but Celestion's current Alnico Blue is a great reissue of the original and a fantastic sounding speaker by any standards, even if very expensive itself.

The whole matter of speaker efficiency deserves a little more consideration. Note that a 35W AC30 with loud, plummy Vox Blues in an open-backed cab will easily be as loud as, or even outperform, a 50W-60W combo with a pair of middling 93dB-95dB drivers (a range into which many fall, while plenty of others even fall below it). These speaker efficiency figures aren't often quoted in plain sight of the consumer – unless it's a point the manufacturer is keen to brag about – but you can see that players who feel they need a 50-60W 2x12″ to suit their gigging needs can come home with amps offering very different maximum volume levels, depending upon speaker type and efficiency, and not even know it until they take that combo out and find it is underperforming the rhythm guitarist's old 30W AC30. Dig a little deeper, and any major speaker manufacturer will publish its models' efficiency specs, somewhere. Those for Celestion, the Jensen Vintage Reissues, and the Eminence range are all pretty easy to come by in their product literature.

Cabinet design deserves a mention, too. The AC30's plywood cabinet, with its semi-open back, has a punchy yet warm presentation that is well suited to its use. With a firmly fixed and relatively thick speaker baffle, it's prone to less baffle and cab resonance than, for example, a tweed Fender, but at higher volumes the relatively compact 2x12″ cabinetry certainly gets humming and singing along, too. Even so, it offers more punch and quickness in its delivery than the solid pine/floating baffle construction of a Bassman or a Super Amp, to name a couple, but has a similar 'surround-sound' dispersion to the Fenders, thanks to the opening between upper and lower back panels. The same also makes for a rich, singing high end (with that slight blurring, mentioned before), and a more open sound than that to be had from closed-back cabs.

Of course the closed-back AC30 Super Twin bottom cab – part of the rig frequently used by The Beatles on stage, for one – would sling this tonal shoe onto the other foot, and yield a woofier, more directional presentation with less singing highs. Neither is an especially deep cabinet dimensionally, and a little more girth would have given a slightly more muscular low-frequency performance to those who desire it, but that's the way it is. Anecdotally, stick a reissue Alnico Blue in a significantly deeper cab such as that of TopHat's Club Royale combo – essentially half an AC30, on steroids – and the low-end oomph is impressive, especially considering its open-backed design.

As ever, the variables contained within this classic piece of kit are many, but most players would agree that they add up to create a stunning whole that easily outreaches the sum of its parts. And hell, most of us would be delighted to scrape together a few of those parts.

As ever, vintage prices associated with attaining an original of this rig can put off plenty of potential jangle-rockers. Rickenbacker offers some good reissues of many of its classic models, however, including the 360/12. One complaint offered by reissue players seeking a truly vintage sound is that the reissue toaster-top pickups are far hotter than those of the mid 1960s. Otherwise, the materials in the pickups are much like those of c1964, so some of these same players are solving the problem by literally unwinding the pickup coils – or having it done for them – until they approach the approximately 7.5k ohm reading that seems to attain the sweet spot for 12-string sparkle and chime. Don't launch into such an operation without experience and the proper instruction. Or better yet, get a pro to undertake the work.

Similarly, Vox offers its own reissue of the AC30TB, and it is a sturdy and good-sounding version of the original. It is built somewhat differently, of course, using PCBs and other modern components for cost efficiency, but still gets close to the sound. Any vintage example you track down will always sound a little different to the reissue – as it will to any other vintage example – as these have had some 40 years to age and loosen up. But The Beatles weren't playing 40-year-old AC30s in 1963, so who's to say the reissue doesn't sound closer to the original in its birth year than a 40-odd-year-old and potentially very tired out original does today? The AC30 rivals the tweed Fender Bassman in being a much-copied amp in the boutique world, and that's not a bad thing. This trend has provided countless players with good working and sounding versions of the Vox magic at lower (well, slightly lower, at least) prices than those of a healthy 1960-'67 AC30. In truth, one of these – through the right cab with a pair of nicely broken-in Alnico Blues – might get you as close as possible to fresh and toothsome sounds of an original AC30 c1965 – or sound so damn tasty in trying that you just won't care anyway.

Clean-cut kid Dick Dale – making a mean sound with a Strat into Reverb into Dual Showman.

SETUP 5
SURF'S UP

The sound of instrumental surf music is easily defined by tracks like the Chantays' 'Pipeline,' Dick Dale and the Del-Tones' 'Let's Go Trippin'' and 'Misirlou,' and the Surfari's 'Wipeout.' It never strays very far from these templates. The gear used to achieve it is equally simple to identify, and easier to pin down than that required for other classic pop and rock sounds. In the late 1950s and early 1960s, when the surf craze swept the west coast, Fender Musical Instruments was *the* California electric guitar brand. Although the saxophone makes an occasional appearance, surf music is guitar music, and the surf guitar sound is Fender all the way.

Deciding on one single artist to credit with the surf sound isn't quite so easy, however. Dick Dale is frequently hailed as 'King Of The Surf Guitar,' and he arguably created the most sensation for the sound by filling the Rendezvous Ballroom in Balboa, and later the Pasadena Civic Auditorium, with standing-room crowds of 3,000 to 4,000 every weekend night of the year in the early 1960s. He also arguably generated the most energy, with his furious vibrato-picked solos and frenetic musical embodiment of the whole surfer lifestyle. But some fans of the music would credit the obscure garage band The Northern Lights with recording the first surf tune, 'Typhoid,' in 1961, or The Bel Airs with being the first genuine surf band; their 'Mr Moto' single of 1961 is also certainly archetypal (although their sound contained heavy elements of sax and piano, so they're not appropriate for our purposes). The entire genre was certainly prefigured by instrumental rock'n'roll and pop tunes from artists such as Duane Eddy, The Ventures, The Shadows from Britain, Link Wray, Johnny and The Hurricanes and others, but many of these were tamer and, crucially, existed before the 'surf' tag was coined – and didn't entirely capture what we now think of as 'the sound.'

When pop music was going clean and respectable, the surf bands inherited rock'n'roll's rebelliousness

It's easy to see how the music evolved from rock'n'roll instrumentals, garage bands and the wilder fringes of rockabilly, with elements of country, Latin, film score, R&B and other genres blended in, although it burst forth in a style all its own. When pop music was going clean and respectable in the early 1960s, the surf bands inherited rock'n'roll's rebelliousness of half a decade earlier, set the west coast and occasionally other parts of the country alight for a few years, then – surprisingly quickly – died away.

For the above reasons, rather than trying to encapsulate the sound and rig of a single guitarist, let's frame the music with a few alternatives of guitars, amps and effects, all of which can excellently capture the sound, and have proven definitive in the hands of various artists.

Titan Of Twang

It still warrants turning to Dick Dale for the entire picture, but since his guitar of choice – the pre-CBS Fender Stratocaster – has already been covered, we won't dwell on that part of his rig. For looks almost as much as for sound, Fender's Jazzmaster and Jaguar have been the dual lodestones of the retro surf crowd, but Dale's Stratocaster, blonde Fender Dual Showman Amp, and outboard Fender Reverb define one direction of the sound as precisely as any rig could hope to.

That said, Dale's sound and style was and is heavier and more aggressive than that of many other surf instrumentalists. Like most studio efforts of the early 1960s, his recorded sound was somewhat reined in by old-school engineers, but his live assault has always been breathtaking, and probably more representative of his energy. Even before he had scored his early hits, Dale was trying to craft a sound that recreated the thundering, swirling frenzy of the actual surfing experience – and volume, speed and motion were a major part of that. He was already playing a Fender Stratocaster by the late 1950s, and, from their introduction in 1960-61, the Fender Showman and Dual Showman amps – which Dale helped Fender to develop – proved the best possible way to bring that experience to a packed crowd of 4,000 dancing fans.

While the cranked Showman at the end of Dale's Strat definitely had some growl to it, the objective was always to achieve maximum loud, clean punch and cut. A firm, tight, atmospheric surroundsound of twang that could transmit gut-thumping lows and shimmering highs. While the Stratocaster gave the Showman a bright, snappy, full-frequency signal that was unlikely to overdrive such an amp by itself, other recently introduced Fender guitars were even more suited to the clean, sharp, and oft-vibratoed sound that defined the surf bands, the majority of whom played with somewhat less aggression than Dale. For many others, the Fender Jazzmaster and Jaguar offered the epitome of west-coast twang; and while the two are outwardly similar, they have a few crucial differences of design that make them more second cousins and siblings.

Both of these guitars have pickups with a slightly lower output than those of the Strat, but their sounds differ distinctly. The Jazzmaster was introduced in 1958 in a bid by Fender to broaden its guitar roster and, as the name suggests, appeal to the jazzmen who were then and now the least likely of all electric guitarists to pick up the radical bolt-together solidbodies of this Californian upstart. The Jazzmaster was still bolt-together in design, and arguably even more radical in look and function than a Strat or a Tele, but it was Fender's top model at the time, retailing at $329 verses $274.50 for a 1958 Stratocaster with tremolo. A couple of significant points of its design did genuinely aim to address the jazzer's needs – but history would prove these not enough for the intended upmarket clientele.

The Jazzmaster was built to the same 25 ½" scale length as the Telecaster and Stratocaster, with body woods of ash (sunburst or blonde) or alder (opaque custom colors), and a 21-fret maple neck with a headstock similar to, but subtly different from, the Strat's. This neck carried, however, Fender's first

Another gem from the long-running ad series. Looks like some mighty polite waltzing for one nasty surf guitar.

rosewood fingerboard – originally an unbound version with white 'clay' dot markers – that was intended to give the guitar a more traditional look and feel. Strangely, a bound-fingerboard model only came along in 1965, after the guitar was already arguably failing at its intentions, although you would think this might be a feature that would appeal to jazz players more familiar with traditional hollowbody archtops.

While the woods and solid but contoured/routed construction were the same, the Jazzmaster's body differed significantly from the Strat's in shape – echoing the form of its predecessor, certainly, but looking much like it had been held too close to the fire and melted. The radical offset-waist design had the appearance of a guitar that had been sawn down the middle and the two halves 'slid' slightly away from each other. It was a groovy shape, for sure, hip, even stylish by most standards, but yielded a slightly cumbersome feel in itself, and was spoiled visually by the oversized pickguard required to carry its collection of odd, mismatched controls. Still, it was a pretty ergonomic shape, and comfort and balance were both good.

In fact the Jazzmaster's electronics are clever in concept, offering different presettable lead and rhythm sounds accessed at the flick of a slider switch mounted near the bass-side horn, beside roller pots for setting the rhythm sound Tone and Volume. More traditionally mounted and styled Volume and Tone pots and a Gibson-like three-way toggle switch mounted on the stumpy treble-side horn for pickup selections and levels for the lead sound. It was a versatile package, but never looked quite right, was a little awkward for many guitarists to use, and for most was probably just surplus to requirements.

The pickups themselves were probably the most significant part of the new instrument and, along with the rosewood fingerboard, were the second feature hotly tipped to snare the jazz player. These are as wide and even longer than Gibson's then-new humbuckers, but were in fact still single-coil units, wound with wide, flat coils that produced a smooth, full-throated sound that was warmer and thicker than the Strat's or Tele's thanks to its wider magnetic window. The bridge pickup could still be bright and snappy, but the neck pickup definitely tended more toward 'the jazz sound' than anything Fender had produced before… yet players of that genre almost unanimously ignored it, outside a few well-placed (and usually fairly short-lived) endorsees. For many guitarists chasing the hot new west-coast craze, on the other hand, the Jazzmaster's electronics proved just the thing. You could flick from sharp, trebly lead runs to smooth, staccato bass-string lines in a semi-quaver, the guitar resolutely refused to overdrive most larger amps, and its lack of sustain and diminished resonance further thinned out the sound in a way that was often appealing to the genre.

These latter design drawbacks – or pluses, if you're a surfer (or, later, grunger or indie rocker) – can largely be attributed to the new 'floating' tremolo system first fitted to the Jazzmaster. This piece of hardware differed greatly from the Stratocaster's tremolo tailpiece with bridge saddles mounted on a single, integral unit, and multiple long springs mounted in a cavity at the back of the guitar. Instead, the Jazzmaster's vibrato employed a tailpiece with the mechanical workings and a single, shorter, wider spring mounted beneath a stubbier steel plate, from which the string anchor piece and vibrato arm protruded. A

The 'floating' tremolo system was a clever design but it inhibited the instrument's acoustic qualities

separate 'fulcrum' style bridge was mounted on a small, pointed allen screw at either end which allowed it to rock back and forth slightly with the vibrato motion, thereby increasing tuning stability. It was a clever design, resulting in a shorter but arguably smoother travel than the Strat's tremolo. But it also inhibited the acoustic qualities of the instrument in a number of ways.

First of all, the Jazzmaster's strings are more lightly anchored than those of a Strat, and simply pass through the moving metal tailpiece plate of the vibrato unit rather than being threaded through a weighty inertia block. The considerable string length from bridge to vibrato anchor point and a fairly low tension

This gorgeously yellowed olympic white 1959 Fender Jazzmaster and 1965 Dual Showman make as big and bold a sound as any surf fanatic could hope for. Just add reverb as desired.

over the saddles can result in some buzzing at extremes, and generally poor transfer of the strings' vibrational energy into the bridge – and therefore the body – in most setups. The fulcrum bridge itself succeeds well enough in its own intentions, but isn't the most solid design you'll find, and it further weakens the transfer of acoustic vibrations. The new vibrato unit carried another extra: a sliding button that locked off the tailpiece to prevent the guitar from shifting out of tune when a string broke. It was a fiddly feature at best, and it was often difficult to get the thing working consistently.

All of this results in a tone with less 'woodiness' and body-generated acoustic warmth than is present in more solidly-strung designs, and a shorter sustain, too. However, this can also up the twang factor to some extent, yielding a percussive jangle that works well for surf and some older rock'n'roll styles. An after-market part designed to combat these string-tension drawbacks on Jazzmasters (and Jaguars) has been available for a number of years, in the form of a tension-bar mounted to a metal plate that screws directly to the top of the original vibrato plate. The strings pass under this bar on their way to the bridge, which they reach at a sharper break angle, which in turn increases the pressure of strings upon saddles and improves both stability in the slots and the transfer of vibrational energy.

Upon its introduction in 1958, the Jazzmaster carried black pickup covers and a gold anodized scratchplate – both gone by the following year.

An Upmarket Short-scale

Fender's Jaguar of 1962 was another bid to broaden the range, and the next candidate for top-of-the-line Fender. It carried the same body shape and similar pickguard lines as the Jazzmaster, but a few crucial changes were onboard. The Jag was built with a shorter 24″ scale-length for easier fretting and bending (although these were never really blues-bender style guitars), and a less full-frequencied voice. This neck was unique among Fenders of the time, too, for carrying 22 frets rather than the usual 21. Also, it carried new pickups designed both to combat some of the noise and occasional microphony of the Jazzmaster's pickups and to offer a brighter, tighter sound. These were thinner than those of its cousin, and looked much like a Strat's pickups but with added notched steel frames on the sides and another unseen on the bottom, intended to help shield the single-coil units from hum.

Like the Jazzmaster, the Jaguar carried switching for separate rhythm and lead sounds, with the same slide switch and roller controls on the bass-side horn, but featured three more slider switches near the treble-side cutaway for pickup selection and a 'strangle' tone created by a low-end filter. All were mounted on metal control plates, too, rather than directly on the pickguard as on the Jazzmaster. Overall it was clearly an effort to create an even more upmarket, 'deluxe' guitar than the Jazzmaster, but the result was mainly an instrument that was even more confusing for players to get to grips with.

The Jag carried the Jazzmaster's vibrato tailpiece – with all of its inherent lightness of tone – but with an added mute mounted to the bridge, constructed of a foam-rubber strip attached to a spring activated metal plate that the player could flick up into contact with the strings to affect a damped, palm-mute-like tone. The 'ticky-ticky' muted sound was popular at the time (again, plenty of guitar instrumentals carried at least one muted lead passage). But the effect was easy enough even for most novice players to accomplish with the edge of the picking hand, and for most this bridge mute got in the way more than anything. Also, a few years down the road when the foam-rubber hardened up and lost its elasticity, flicking this mute into position would often merely raise the guitar's pitch by a half-step rather than yielding the desired 'ticky-ticky' sound. It's not uncommon to find vintage Jags today that long ago had these mutes removed from them.

It isn't clear whether the Jaguar was designed specifically for the surf crowd, but it suited the music perfectly. The guitar enjoyed a few years of popularity when first released, but ultimately proved less versatile – and certainly more labor-intensive to play and switch – than either the Telecaster and Stratocaster, and has never rivaled these twin Fender flagships. The prices of both Jaguars and Jazzmasters on the vintage market certainly bear this out, and original vintage models sell for only a fraction of the prices commanded by Strats and Teles from the same era, although the former were more expensive guitars when bought new in the late 1950s and early 1960s. (The author's first serious guitar as a kid was a 1964 – ie, pre-CBS – Fender Jaguar bought in 1975 for $200, when Strats of the same year were already commanding upwards of $1,000. A second Jag, an all-original sunburst debut-year model from 1962, was bought in 1995 for only $500 – what would an original '62 Strat have cost you even ten years ago? Neither stayed in the arsenal for long.)

Sonics aside, the Jag and Jazzmaster look is somehow just right for warm California evenings, breaking curls, and a sandy shindig stage – especially when they come clothed in a custom color. Fender custom colors were just coming into their own in the early 1960s, and the sweeping automotive lines and sparkling chrome of a Jaguar seems to demand a fiesta red, surf green, daphne blue or burgundy mist finish even more than any Stratocaster ever did. They are cool guitars, however you slice 'em, and although their workings slide somewhat outside the usual utilitarian Fender envelope of simple functionality, they are surf machines all the way.

Whatever the color, a Jazzmaster or Jaguar into a late 1950s tweed Bassman, Super or Deluxe amplifier with the volume cranked toward full yields a crunchy, bluesy wail. But this is far from the desired effect for surf music. Jack it through the Tolex-covered Showman that came along just a year later, however, and you've got a chunky, bright, thundering and pretty damn clean assault on the ears and gut – and this is just what's needed to reproduce the feel of that surging swell and breaking curl.

The Fender Showman Amp introduced in 1960 blended the output section of the high-powered tweed Twin and the preamp and tone controls of the larger new Fender Tolex amps, so in its constituent parts it was nothing particularly new. In the execution of the whole package, however, it was a revelation – a concerted effort to corral these new high-powered capabilities and really make them roar, and it was an enormous success as such. It was also historical in being Fender's first production model 'piggy back' amp. Born the same year that the tweed Bassman examined in Setup 4 died, this was a very different amp indeed, and a major step forward toward the powerful amplification of the future.

Silicon (solid state) rectification delivered a steady, low-sag DC power supply to four 6L6 or 5881 output tubes and a hefty, redesigned OT that together were capable of putting out a steady 85W of low-

FLOATING TREMOLO / FENDER MUTE / SHORT SCALE NECK
22 FRETS / OFFSET WAIST DESIGN / SPECIAL DESIGN PICKUPS

the Sensational new

FENDER
JAGUAR

The Fender Jaguar is believed to be one of the finest
solid body electric guitars that has been offered to
the public. Every serious guitarist is urged to try
the Jaguar and discover its many new
tone and playing characteristics.

distortion power, with peaks of upwards of 150W. The high-powered Twins of the late 1950s had the same output-tube configuration, but a less efficient OT, and in other way – as we shall see – the new Showman was an entirely new concept in clean, high-volume playing, rather than just another amp that doubled the output power and hoped for the best. This amp's preamp and tone stack were all new, and its phase inverter was state of the art for the time, as were these stages in all of the new piggy-back 'Professional Amplifiers' series of blonde Tolex amps, which included the Bandmaster, Bassman, Twin and Tremolux along with the two Showmans.

Preamp tubes were now the higher-gain 12AX7s (or equivalent 7025s), and the circuit surrounding them was changed significantly. The volume and tone controls – just Bass and Treble on the Showman – were now placed between the plate (anode) of the preamp tube's first gain stage (or triode) and the grid of its second, which yielded a tighter, more high-fidelity, and some would argue less touch-sensitive response than the cathode-follower tone stack of the tweed amps. The result was more headroom in the preamp's overall response, and tone controls that acted more precisely as such, without also doubling as

Tan and early blonde Tolex amps carried one of the most advanced tremolo circuits ever seen

gain-tweakers the way those on many tweed amps did. The 'long-tailed pair' phase inverter was also an extremely efficient design, and introduced a minimum of its own distortion into the signal. For all this, however, the relatively low voltages fed to the preamp tubes, along with DC levels fed to the power tubes that were not pushed as high as they would be in coming models, meant these blonde and tan Showmans were a little juicier and more tactile, and not entirely as clean, as the blackface versions that would follow.

Tan and early blonde Tolex amps still employed the Presence control of the larger tweed Fenders, which offered a little extra high-end sparkle, tapped from the negative feedback loop around the output section. They also carried one of the most advanced tremolo circuits ever seen on popular tube guitar amps (conversely named 'vibrato,' in a continuation of the Fender company's efforts to confuse the two effects), which used a full two and a half preamp tubes (verses the one tube of blackface Fenders and many others) to produce its deep, rich, hypnotic wobble. To top off what lay inside, the amp's front-mounted control panel was a revolutionary, forward-looking feature in its day and a bold step from Fender, and as revered as all things tweed are today, the rugged, wipe-clean Tolex covering was a major improvement in cabinet protection. You better believe that in 1960 those gleaming ivory amp stacks with controls in full view were a sight to behold on the guitar store floor, or surf-gig stage.

As much of a wonder as the amp itself was, the Showman's speaker cabinet was the product of intensive and well-focused R&D. These make an excellent example of an early equipment manufacturer going to great lengths to recognize the importance of the role that a speaker enclosure plays in an amplifier's performance, and were the product of some clever notions of how to cleanly and efficiently reproduce the energy of a high-powered, relatively low-distortion output section, without introducing too much of the speaker distortion that was almost omnipresent in any cranked tube amp up to this day. While the tweed and tan Tolex Twins carried the same output rating as would the Showman, along with two heavy-duty Jensen P12N or C12N speakers, their open-backed cabinets never quite maximized the amps' volume potential; something entirely new was needed.

Original Showman speaker cabs of 1960-'61 were closed-back enclosures carrying either a 12″ or 15″ high-powered JBL D120 or D130 driver, mounted to a metal 'tone ring' and an elaborate ported false-baffle arrangement mounted behind the cabinet's fixed front speaker baffle. The closed back dampened low-frequency resonance and thereby helped the driver's cone handle the heavy work of loud bass reproduction without straining, and the complex ported baffle arrangement served to decouple the speaker slightly from the cabinet to further aid efficient reproduction of the low end. The seemingly odd tone-ring, or 'Speaker Projector Ring' in some Fender literature, served to decouple the speaker somewhat from the inner baffle, and thereby to reduce the phase-cancelling effects experienced in the clash of sound projected from the front and back of the cone. All of this meant that players seeking a real gut-thumping response from their low-string runs and power chords didn't have to lean too heavily on the amp top's own Bass control, or demand as much from the output tubes and OT in low-frequency-handling duties, so there was more on tap for midrange punch and high-end sparkle. On top of this, the cab's tilt-back legs offered a simple but effective aid to sound projection. In short, a few clever twists in the speaker cab meant a better overall performance from the amp itself.

Dick Dale Turns Amp Designer

The Dual Showman model that followed the originals went so far as enclosing two 15″ JBLs in a single cabinet with individual baffles but without the elaborate dual-baffle and tone ring arrangement of its predecessors, for a truly eviscerating aural assault with positively bovine low-end content. As for design considerations, however, the single-15″ Showman of 1960-'62 is arguably a more impressive beast, and illustrates an amp-maker's foresight in using speaker enclosure design to greatly determine how the amp's electrics perform – a truly interactive coupling of the top and bottom of the piggy-back set.

It's worth noting, also, that the Showman is significant as this chapter's amp of choice – the only possible choice, really – because the young Dick Dale himself put considerable thought into the model's development. As mentioned near the top of this chapter, the lefty surfer had been a Stratocaster player since the mid 1950s (originally playing a right-handed guitar upside down without reversing the strings), and was seeking an amp that would fulfill his dreams of creating a room-filling surf-sound sensation. He had met fellow Californian Leo Fender on a number of occasions, conveyed his desires to him, and was eventually asked to test a range of prototypes for a new high-powered Fender amp model. Legend has it that Dale's full-throttle assault blew up nearly 50 test efforts before Fender wired up a design that could take the heat, partly, it would seem, thanks to the new and specially-designed heavy-duty output transformers commissioned from the Triad company (part number 125A4A). We have already discussed elsewhere how an OT's power handling abilities and low-end response are in direct proportion to the size of its core, and these new Showman 'Dick Dale' transformers had girth in abundance.

Legend has it that Dale blew up nearly 50 amps before Fender wired up a design to take the heat

Dale also made suggestions for the speaker cabinet, and purportedly played a role in specifying the custom-order JBL speakers that would become the D130F ('F' for Fender), the last link in the power chain. The new JBLs had heavy magnets, ruggedized frames, and thicker and sturdier paper cones with rubber reinforcement around the edges to keep them from flapping and tearing in the basket. However involved his developmental role actually was, Dale was clearly happy with the eventual results, and continues to play blonde Fender Dual Showman amps to this day.

JBLs of this range are both powerful and sweet, thanks to an efficient design that employs larger-than-

FENDER QUALITY . . . . . . INSIDE AND OUT!

These are a few of the latest developments and design features of Fender Professional Amps. They combine with those features described on the opposite page to provide you with the tops in amplification qualities, plus complete satisfaction of ownership.

DUAL CHANNEL CIRCUITS

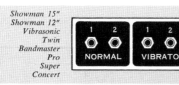

Showman 15"
Showman 12"
Vibrasonic
Twin
Bandmaster
Pro
Super
Concert

Bassman

Tremolux
Vibrolux
Deluxe

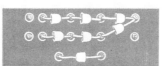

Modern silicon rectifiers are used rather than glass tubes. This feature reduces chassis heating and reduces servicing problems.

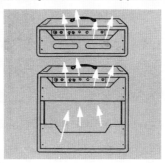

Vented cabinet design provides air circulation around chassis. Components operate at cooler temperatures thus prolonging amplifier life.

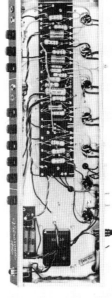

FRONT PANEL CONTROL. More convenient to use; control settings easier to read.

Attractive "Tolex" vinyl covering material resists abrasions and scuffs and is unaffected by climate variations.

Solid wood ¾ inch cabinet stock is lock-jointed at corners providing rugged construction and adequate chassis support.

Component layout and chassis design eliminate circuit interaction, facilitate servicing. Note unit parts panel . . . all small parts are securely soldered eliminating vibrations and rattles.

Modern cabinet styling is striking in appearance and is enhanced by the textured Tolex covering material.

Fender flaunts the design virtues of the Professional Series amplifiers.

usual alnico magnets and a thick and relatively shallow pulp-paper cone that is able to withstand a lot of pumping. The whole thing is mounted in a heavy duty die-cast metal basket that even at first glance offers a more robust and roadworthy package than plenty of other fine speakers in production, including the quality Celestion and Jensen drivers of the day. In an open-backed cabinet these speakers can be extremely bright; many people find them a real icepick-to-the-ear in the Fender Twin Reverbs they occasionally came in as an upgrade. But what sounds super-bright in the studio or in a reflective rehearsal space can be just the ticket to cut through on a large stage, where your warm, smooth, lush tone might only get eaten alive by the snare, cymbals and horns, for example. For that reason, these JBL-loaded Twins were perfect for guitarists in big show bands or touring country artists. Put them in a closed-back Showman cab, on the other hand, and the potentially harsh highs are tapered by a fuller overall performance. Their power handling abilities and full-frequency performance makes them a speaker that will push out meaty lows and muscular mids when coupled with an amp that can deliver the goods, and they really do sound their best when pushed hard.

The heavy, luscious tremolo of the Showman was often employed in the surf sound, along with, of course, liberal vibrato-arm dips and waggles, but the effect now inextricably linked with the style is the spring reverb unit. Other companies had marketed both onboard and outboard tube-powered spring reverb units prior to Leo's boys, and they'd been a feature of console organs like Hammond, for example, for years, but since Fender was the first and last word in surf gear, it was the Fender Reverb Unit of 1962 – prototyped in 1961 – that set the standard.

Both Dick Dale's first single, 'Let's Go Trippin',' and first album, *Surfer's Choice* (1962) were cut without any reverb on the guitar, and when he first sought out the effect it was to enrich his voice. It's surprising with hindsight, but the 'King Of The Surf Guitar' launched his career as a country singer, but evolved naturally and inevitably toward the wild surf instrumentals that became his stock in trade. Legend has it that Dale first sampled reverb after disassembling a Hammond unit to sing through in an effort to make his voice sound like Elvis Presley; when he eventually stuck the thing between his Stratocaster and his Showman, the sound of surf guitar was changed forever.

Let's Get Wet

Any good onboard amplifier spring reverb effect will do a good approximation of the sound, but the Fender Reverb Unit was the sproing of choice from early 1962. It had more depth and a springier tone than most amp-based reverbs, and provided the best version of the rolling, sustaining, ultra-wet sound that partially defined the west coast craze.

Compared even to Fender's own onboard reverb stages, the Reverb Unit is a complex affair. As seen in blackface amplifiers, the reverb stage uses one preamp tube as a driver, a small OT feeding a spring can, and a second preamp tube as a recovery stage. The outboard Unit of course required its own power transformer, used a 12AT7 as a preamp stage, a 6K6 output tube (similar to a 6V6) as a driver, the required small OT and spring can, and a 7025 (12AX7) for both recovery and dry signal mixing duties. Rather than just the Reverb depth control of the amps, the Unit carried controls for Dwell (echo length), Mix (wet/dry mix, or depth), and Tone – the latter a treble-bleed network affecting the wet signal only.

I say 'driver' above in referring to the 6K6 tube, but it is actually functioning as a straightforward output tube, as are the 6V6 in the Reissue '63 Fender Reverb and the 12AT7 in the blackface and silverface amp circuits, but they are setting the springs in the spring can vibrating rather than pumping a speaker. In fact you can rig a speaker connector to the RCA-style output running from the chassis' underside to the input of the spring can, hook this to an 8 ohm guitar speaker, and use it as a decent little recording or practice amp of about 1W.

The Reverb Unit's sound and function also differs slightly from that of amp-based reverb in that it was (and in its Reissue form, is) placed between guitar output and amp input, rather than patched in an effects loop between the amplifier's preamp and output stages, which is where the onboard version of the effect lives. This placement yields a more all-encompassing reverb sound, and a little more touch-sensitivity in the wet, sproingy wash of the springs' response. It also makes good sense when the amp used – a Showman or other large, clean amp in the case of classic surf music – is reproducing a big, bold, undistorted (or little-distorted) version of the guitar. Into a dirtier vintage amp, the reverb-before-input setup changes the tonal relationships somewhat, and isn't always ideal.

With a trio of Jazzmasters, a early Showman, and an early Tolex-front Reverb Unit, this catalog shoot is clearly ready for the shindig.

As for period-perfect, hard-core surf, that about does it. You will occasionally hear other effects added, and see other gear used, but the original surf wave of the late 1950s and early 1960s was starting to recede by 1963 (only a year after the Fender Reverb Unit's release), and virtually died altogether by 1964 in the wake of the British Invasion. Up to that point, the gear options were pretty simple and limited, and there wasn't very far anyone could stray anyway. It's worth mentioning one other aspect of the sound, though: the strings. We have visited this stop before, but of course surf guitarists of the early 1960s would still have been playing relatively heavy gauge, pure-nickel flatwounds with a wound G-string. These gave a rich, gristly, shimmering and slightly percussive response, with tamer highs than the more familiar nickel-plated roundwounds of today.

These are still an essential ingredient in the sound, and since surf guitar doesn't require much finger bending beyond the occasional half-step flicker, the heavy gauge is more a tonal bonus than the finger acher it was to blues and country players of the day. Loud, clean, biting, wet, frenetic and wild – surf's up, so hop aboard.

A young Mick Taylor wrangles fat riffs from a Les Paul 'Standard' with the Rolling Stones.

SETUP 6
BRITISH BLUES

This setup is just about as far from the surf sound of our previous chapter as you could get in the mid 1960s – a hot, warm, sultry, sustaining and bend-friendly blues rock voice that would set guitarists' dreams on fire, and change the sound and direction of rock music more than probably any other sound to date. Eric Clapton had been searching for his own voice as a guitarist while playing with the R&B-influenced pop-rock outfit the Yardbirds, using mostly a Fender Telecaster and a Vox AC30 amp – sometimes augmented by a Tone Bender fuzz box. But he found it in spades a year later playing with John Mayall and The Blues Breakers when he plugged a 1959-60 Gibson Les Paul into a Marshall model 1962 JTM45 2x12″ combo amplifier – aided by a Dallas Rangemaster Treble Booster – and coined one of the most inspired and inspirational tones in all of rock music.

Both Marshall amps and Gibson Les Paul guitars had had their followers before this time, although both were still just youngsters on the scene (hard to imagine now, eh?), and neither had really come into its own quite yet. By the mid 1960s plenty of artists had moved on from their Vox AC30 combos to bigger Marshall JTM45 half-stacks, which had quickly become more popular (if not necessarily louder) than Vox's own 50W AC50. Pete Townshend was an early devotee, although in early Who photos he is as often seen playing a Fender or other head through a Marshall cab, and the others lining up to buy them mostly included scads of long-forgotten British pop and show bands who needed the power to get them across on large dance hall stages. Early Marshall ads touted endorsee names like Eden Kane, The Mark Leeman Five, and Brian Poole and the Tremeloes – remember them? Thought not. And none of these was using them in the manner for which they would soon be famed, arguably not even the thrashing, flailing limbed Peter Townshend, always more a bold, punchy rhythm guitarist than a vocal-toned lead man.

Much the same was true of the Gibson Les Paul up until the mid 1960s. The guitar had sold in respectable numbers in the three brief years of its original production in this archetypal form (sunburst finish, humbucking pickups), but hadn't set the guitar world alight. The Les Paul just hadn't really found a home: it wasn't much suited to country, was too warm and fat for surf, didn't quite suit most traditional jazzers, was a little serious and heavy-duty for rock'n'roll… Pre-1965 users mainly included a range of inconsequential crossover jazzers and studio session men and, well, Les Paul, along with Keith Richards, the only rock star of note at this time, who picked up a Bigsby-equiped Les Paul while on tour in the States in 1964 but, like Townshend and his early Marshalls, never quite used it in the manner for which the guitar would make its name. Aside from that, it really wanted a smooth, agile lead wizard – and not a lissome, wiry, R&B riffster like Keef – to show what this low-action, easy-bending, sustainful upstart of an instrument could do.

And aside from these musings on the middling popularity of each as an individual piece of kit, they really wanted to be matched to do their best work. At the dawning of 1965, no one of note had put the two together – and the Les Paul 'Standard' and Marshall amp really, really wanted to play together. Clapton used the combination of Les Paul and Marshall combo together for slightly less than a year, but it was enough to set the tone in stone for eternity. Within a couple of years Jimmy Page, Peter Green, Paul

Eden Kane

Brian Poole and The Tremeloes

Go over big with
MARSHALL

The Nashville Teens

Go over big with

MARSHALL

This sunburst Gibson Les Paul and 1966 Marshall Model 1962 'Bluesbreaker' combo together offer the fat tones and singing sustain that helped define the blues-rock sound. Their use by Eric Clapton and other British blues stars helped to save both from possible obscurity. The Les Paul had only achieved mediocre success before its deletion in 1960, and Marshall endorsees prior to Clapton make up a mostly forgotten bunch today.

Kossof, Jeff Beck, Mick Taylor and plenty of others would also make the pairing famous. And in the USA, Mike Bloomfield's Les Paul playing on the Butterfield Blues Band's *East-West* album of 1966 – released shortly after Clapton's *Blues Breakers* LP/Marshall foray in the UK – went a long way toward increasing the guitar's popularity over there too. Rather than the Marshall combo, however, Bloomfield's amp of choice was a blackface 100W Fender Twin Reverb.

So much has been written on Clapton's hot, singing, slightly howling tone on the John Mayall album *Blues Breakers With Eric Clapton* that it is virtually impossible to say anything new about the sound. It's probably better to just imagine the sweetest fat, juicy, humbucker-loaded Gibson-through-cranked-tube-glory kind of tonal dream you can conjure up, and be done with it. Or, of course, get the album and give it a spin, and let tracks like 'Hideaway,' 'All Your Love,' 'Steppin' Out,' and 'Key To Love' speak for themselves. Nearly every rock-leaning player has yearned to sound like this at least once in his playing

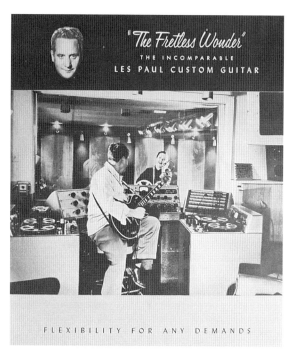

"*The Fretless Wonder*"
THE INCOMPARABLE
LES PAUL CUSTOM GUITAR

FLEXIBILITY FOR ANY DEMANDS

Les Paul in the studio with the new Custom model of his namesake, dubbed 'the fretless wonder' for its low, wide frets.

career, so this rig is lodged near the very heart of our universal conception of 'great rock tone.' The sound is undoubtedly a far, far cry from anything Gibson – or Mr Les Paul himself – could have conceived of when they brought the guitar off the drawing board and into the music stores early in the previous decade.

The sunburst-finished model of 1958-60 with humbucking pickups is easily the zenith of the model, but the Les Paul was born in quite a different form and evolved considerably to arrive at its position as the object of so many players' and collectors' desires. In shape and general appearance, at least, it started off as much the same instrument, but the famous Gibson's birth just six years before the 'bucker-'burst combo arrived was a labor born right out of the origins of the solidbody electric guitar.

Laughed at. Hooted down. Scorned. Chided. Jeered. Derided. Subject to such utter disdain, it's almost hard to believe the solidbody electric ever came to be. The ridicule and mockery would have been enough to send a less self-confident inventor running for the hills. With the benefit of hindsight, however, we know it just had to be. A world without the solidbody guitar? Moreover, without the Gibson Les Paul? Unthinkable.

Of course Gibson didn't bring us the first of the breed. Rickenbacker had marketed its 'Frying Pan' in limited numbers since the early 1930s, guitarist and inventor team Merle Travis and Paul A. Bigsby produced a few forward-looking single-cutaway solids in 1947-48, a handful of others had dabbled, and that upstart lap steel and amplifier maker from southern California put the first commercially successful production solidbody on the market in 1950 as the Fender Broadcaster (later Telecaster). But Gibson was no surf'n'sunshine tearaway company; these guys had a reputation – hell, Gibson had invented the hollowbody archtop guitar... in a previous century. Gibson had an enormous reputation in the jazz world, was an iconic producer of flat-top acoustics, mandolins and banjos, and had a history and a reputation to consider. Little wonder its execs told young inventor, recording artist and radio star Rhubarb Red to take a hike when he first started pestering them to turn his solid-cored electric into a reality in the early 1940s.

Through the immediate postwar years, fledgling solidbody efforts were almost universally laughed at as 'planks,' 'logs' and 'broomsticks with strings' by players and guitar-makers alike. But you can't stop progress, and the reality eventually dawned: formerly buried amid the rhythm sections of large orchestras vamping to beat the band (as it were), guitarists were stepping to the front of the stage, and they wanted to be heard. Bright, cutting, feedback resistant – the solidbody electric was the way to do it. "Uh, Mr Paul? This is Gibson. We were just wondering if you wouldn't mind popping back in for another little talk about that 'log' contraption of yours…?"

Going For Gold, Getting A Neck-Ache

The debut Les Paul of 1952, forever after known as the 'Goldtop,' employed many of Paul's ideas in a format that included tested elements of Gibson's own build quality, such as the set neck and carved maple top. Thanks to these and the major effort of leading Gibson designer Ted McCarty, the Les Paul Model was a far classier proposition than Fender's slab-bodied, bolt-on affair. Its near-identical resemblance to descendants in production today is indicative of how much Gibson got right the first time out of the box. Amazingly, though, they got one big, big thing wrong: attaching the neck to the body at too flat an angle meant the strings had to be wrapped under rather than over the trapeze tailpiece, the reverse of the way the guitar's namesake and contributing designer had intended it. It's still hard to imagine how such a mistake was made; it meant manual palm-edge string muting at the bridge was nearly impossible for the player to achieve, and the tone suffered too, as did the stability of the strings' anchoring against side-to-side movement.

The guitar should have gone back to the drawing board , but production went ahead for a year

The guitar really should have gone back to the drawing board – and Les Paul himself has said he was amazed that it didn't – but production roared ahead for more than a year.

After the sale of nearly 4,000 seriously flawed guitars, the Les Paul Model was corrected in late 1953 with a steeper neck angle and a new wrapover stop-bar bridge-tailpiece, the latter a basic but solid unit that many tonehounds still swear by. With this change the Goldtop finally lives up to its potential; these models are light of weight but fat sounding, with gritty, hot, roaring P-90 'soapbar' pickups and chunky but beautifully playable necks.

Our Les Paul Model of choice for this chapter evolved in pieces represented by earlier models over the course of the five years preceding its own arrival in 1958. When Les Paul the guitar star requested a classier version of Les Paul the instrument, Gibson brought out the Custom of 1954, with sleek black finish, block abalone inlays, deluxe binding, a Seth Lover-designed 'alnico' neck pickup that differed somewhat from the standard P-90 and, most significantly, the latest clever piece of hardware from Ted McCarty: the tune-o-matic bridge.

The latter was the first on a Gibson to offer fully independent intonation adjustment on each of the six saddles, along with points for overall height adjustment achieved by thumbscrews at either end. It appeared on the 'Standard' Les Paul in 1955 (note that the original Les Pauls of the 1950s never carried the word 'Standard' as an official designation, but were merely the Les Paul Model, Custom, Special or Junior). As well as helping the player to keep the guitar at accurate pitch, this was a solid anchor in the signal chain, the notched saddles gripped the strings firmly, and an impressive portion of the strings' vibrational energy was passed along into the body, resulting in fine acoustic resonance and excellent sustain. The tune-o-matic bridge's continued use today in a range of near-original and slightly adapted forms attests to its ingenuity.

In 1957 the model took its most famous incarnation hardware-wise, although it was still painted in the flashy metallic gold in which it was born. In an effort to produce a pickup that would resist electronic hum, Lover now came up with the famous humbucking pickup, a unit with two near-identical coils wired together, but out of phase and with reverse magnetic polarities. The out-of-phase nature of the dual coils serves to reject electronic hum, while their side-by-side positioning makes for a wide 'magnet window' in which the strings' vibrations are captured, and an accordingly fat, warm, even slightly sophisticated sound. Partnered to the Les Paul's solid, multi-wooded body – which we will dissect below – this made for a punchy guitar with throaty, singing sustain.

The humbuckers of the original run of Les Pauls, which have become known as PAFs because of the 'Patent Applied For' stickers found on their undersides, are widely considered the first pickups with the

The humbuckers of the original run of Les Pauls, which have become known as PAFS, are widely considered the first pickups with the power to rock

power to really rock. In fact, electronically, PAFs aren't especially hot pickups; they are usually no more powerful than the vintage P-90s that preceded them and many of each type have very similar resistance readings in the 7.5K to 8.5K ohms range. But these humbuckers' broader sonic window sends a meatier spread of frequencies to the amp, which more easily drives it into distortion. Because string vibration is sensed at two points, one above each of the pickups' two coils, the signal naturally has a little less of the harmonics-rich sparkle of a single coil pickup with a narrow magnetic field, such as that of a Fender Stratocaster. The result is a fatter signal, that often can behave as if it is more powerful than its actual resistance reading would belie.

Acquiring Alnico

For all this fatness, however, alnico magnets and judicious winding kept these PAFs sweet and vocal sounding, and far less muddy and barking than many over-wound, ceramic-magnet replacement humbuckers that followed in later years. Many players talk simply of 'amazing Gibson PAF pickups,' but there were quite a few different PAFs made even within the brief span of their original issue, from 1956 (initially on lap-steel guitars) to late 1962. Although Seth Lover's original design for the units specified alnico V magnets, throughout the first five years of the pickup's existence Gibson used whatever stocks were already on hand for its P-90s, which generally consisted of whichever of the alnico II through V blends the company could lay its hands on in good supply at any particular time.

Post-1961 Gibson stuck consistently to alnico V magnets. A greater consistency of windings from this period, combined with the fact that it used slightly smaller magnets than previously to compensate for their greater strength combine to yield pickups that are generally closer to a spec of 7.5K ohms. This holds for the last of the PAFs, early 'patent-number' pickups with very PAF-like construction, and the standard Gibson humbuckers which followed. While these constructional factors became more standardized, other components changed through the years, so that by 1965 these pickups, though still very similar in appearance, were already sounding noticeably different, and by the late 1960s and early 1970s they were a long way from the hallowed PAFs of 1956-61, or even 1962.

Clapton had also removed the 'nickel' covers (actually German silver, a copper/zinc/nickel alloy) on his PAF pickups. These metal covers raise the capacitance of the humbuckers and darken the tone somewhat, and it became popular to remove them in order to gain slightly more high-end definition from the units – although doing so without due care can short out a very expensive pickup. Discovering what color 'bobbins' lay beneath these covers also became something of a craze. When Gibson ran short of the black plastic coil formers it bought in cream stock, so double-cream or black-and-cream PAFs – dubbed zebra stripes – can be found. All sound the same, of course, but the latter two are highly desirable to collectors – although these same collectors would generally prefer a vintage Les Paul in original condition (ie with nickel covers still in place), so go figure the logic there.

Tube amps of the late 1950s that were designed for thinner-sounding and less powerful pickups, such as those on Fenders of the day, can really be made to scream when shown a humbucker-loaded Les Paul and a little volume. Before this classic British blues tone was even a glimmer in Eric Clapton's eye, plenty of American blues originators were creating ballsy, singing sounds with P-90 and PAF-equipped Gibsons plugged into tweed Fender amps.

Our Les Paul 'Standard' came entirely into its own in 1958 thanks merely to an incidental change of cosmetics. A new cherry sunburst finish revealed what was often a bookmatched, sometimes dramatically so, carved maple top. It was only a change of paint, but it marked the final evolution to the all-time classic Gibson solidbody. Sonically, the ingredients that came together – culminating a year before, really – are what matter most.

Looking at a good, late-1950s Les Paul as a cleverly wrought signal chain, many significant points spring into view. The guitar's maple top lends the benefit of sharp, well-defined attack to the good sustain and round, warm, open voice of the mahogany body and glued-in mahogany neck combination. A rosewood fingerboard contributes a slight sizzle to the brew, while a relatively steep neck and headstock pitch, paired with that excellent anchor point at the tune-o-matic bridge and stop tailpiece, offer excellent stability for solid, buzz-free string vibration (as ever, when properly setup). The LP's headstock pitch holds the strings firmly in the nut slots, negating any need for string trees or retainers, although the sharp sideways break-angles from the middle four strings to the tuner posts can sometimes lead to hitching and, therefore, tuning problems, unless these slots are kept clean and well lubricated. Even in the late

John Entwhistle and Pete Townshend of The Who go over big with Marshall... and, soon after, even bigger with Hiwatt.

1960s, many players of 1957-60 Les Pauls replaced the original Kluson tuners with heavier, encased Grover machineheads. There was a long-standing school of thought that the latter were simply superior, and perhaps they are more durable in some ways, but the original Klusons are an efficient tuner when kept in good shape and, what's more, helped to keep weight down at the headstock end, which sometimes contributes to better balance between neck and body when the guitar is strapped on.

Feel-wise, the neck pitch also makes the guitar seem to 'hug' the player, creating a more 'wraparound' angle between body and neck than the parallel planes of the slab-bodied Fender Telecaster and Stratocaster and putting the neck within easier reach of the left hand. The flatter fingerboard radius of 12″ makes these Gibson necks feel less embedded in the hand to some players than the rounder Fenders, but means smooth fingering across the 'board and less choking on heavy bends. The excellent action achievable on many of these guitars is also a revelation to many who pick one up for the first time, and they were impressively fast-playing beasts compared to most everything else that was out there in the late 1950s.

In addition, of course, a Les Paul's 24 ⅝″ scale-length contributes further to a more bend-friendly playing feel than Fender guitars offer, although it also rounds out the voice somewhat, offering less of the shimmering array of high harmonics of the Strat and Tele – a further positive in itself for many players who enjoy the thicker, fuller Les Paul tonality. Another element found at the neck, its full complement of 22 frets, was a 'deluxe' feature of the day, and compared to most of the competition of the late 1950s this guitar offered good access to all of them.

Sunburst 'Standards' of 1958 debuted with chunky necks that some players even refer to as 'clubby,' and narrow frets more akin to the traditional Fender wire gauges. Wider frets arrived in 1959 – further upping the easy-bend feel, but taking the guitar's noting precision down a notch (not always a major concern during flurried lead breaks through a cranked Marshall stack) – and the evolution to super-slim

As ads of the day clearly show, Gibson exploited Les Paul's endorsement from every possible angle, although the man himself was rarely entirely happy with production models. Keith Richards, far right, only occasionally donned the big Gibson.

THEY'RE TOPS...LES PAUL, MARY FORD AND THEIR GIBSONS

Les Paul series

necks in 1960 completed the Les Paul's journey. In 1961 the model remained in name, but became the guitar we otherwise know as the Gibson SG, a very different beast.

Plenty of players feel the bigger early necks contributed to a bigger tone, and there is some logic to that, considering the greater mass of wood available to transfer resonance picked up at the nut. Others will say that's nonsense. It's a difficult, perhaps impossible, point to prove, since any two Les Pauls that came out of the Gibson factory even in the same month of the same year will sound slightly different today, and most likely did so even when they were born. Feel-wise, the slimmer necks of 1959 and 1960 quickly became the favorites of many players, and rock lead guitarists especially. Eric Clapton has always said that his Blues Breakers Les Paul had an especially slim neck, so it was most likely one from late 1959 or 1960. He himself wasn't aware of the guitar's exact year when he owned it, and since the instrument was stolen in the summer of 1966 during rehearsals for the first Cream tour, there's no way to find out now.

Despite all of these tone-affecting ingredients, the Les Paul's sunburst finish – and what lies beneath it – has become one of the biggest factors in determining its collectable status among vintage guitar buyers.

A 1957 Goldtop might still have the PAF humbucking pickups, tune-o-matic bridge, and otherwise identical construction to a 1958 'burst in the same condition, but the latter easily fetches two, three, or even four or more times the price on the vintage market. Perverse? In some ways, yes. But it just goes to show what elements can become more important to collectors than to players while, sadly, the whole phenomenon inevitably means fewer and fewer players can get their hands on the things at all. Even the degree of flame or quilting in the maple top visible beneath the inner area of the finish, something of an afterthought during original production, can mean a great variance of value between two otherwise identical sunburst Les Pauls, and the way in which the finish has faded – its cherry red element especially – can further enhance its desirability. For those more concerned with tone and playability, however, the real magic comes in closing your eyes, picking up the thing, and letting it sing.

Sharp Points And Radical Departures

When Gibson changed to the slimmer, rather slab-bodied, all-mahogany double-cutaway Les Paul in 1961 – which then became the SG in 1963 when Les Paul failed to re-sign his endorsement deal – it changed the guitar completely. This major model transition in itself makes a great lesson in how woods, body shape and neck attachment affect a guitar's tone relative to hardware and electronics. A 1961 Les Paul carries the same pickups, nut, tuners and bridge as a 1960 (although the SG/Les Pauls were given the vibrola tailpiece, often something of a tone dampener in itself), has the same scale-length, and is built with near identical neck and heastock pitches. But the guitars sound very different. There is a similarity, sure, but the SG variety of Les Paul is just slightly thinner, blurrier, and less complex sounding. Most 1957-60 LPs really beat them for sustain, too. It's amazing to consider that original sunburst 'Standards' have gone for upwards of $250,000 in recent years, while you can pick up the same-name guitar built in 1961 or 1962 for $10,000 to $15,000 (all of these are obviously guesstimated at the time of writing, and of course these prices can sometimes change quickly). Then again, just fewer than 1,700 of the sunburst Les Pauls were made between 1958-60, so the laws of supply and demand apply here in the extreme.

Not that SGs can't sound full and fat. After trying a few other 'Standards' Eric Clapton eventually settled on an SG/Les Paul with a colorful 'hippy's acid dream' type paint job as one of his main guitars with Cream, and this is the instrument responsible for much of his famed 'woman tone' – a deep, warm, bassy sound created by playing on the neck pickup with the tone control wound down, with a 100W Marshall stack floored to 10. Clapton no longer has this SG/Les Paul either, having traded it years ago to Todd Rundgren in a gear swap.

Watts In A Name

Many amplifiers have played essential parts in classic tonal combinations – whilst usually being less recognized for their roles than the guitars with which they were partnered – but the 1965 Marshall model 1962 combo is among the most crucial, inseparable really from the Blues Breakers-era Clapton sound. So much so that Clapton's use of the amp on the Mayall album gave the model the name by which it would ever after be known. And although we are talking about an amp manufactured in Britain in the mid 1960s, we have already discussed this piece of gear's

In the early 1960s, Fender amps were highly regarded in Britain, but rare and expensive

roots in a seminal late-1950s American design. (As we proceed, remember that many Marshall model numbers rather confusingly look like year designations, but bear no relation to the year in which said model was introduced. The model 1962 first appeared in 1964, while the model 1987, for example, was born around 1963.)

In the early 1960s Fender amps were highly regarded in Britain, but very rare and extremely expensive. London music shop owner Jim Marshall seized on an opportunity to build his own versions of the great Fenders that so many British musicians were dying to get their hands on, and used the powerful, versatile 5F6A tweed Bassman as his template. A look at the Bassman and original Marshall JTM45 control panels shows you their functions were the same, and a peak inside at the circuit would reveal a clear kinship of internal design, too. Marshall and colleagues Ken Bran and Dudley Craven prototyped a few near-identical models – which differed more in their use of British components than in anything else – and a rock legend was born.

Marshall's first proper production JTM45 arrived in 1963 as the 'salt and pepper' model (ie, textured blonde front) and then 'sandwich fronts' (⅓ black vinyl, ⅔ textured cloth) of later the same year. The amps used the same preamp stage, cathode-follower three-knob tone stack (shared by both channels), phase inverter, tube-rectified power stage, and negative-feedback loop tapped for Presence control as did the Bassman of 1958-60. Many players – even fans of later Marshalls – fail to realize that the JTM45 initially used US 5881 output tubes too (a ruggedized version of the 6L6), rather than the Brit-voiced EL34s, with occasional substitution for the electronically equivalent but slightly different sounding European KT66s, which were more readily available in Britain at the time.

As you might expect from all of the above, put an early JTM45 and a tweed Fender Bassman side by side, patch them through the same speaker cabinet, and there are certainly many sonic similarities. The main differences that give these early Marshalls their own sonic signature come in the form of the UK-spec output transformer and, to a greater extent, the speakers and speaker cabinets. Rather than the four low-powered 10″ Jensen drivers of the Fender, Marshall used four 12″ British-built Celestions, but put them in a heavier closed-back cabinet to help the low-powered speakers take the strain from the amp at full-tilt. Rather than the cranked Bassman's surround-sound dispersion, which comes both from the front of the amp and out from the rear of its semi-open backed cabinet, the JTM45 head with 4x12″ cab has a more unidirectional and somewhat punchier response, with a little more of a boxy compression in its midrange. The Bassman's thin plywood speaker baffle and light, solid-pine cab vibrated like crazy and could even start to shimmy across a smooth stage floor when the amp was cranked, and that cabinet-wood resonance also contributed to its sound. The Marshall's heavy-duty, closed-back cab and sturdier baffle sat more firmly, and blasted out a greater proportion of speaker sound

While it is, in so many ways, merely 'half a JTM45 half-stack,' the Bluesbreaker's partially open-backed cab elicits an entirely different response from its Celestion greenbacks.

vs cab resonance. That said, it is still a far bluesier sounding amp than the EL34-based 'Plexi' model that followed, and somewhat apart from the characteristic 'Marshall sound' as most players understand it today.

But that's the piggy-back JTM45. Come late 1964, Marshall saw the need for a slightly smaller, more easily transportable combo version of the same amp. Something that would appeal to fans of both Vox AC30s and Fender Twins. The model 1962 2x12″ combo essentially consisted of a JTM45 amp chassis with added tremolo, bolted side-on to a semi-open-back cabinet. The cab was at first relatively deep, but shallower by mid 1965, and was made of thinner plywood than that used in the big 4x12″s. It carried two 16 ohm ceramic-magnet Celestion G12M 'Greenback' speakers, which were rated at 20W at the time rather than the 25W of later units, wired in parallel to an 8 ohm output from the amp. Celestion Greenbacks were never a driver capable of tight, firm low-end reproduction. Put four together to spread the load in a big, sealed box and they manage to thump it out pretty well, but two in a thinner, shallower, open-backed cabinet start to suffer when hit by any low-down riffs on a fat Les Paul. They will also start to break up a lot quicker than the 4x12″, with less acoustic dampening to keep cone-travel in check, and only 40W power handling as opposed to 80W to handle the blast from the cranked JTM45 chassis.

The result is a smoother, more saturated tone than that characteristic of the early Marshall half-stacks, and one with a crisper and slightly Fender-ish high-end response, too. A great combination of roar and howl, and perhaps a useful rounding-off of a Les Paul's tendency toward low-end muddiness in some amps, which could be especially helpful in an effort to record loud electric blues in a traditional studio.

When they were setting up to record the Blues Breakers album, Clapton famously told the engineer – who was about to place a mike close in on the Marshall combo – to set the thing across the room because they intended to "play loud," and all of his recollections of the sessions state that the amp was on or close

to max throughout. That said, 10 on a JTM45 or Bluesbreaker combo (note the band and album are two words, 'Blues Breaker,' while the amp is usually referred to with one) is not quite like 10 on a 50W Plexi or later Marshall amp. The '45' in the model name was only ever that – a name – and these amps actually put out something close to 35W. Originals are still surprisingly loud beasts, but they are somewhat easier to control in the studio or on the club or small-hall stage than most true 50W half-stacks you'll come across. The tube rectification from a sturdy GZ34 also gives these amps more compression and sag than the later silicon-rectified Plexis, and this characteristic is especially evident in a roaring open-backed 2x12″.

Along with the British speakers and other notable component variations, those KT66s, even though they were a straight-swap alternative for the US 6L6s, yielded a somewhat rounder, smoother, more full-throated tone than the output tubes appearing in American amps at the time. The Bluesbreaker combo is probably the most closely allied of all vintage Marshalls to what you could call their 'genetic roots' at Fender, but it is still a distinctively different amp. That said, about the closest I have come to eliciting a Bluesbreaker sound on a non-Bluesbreaker amp was with a late

The rare three-PAF Custom and sunburst Les Paul represent the model's zenith – but the man wouldn't lend a name to the headstock for much longer.

1950s low-powered tweed Fender Twin, with its RCA 6L6s swapped for a great pair of NOS (new old stock) GEC KT66s. Despite the sturdier and sonically different Jensen P12N speakers and other variables like a slightly different tone stack and phase inverter than its sibling Bassman carried, that Twin sounded surprisingly British when cranked toward 12 with a Les Paul injected.

By the time of the Bluesbreaker combo's birth, however, Fender had already changed to the very different blackface circuits, and even Marshall's own tube-rectified, KT66-powered models would only survive another couple of years. Plenty of great amps followed, but for touch-sensitivity, bluesy smoothness and a more-ish compression that wants to let you play all day, those JTM45-based Marshalls and tweed Fenders are still hard to beat. With Cream, Clapton moved over to SGs and ES-335s through 100W Marshall stacks and, while he coined another legendary tone, he never sounded quite the same again. Interestingly, his use in recent years of vintage tweed Fender Twins (and closely-duplicated boutique replicas from the likes of UK amp-maker Denis Cornell) almost brings him full-circle in amp terms – but the stolen 1959 or '60 Les Paul is still missing without a trace.

High And Mighty

The final link in the Blues Breakers tone chain is the rare, now highly prized Dallas Rangemaster Treble Booster. This simple 'pedal' predates most other small-box transistorized effects, and isn't really a pedal as such since it was designed to sit atop the amplifier, with a jack to plug a guitar into the front and a built-in lead running from the back of the unit to the amp's input. The idea was to provide a significant level boost, but more in the upper-mid and high frequency range than in the full frequency spectrum. To many players today the idea sounds daft; modern amps, partnered with efficient connecting cables (cords) and well-made effects pedals that don't suck too much tone, have more than enough treble for most of us, and if anything the tendency today is to switch out any Bright switches and turn down Presence and Treble controls a bit to warm things up. Back in the day,

The Dallas Rangemaster Treble Booster provided the gain-lift to knock many a Marshall or Vox into overdrive.

The final link in the Blues Breakers tone chain is the rare Dallas Rangemaster Treble Booster

however, this wasn't always so, and treble was often highly sought after, and too easily lost. The treble booster, then, was simply a level-boosting preamp with an intentional upper-frequency emphasis.

In the early 1960s, when the Rangemaster arrived, treble boosters provided a means of getting that extra bite and cut-through potential into an amp that might otherwise be too dark to pierce a foggy mix. They were used at one time or another by plenty of great players, in Britain in particular, including Jimmy Page (another Rangemaster into Marshall combo), Ritchie Blackmore, and later Brian May (who'd have thought a single-coil-loaded solidbody into a stack of cranked Vox AC30s needed *more* treble? Obviously Brian May did).

Dallas was a British music electronics manufacturer that eventually joined forces with the distributor Arbiter to form Dallas-Arbiter, home of the even more famous Fuzz Face and plenty more besides. Years before the Fuzz Face was born, however, the simple Rangemaster was doing the biz for plenty of satisfied customers. The circuit inside the gray metal box is a simple one, at the heart of which lies a single germanium transistor (usually either a Mullard OC44 or an NTK275) along with four capacitors and four resistors that help the thing do its job. On the outside there is simply a Boost on/off switch, a level knob,

Gibson SOLIDS

- Ultra thin, contoured, double cut-away body.
- Slim, fast, low action neck—with exclusive extra low frets—joins body at 22nd fret.
- One-piece mahogany neck with adjustable truss rod.
- Rosewood fingerboard, pearl inlays.
- Adjustable Tune-O-Matic bridge.
- Twin powerful humbucking pick-ups with separate tone and volume controls which can be pre-set.
- Three-position toggle switch to activate either or both pick-ups.

24¾" scale, 22 frets.

12¾" wide, 16" long, 1⅜" thin.

No. 5432/02. Les Paul Standard Cherry .. **125 gns.**

No. 5432/66. Plush-lined slimline case for above .. **£8 0 0**

LES PAUL STANDARD

An established favourite with completely new modern styling . . . with thinner light weight contoured body, and deep double cutaway that provides easy access to all 22 frets. The extremely slim, fast, low-action neck makes this guitar a joy to play. Tone is clear and bell-like throughout its entire range. The perfectly balanced solid body makes playing comfortable in any position, sitting or standing. The Tune-O-Matic bridge permits adjusting string action and individual string lengths. The finish is a beautiful cherry red with nickel-plated metal parts and individual machine heads with deluxe buttons. Deluxe padded leather strap included.

Bigsby True Vibrato Units can be supplied fitted to any Gibson Solid Guitar at a supplementary charge of **12 gns.**

Cases, see page 16
4

For two years it was a Les Paul, but an SG by any other name is still an SG.

and the aforementioned jack input on the front and hardwired output cable at the back. There's no on/bypass stompswitch, so the thing is either in circuit or out… unless you hop to the back of the stage and flick it on for your solos, not a practical option really. Given a thimbleful of the right parts most electronics hobbyists could whip one up – while originals nevertheless go for anywhere from $500 to upwards of $1000, depending on condition and originality.

The little dose of magic that these things possess lies mainly within that germanium transistor, siblings of which are responsible for many great early fuzz box sounds elsewhere – the Fuzz Face again, Maestro's Fuzz Tone, the Vox/Sola Sound/Colorsound Tone Bender, and others. Germanium transistors were less powerful than the silicon transistors that took their place in the late 1960s, but they had a softer, smoother distortion characteristic, which makes them favorable to many players in a range of applications. As embodied in the Rangemaster, the booster is a very different beast from the 'transparent' and 'linear boost' devices advertised by many quality pedal builders today, which aim at a goal of pure level boosting with no tonal coloration. A Rangemaster – or most any other crude early germanium treble booster – most definitely colors your tone; it thickens, softens, fattens and even furs it up some, and for many uses sounds gorgeous in the process. Their intention was always to provide a 'clean' boost, but when that clean, frequency-selective germanium boost hits an amp's preamp tubes (and that higher-gain signal is subsequently passed along to the output stage) a slathering of sweet distortion certainly results.

With the Les Paul and Marshall JTM45 model 1962 combo the Rangemaster makes a great means of adding crunch and sustain in the more desired frequency range, and a little punch in the mids, without contributing to boominess in the low end, which could have been a problem with a full-frequency or bass-emphasizing booster. It's impossible to know just where and when Clapton used a Rangemaster; throughout, possibly, just turning the guitar's volume up and down to make lead-rhythm transitions, or perhaps just on selected tracks. Because there's no stompswitch to bring the booster in for solos we don't have any instant 'stomp-solo' jump to listen for on the records, but legend tells us it's there, and much of his juicy, rich, singing tone just screams germanium booster.

Treble boosters faded from popularity over the years, mainly as more wide-ranging boosters and overdrives and fuzzes became available, and as rigs became more efficient at high-end retention. Versions of the classics are available again in various forms, though, with 'boutique' pedal builders like Analog Man, RM and Tube Amp Doctor building component-perfect replicas of the Rangemaster (though usually housed in somewhat different boxes, complete with stomp switches and sometimes even tone controls or switches), while Roger Mayer builds the more flexible Concorde+ Treble Booster, which has an AC128-based germanium drive stage coupled to a silicon output stage and a thin-to-fat Tone control. Compared to many of the modern renditions some original Rangemasters can even sound a little harsh and rasping to many ears – and certainly noisier – but they still possess a certain raw magic.

For those with shallower pockets – or who need to apply their mortgage toward a house, not a rock setup – there are other version of this rig available. Gibson's Les Paul 'Standard' model has of course been available in a range of 'vintage reissue' and contemporary versions over the years, of varying quality and period-accuracy, so a relatively affordable dose of that PAF-loaded 'burst sound isn't too difficult to get your hands on. Marshall originally reissued the Bluesbreaker combo back in the late 1980s, and it's a good sounding version of that open-backed combo. Certain components have changed, and the 5881 output tubes replace the KT66s, but basic upgrades are easy, and these can be made to sound pretty close to the originals. Or just take a second shift, start saving your pennies, and keep dreaming.

Jazz star Pat Metheny and much-modified Gibson ES-175, with nifty toothbrush strap-anchor.

SETUP 7
CLUB JAZZ

The 'jazz tone' – known as 'the jazz *lack* of tone' to its detractors. To some who aren't fans of the music (and a few who are), this thing that has evolved as the traditional small-group electric jazz guitar sound – forged in clubs and on records all through the late 1950s, 1960s and 1970s – is a dull and lifeless simulacrum of what the electric guitar can do. But listen to any of the great players, and they all have fantastic tone: Wes Montgomery, Jim Hall, Kenny Burrell, Joe Pass, Grant Green, George Benson. I mean listen closely, to the richness, depth, warmth, color and dynamics their sounds exhibit. Warmth, sure, but no dullness there – and this is where we find the 'club jazz' sound worth emulating. Also, while there are some similarities of guitars and amps being used by these players, there is probably as much variety in makes and models as found among any half-a-dozen country or metal or blues players, although the designs of the classic jazzer's tools of the trade are likely to share more touch points.

Jazz guitar's signature sound stems from the early electric guitarist's pursuit of the horn players' place in the spotlight, and in the 1930s and early 1940s was often valued particularly for its ability to sound 'hornlike.' Also, the early guitar/amp combinations pretty much sounded the way they sounded. Solidbodies weren't commonly available to brighten things up, and makers still felt a single pickup placed near the neck or about midway between neck and bridge was enough to capture the instrument's range (hey, you don't get two or three sounds from a horn, do you?). Wire up the old rigs, and that was what you got – and for a time, it was pretty much all the range and variation that electric guitars were capable of. Warmth and darkness therefore became benchmarks, but players who aim for this timbre without regard to other enriching subtleties of

Warmth and darkness became benchmarks, but players who aim for this timbre without regard to other enriching subtleties often make do with a muddy, dull sound that apes 'the jazz tone'

frequency and harmonic considerations often make do with a muddy, dull sound simply because it apes what is commonly considered 'the jazz tone.' Dark, serious, but too often quite dull. Listen back to the CD's first example of Setup 1, and you will hear plenty of tonal depth and dynamics there, amid the slight boominess and low-end emphasis of the rig; as the jazz tone advanced in the hands of its greatest practitioners, such as those named above, it became far more sumptuous and refined. Yet a sense of dullness still pervades the 'sonic visions' of those who don't look – and listen – beyond the obvious outward characteristics. It has also too often been accepted by many decent players as the sound to emulate.

For this setup, then, let's combine two of the most common ingredients, but ones which also raise some debatable points about the convergence – or otherwise – of 'best jazz tone' with 'classic jazz tone.' For our guitar, Gibson's ES-175 is a clear choice, and let's plug it into 'the McDonalds of jazz guitar amps,' a Polytone Mini-Brute MkII… with reverb, of course. Two of our earlier list of players who epitomize this jazz sound, Jim Hall and Joe Pass, regularly played the ES-175/Mini-Brute combination, and most of the others and many more besides occasionally turned to one or the other. Of course Polytone didn't arrive until 1968, and its most played models some years after that, but not long after that many players pursuing this sound turned in droves to Polytones to get it.

Few will debate my selection of the ES-175. It doesn't have nearly the refinement or acoustic splendor of a vintage Gibson L-5 or D'Angelico New Yorker, or a contemporary Benedetto Cremona or the like; but

An early-1960s Gibson ES-175 and late-1970s Polytone Mini-Brute. Solid state, hollow ply – and together they epitomize the classic warm, smooth club jazz tone.

it is probably the single most-played jazz box out there (in original or copy form), and for many it defines the tone from the guitar's standpoint. Gibson estimates that not far short of 40,000 ES-175s were sold in the first 40 years of the guitar's production; it was the company's first truly successful venture into the new world of electric guitar, and it remains in the catalogue today. The sheer near-omnipresence of the Polytone on the jazz club stage gets it its first vote for inclusion here. Let's give credit where credit is due: when talking entire rigs, even more than the ES-175 this amp has a good case for being the single most common ingredient in the jazz setups of the 1970s and 1980s, so it's the easiest point of commonality. A

range of vintage style tube amps was always used by great players, too, including mainly Fenders, Gibsons and Ampegs but a few others as well (sometimes Magnatones or Gibson-made Maestro and Epiphone models), but the Polytone Mini-Brute has long been the workingman's standby. It's inclusion also gives us a chance to examine solid state amps briefly, which otherwise don't make an appearance in this book, and to open up that whole 'tubes vs solid state' can of worms that can get so heated among some players. However you slice it, I'd be willing to bet that this pair has romped the changes in more Village Vanguards and Tiki Lounges and 100 Clubs and Howard Johnsons and Blue Whisps than any other combination of jazz guitar and amp ever put together.

Adapting To Amplification

Gibson epitomized the art of fine archtop guitar building in the 1930s with models like the L-5 and Super 400. These were carefully crafted instruments with hand-carved arched, solid spruce tops, bookmatched carved solid backs, and a myriad design and constructional considerations for acoustic tone. But the snowballing of the electric age soon proved that in certain circumstances a lot of this effort was wasted once a pickup was bolted onto the guitar and it was played through a blaring amplifier behind a swing orchestra on a crowded bandstand. Plenty of players still wanted the high-end product, and the option of sweet, rich tones either unplugged or amped up, but when full-volume playing was the goal, it made a lot of sense to cut to the chase and concentrate on the features that emphasized the amplified performance,

Wes Montgomery with a mid-1950s Gibson L-5CES. With its carved, solid-spruce top, this is a more studiously crafted guitar than the more common ES-175.

while eliminating many of those that detracted from it.

Great acoustic and great electric performance do not go hand in hand. Plenty of gorgeous, handmade, solid-carved-topped jazzboxes can sound phenomenal when plugged in with the right pickup attached, certainly. But rigged up without consideration of the nuances of tone reproduction, frequency emphasis and feedback, plenty can often sound boomy, muddy and howly, too. With the introduction of the ES-175 in 1949 – the company's first laminated-top archtop guitar, and also the first with a pointed cutaway

– Gibson went a long way toward eliminating these variables, and offering a consistent performing and sounding instrument to the guitarists of the amplified age.

The ES-175 was born with a single P-90 pickup in the neck position and single Volume and Tone controls. The 16 ¼″ wide and 3 ¼″ deep body was, and is, constructed of maple-fronted plywood which consists of maple front and back veneers with basswood or other 'filler' in between. These are pressed into their arched shape for the guitar's front and back, rather than carved like the costlier solid-wood tops, and the pickup(s) and controls are set into cutouts in the top itself, rather than mounted 'floating' as on more traditional solid-topped, acoustic archtops (which is to say, pickups mounted to the end of the neck or pickguard so as to not touch the top of the guitar or affect its vibration). The plywood yields less to the feedback-causing vibrations that can plague more refined jazz boxes, though make no mistake, these wide hollowbodies can still howl. But the tradeoff is less acoustic resonance in the instrument overall, and therefore a far less toneful acoustic sound.

Given this, Gibson designers reckoned there wasn't much harm in cutting right into the instrument to mount the electronics, and they were probably right. If anything, the coupling of the pickup to the guitar's face adds further character to this archetypal sound as the unit vibrates in conjunction with – though not, technically, in harmony with – both the strings and the wood of the guitar. In such a case, the vibrational energy is passed into the sound chain at many more points than on an acoustically-designed archtop with floating pickup, and the ES-175 offers a sound that is more in the electric than the amplified-acoustic realm, even if this is still a far cry from the solidbody. The combination of the top's greater stiffness and the body woods' maple content also helps to brighten up the voice of the model, which was another desirable factor in Gibson's efforts to move toward a cutting, rounded, easily-heard electric instrument, as distinct from its double-duty L-series and Super 400 archtops and others.

Plummy Mids, Sparkling Highs

While most high-end archtops carry maple necks with ebony fingerboards and ebony bridges, the ES-175 was given a mahogany neck with a 20-fret rosewood fingerboard and rosewood bridge. Mahogany is an equally stable wood to solid maple – if not more so, as some guitar-makers tell me – while rosewood is considerably softer and less dense than ebony. Both are generally 'down market' alternatives in this application, but in fact work to enhance the sonic character of the guitar. The combination helps to round out the snap and precision of the firm, maple-rich body, which might be just too tight and

The combination of mahogany and rosewood helps round out the snap and precision of the maple-rich body and contributes to warm mids and lows

punchy with the maple neck/ebony 'board options, and contributes to warm, plummy mids and lows with highs that are sparkling without being cuttingly bright. In the description alone, you can already 'hear' the archetypal jazz sound emerging. In feel and profile, these necks have always been well rounded and tending to the fuller side of medium-depthed, without ever being too clubby. It's a shape that has always been popular with jazz players, and Gibson has altered it far less in 45 years than, for example, it did the Les Paul's neck profiles just between 1956 and 1960.

The 24 5/8″ scale length has already been discussed in a number of places, and the ES-175 shares this Gibson standard. These guitars don't need the bend-friendliness that bluesers and rockers enjoy from this

scale on solidbodies like the Les Paul or SG, but it does also afford the easy fretting and plummier, less harmonically saturated tonality that jazz players appreciate too. These features make it a very playable instrument, while that deep Florentine cutaway contributes by offering easy access up to about the 18th fret, and even a stretch to the 20th if you keep that pinky limber.

Many noted archtop-makers in earlier years followed a longer 25 1/2" standard (along with some early Gibson models), while the compromise of 25" has become an oft-used scale of contemporary luthiers specializing in jazz boxes. The differences between all of these are subtle, but considerate and experienced guitarists are usually able to express clear preferences between them. Play with guitars of three different scale-lengths for a while, and you will soon notice the differences. The 17-degree headstock break angle used by Gibson up until 1965 makes for excellent downward pressure on the strings in the nut slots, and many players say this is one of the magic little ingredients of the best sounding Gibsons, whether ES-175s or Les Pauls or whatever. Shallower angles followed in the years after, introduced for reasons reportedly having to do with anything from efforts to decrease incidences of headstock breakage to a mere simplifying of the manufacturing process.

Some players swap the carved, one-piece top saddle section of the model's two-piece rosewood bridge for a metal tune-o-matic bridge, which contributes to a slightly tighter sound and offers individual setting of the strings for more precise intonation; others, however, feel the wooden saddle is an integral part of the jazz sound. The trapeze tailpiece behind it has changed little through the years. On the ES-175 this is a cruder, simpler affair than the decorative hardware on many more expensive Gibsons, but plenty of top luthiers will tell you that carrying as little non-wood weight in these positions is a good thing in an archtop, letting the body resonate free from too much anchoring down from decorative metal, bindings, inlays, whatever. With this in mind, the ES-175's simple trapeze is as effective as any chunky, ornate, gold-plated pseudo-sculpture, and probably more so.

Pick Of The Pickups

Gibson's P-90 pickups, despite being single coils, are fat and meaty sounding – and in fact I would sling at them many of the same adjectives that the ES-175 itself generally garners. They aren't an overly refined unit, and have a certain grit and blur to their overall reproduction of whatever guitar they are mounted to, plus a pronounced midrange emphasis on solidbodies that translates into a certain appealing rawness in many archtops and semi-acoustics. They also have significantly more output than most Fender-style single coils, and can easily drive a tube amp into early breakup at even slightly advanced volumes. The result can be an appealingly chewy edge at the front of a great jazz tone that simmers with just the slightest hint of distortion when hit hard. Most traditional jazzers playing in the genre under discussion avoid anything that gets close to resembling out and out distortion, though, so these guitars will often be played

For a time, Epiphone gave Gibson a run for its money with jazz players, aided in no small part by star endorsements like this from Al Caiola.

with the Volume control rolled back slightly to keep the pickup's high output reined in. For a blueser, however, this combination can be a fast track to getting your mojo working. This is true for later models with humbuckers, too, and the neck position of either of these variations further exacerbates their tendencies to put a dent in a suffering old tube amp's headroom. Firmer solid state units like the Polytone, however, can withstand these peaks of attack a little better than medium to small tube amps, but can still be driven toward breakup when pushed.

In 1953 the ES-175 was joined by the ES-175D ('D' for 'dual') which carried a P90 at both neck and bridge positions, with independent Volume and Tone controls and a traditional three-way toggle-type selector switch. In early 1957 the model took on the hallowed PAF humbucking pickups then newly developed by Gibson at the hands of designer Seth Lover (discussed in more depth in Setup 6: British Blues). There are plenty of fans of the older P-90 versions of the guitar, but like any Gibson with PAFs, the one and two-pickup models manufactured between 1957 and late 1962 are the most revered ES-175s ever made. Instruments of this era happen to have hit the guitar store shelves at the time when many of the best proponents of this style of electrified jazz guitar were cutting their teeth, and cutting some of their most seminal tracks, and at a far lower sticker price than an L-5CES or Super 400CES these ES-175s would have been one of the first 'quality Gibsons' within reach of the hardworking jazzman. It is probably not entirely coincidence that the guitar and the music were hitting their peak at around the same time. Examples manufactured for a couple years after the PAF finally received its long-applied-for patent – and so carried pickups with patent number stickers on their undersides – are also sought after, as these pickups retain many of the constructional and sonic properties of their predecessors. For this reason, 1962-64 ES-175s with 'patent-number' pickups and other desirable early 1960s features are still among the most highly prized of guitars.

But whatever the era, the humbucker-loaded ES-175 really is the version for our sound. The P-90s can sound great, but the humbucker is just that bit smoother, fuller, rounder and more refined on this instrument – on any, for the most part. The humbucker epitomizes the softened-butter sound of the genre, and nails our Club Jazz tone just that bit more easily. Sonically, these humbuckers naturally went a long way toward doing what jazz players were previously tweaking their gear to achieve. With a wider magnetic window, it eliminated some of the excessive brightness that many players dialed out of the single-coil P-90s, and had a little less bite than those pickups, too. They were more liquid velvet than liquid fire, and completed the instrument's evolution. From here, there was really nowhere for the ES-175 to go, so it has pretty much just hung around.

Few jazzers use the bridge pickup much, whether P-90, PAF or otherwise, but its inclusion makes it a versatile instrument that can also turn its hand to rock, rockabilly and blues. Yes guitarist Steve Howe is one oft-cited ES-175 fan who uses a two-pickup model for his rock-cum-fusion playing, while fusion-cum-jazzer Pat Metheny added a bridge humbucker to his beloved neck-only ES-175, found he didn't use it as much as he had thought he might, and removed it again. Adding the second

Many great jazz players have opted for the ES-175D, even if they rarely use the bridge pickup, simply because it was the more 'deluxe' version of the model and they found they could afford the upgrade when they were out guitar shopping

pickup mounted to a hole near the bridge will certainly change this model's acoustic resonance slightly, and therefore affect the sound even when only the neck humbucker is selected, but because of the constructional aspects of this guitar that have already been discussed, such will be a lot less detrimental than, say, cutting a hole in the top of the hand-carved, solid spruce top on an L-5 or a recent Benedetto or something and weighing down that crucial vibrational point with a heavy magnetic pickup. Minimal – if detectable – sonic differences aside, many great jazz players have opted for the ES-175D over the years, even if they rarely use the bridge pickup, simply because it was the more 'deluxe' version of the model and they found they could afford the upgrade when they happened to be out guitar shopping. And hey, it's always there to flick to if you get called for that short-notice pop session. As far removed as the ES-175 is from the fully acoustic archtops pioneered by Gibson way back in the 1920s and early 1930s, and intentionally so, either version is going to get you pretty effortlessly to that single-malt tone on a smokey Friday night.

Smooth Feel, Smooth Sound

Pure nickel-wrapped flatwound strings would have been the norm on ES-175s from the 1950s and early 1960s, in gauges of from .012 or .013 up to the low .050s, and many jazz players today still swear by their sound and feel. If you have never played flatwounds, are at all interested in dabbling in jazz, and have an appropriate guitar to stick them on, give these things a try. After a little adapting of playing style, its a smooth ride that can quickly become addictive. Many a guitarist who thought he had the setup right but still couldn't nail 'the sound' has discovered that it all finally clicked into place when he got the pure-nickel flatwounds on there. They produce a smooth, round, plummy tone that sits right in there with the vibe we are striving to pin down in this chapter.

The solid-state electronics allowed for savings in weight as well as size, and these were an easy piece of gear to lift and sling into the front seat of a VW Beetle or even heft down into the subway

Given the relative uniformity of 'the jazz sound' it is not surprising that a maker eventually came up with an amplifier designed to produce mainly that. 'Polytone' is an interesting choice of name. It would be unfair to suggest that these amps have only one application – in truth many models are designed to be fairly flexible, and certainly appeal to guitarists and bassists in other genres too – but they have become famed for their ability to fast-track you to one single tone. The company was founded in 1968 by accordionist Tommy Gumina, and soon introduced the Brute line of powerful solid-state amplifiers aimed mainly at the jazz and function guitarist and bassist. With developmental input from Joe Pass, Polytone introduced the compact yet muscular Mini-Brute in 1976. This proved to be as much amplifier as most jazz guitarists ever needed, with more than 100W output into a single heavy duty 12″ speaker, and the Mini rapidly became Polytone's biggie, in sales and reputation terms at least.

One feature that appealed to many a hardworking musician was the fact that Polytone packed all of this punch into a rugged, compact cube of a combo that was not a whole lot bigger in any direction than the dimensions of the speaker it carried. The solid-state electronics allowed for savings in weight as well as size, and these were an easy piece of gear to lift and sling into the front seat of a VW Beetle, or even heft down into the subway, your trusty ES-175 alongside it in the other hand, and onto the train uptown to that night's gig. Players picked them up by the thousands as a standby rig for small or short-notice gigs, and soon found themselves leaving their heavy Fender Twin Reverb and Gibson GA50 tube amps at home for 99 out of 100 calls. Most of these musicians were clearly pleased with the Polytone sound, but the Mini-Brute's convenience often helped to negate any preference for tube tone that might have lingered.

Warm, If Not Glowing

Or to be more accurate – or more objective – maybe the Mini-Brute just proved a quicker, less labor-intensive means of achieving precisely the tone that so many of these players had for years been tweaking and twiddling to achieve. Guitarists talk incessantly of the 'warmth' of real tubes, but listen to tracks 32 and 33 on the CD in quick succession (without checking the track listings or notes, if you haven't already). Which one nails the common definition of 'warmer'? Most will probably agree it's not the tube amp, and note that this tube amp is set to do its best version of 'the sound.' In truth, the tubes types used most in guitar amps are capable of reproducing enormous quantities of the abundant highs and upper-mids that some people hear as the negator of so-called warmth, and they do so in extremely simple circuits, too.

And yes, they can also sound plummy, full and warm, but to categorize tubes as 'the warm technology' and transistors as 'cold' or 'bright' is deceptive, and misleading. Top engineers who have worked in the studio for years with both tube and solid state microphone and line preamps and compressors know this instinctively; there's often a lot of sparkle in those old tube units, while plenty of solid-state models have an abundance of warmth. As usual, if we're not careful, over-categorization and thoughtless simplification can lead us away from a deeper understanding of what makes our tone, and how.

Basic transistor circuits, in the early days in particular, often fell on the side of the smooth and woolly, and if anything required the designers to pull on their thinking caps in order to eak out a little more shimmer and high-harmonic dimension. Done well, they came off as warm; done poorly, they sounded merely dull and lifeless. The latter is what helped to give solid-state guitar amps a bad name in the early days of their insurgence into tubesville, and makers backing the technology – including Polytone – have labored ever since to improve upon this reputation.

Nevertheless, Polytone amps are derided by lots of guitarists. And the fact that so many musicians turned to Mini-Brutes as a quick fix of the jazz tone for a solid couple of decades meant that a lot of players did start sounding very similar, in broad tonal terms if not in nuances of style and technique. This sonic homogeneity further broadened the tube/tranny divide, and fans of the old glowing bottles sometimes point to Polytone use as a compromise toward uniformity. Certainly many players' experiences indicate that solid-state amps are a little less 'playable' than tube amps – which is to say they respond a little less dynamically to the player's own touch and attack – so it is arguable, therefore, that the tube amp is intrinsically primed to better highlight a range of players' individualities. That said, you can't fault the hardworking, underpaid jazz guitarists for wanting a solid, portable reliable combo that he can plug into in a range of rooms and instantly achieve a sound he recognizes.

Polytone's MkII version of the Mini-Brute is among the most popular of the models (there are at least five 'marks' so far, and a few other special versions). It has two channels with active Treble and Bass controls capable of both cut and boost of their respective frequencies, a three position Dark/Normal/Bright tone emphasis switch, Drive control for its distortion circuit, and Reverb. The square, deep, closed-back plywood cabinet offers impressive low-end reproduction for its diminutive height and width (the same models double as compact double-bass amps), while cosmetics emphasize the businesslike rather than the stylish – a fact which doesn't seem to have bothered many customers. Similar 1x15″ models made through the years pump even more air.

Inside, early Polytones exhibit the older style discrete solid state technology, which is to say they were put together from individual components and a few basic opamps, rather than the large ICs used in most

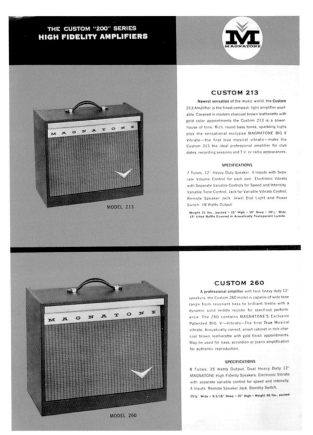

Magnatone was another quality brand of the 1950s and 1960s that was popular with many jazz players. Its rich reverb and deep vibrato suited the genre well.

modern consumer electronics. Fans of transistor circuits in other realms of music electronics swear by the virtue of these more archaic designs, although as with so much of the talk regarding tube amps (hand-wired vs PCB construction, high-end vs bulk generic components, metal film vs carbon comp resistors, etc) this might be equally based on nostalgia as on sonic results.

The MkII's tone controls don't range to extremes, but offer plenty of room to dial in a little more or less bite, sparkle or oomph, and the three-way voicing switch is useful for setting your starting point. The reverb in these amps is generally pretty good, with a little more depth and dimension than some of the cheaper versions of the effect included on many modern 'budget' tube amps, for example. Opinions of the Drive effect, however, range from "vile" to "horrid." The sound is derived from a modified diode-based clipping circuit, and if there's anything about the Mini-Brute that sounds overtly transistorized, this is it. Most of the jazzers who use these amps happily ignore it; hey, they don't want to distort anyway.

Plug many of the same players into a good and appropriately spec'd tube amp, however, and some of them might decide they did enjoy just a little distortion, whether they realized it or not. The edge of breakup and the resultant second-harmonic saturation in even small to medium sized tube amps can help to give them a depth, thickness and – yes – warmth that contributes to a perception of volume that belies their size. Plenty of gigging jazz guitarists have happily filled small clubs with the sweet, dynamic tone of a 22W 1x12″ Fender Deluxe Reverb for years, for example, and wouldn't switch from tubes for anything. Bigger Fenders such as 40W 2x12″ Pro Reverbs, 45W 4x10″ Super Reverbs, and 100W Twin Reverbs have long been popular, too. Surprisingly, the mid-powered 40W-45W amps can sometimes sound thicker and warmer for jazz than the powerful 100W Twins, for reasons we have already discussed elsewhere. A Twin certainly holds firm to its tight, clean performance to higher levels, but – while we're not aiming for a distortion sound as such – that forward edge of distortion, and the attack-manipulated dynamics that it affords, can really fatten up the tone of an ES-175's neck humbucker. Good blues and rock'n'roll 'clean' tones are traditionally found on a vintage-style, non-master-volume amp at the Volume setting that lets you retain clean shimmer with lightly picked passages, but still slide into succulent crunch with a good thwack of the pick. It's much the same with a good jazz sound on the same amps, but back down just another tick from this on the amp's Volume, and often with the guitar's Volume rolled down to 7 or 8 for all but the most heated solos. Pick those meaty flatwounds hard, and you're still going to segue into a greater ratio of total harmonic distortion, and very possibly you'll love the results.

Larger Gibson amps have always been popular jazz blasters too, as have many fine early Ampeg, Magnatone and Standel guitar combos. The latter had an endorsement list to rival Fender's in the 1950s, before the switch to solid-state designs in the 1960s and the subsequent decline of the brand's reputation. Ampeg originated and has remained best known as a bass amp maker (well, even before that as a maker of an early pickup for the upright bass), but many of the company's larger guitar combos offer deep, warm sounds that are ideal for jazz, and they have some of the sweetest sounding reverbs ever heard. The company's use of preamp tubes less seen in other guitar amps of the 1950s and 1960s, but which offer full frequency response and usually greater headroom than the usual 12AX7 preamp types, sets it apart right from the drawing board, too. But that can be a consideration for the vintage-amp buyer who needs to know that replacements will be readily available. Or you can buy a Polytone, and never replace another tube in your life... though any experienced amp tech will tell you that plenty of tranny amps break down too. In all, though, the 'jazz sound' is actually far more polytonal than mere Polytone-al, and the great players who display it best wield sounds that are rich in diversity, if subtly so.

Jimi Hendrix – doing with one finger what the rest of us strive to achieve with our entire being.

SETUP 8
THE JIMI RIG

Jimi Hendrix's sound and the equipment that helped him to make it are more shrouded in myth and mystery than those of any other player in the history of the electric guitar. Compared to most modern rigs, his setup is really pretty simple. There are indeed a lot of little quirks and alterations of particular links in the sound chain that help to make the whole thing groove in a manner that is more soulful than the sum of the individual parts. But then again there are also factors and alterations from the 'norm' of certain elements in the rig that are just there because that's the way Hendrix used them. Copying the oddities to the letter isn't necessarily going to get you sounding like Jimi.

The variables – and a lot of the magic and mystery – come from three different directions: 1) Hendrix played a right-handed Fender Stratocaster upside down, but restrung low-string-highest for standard but 'mirror image' fingering (lefty Strats existed, but he liked the controls at the top); 2) the majority of Hendrix's effects were heavily modified or 'improved' from their factory stock condition; 3) Hendrix was an extremely agile, musical, soulful guitarist with a seemingly magical control over his instrument and all of his gear. Throw all of these into the pot, stir, and simmer gently, and it's not a stew you are easily going to replicate just by assembling the various bits of hardware and plugging them in. That said, hey, this is great sounding gear, and you can employ it to great advantage in crafting your own sound and vibe... which might even come to pay homage to a ghost of the sound of the great man himself.

Like almost every great and adventurous guitarist who has strutted the stage and studio floor, Jimi Hendrix of course used a wide number of guitars, effects and amplifiers over the course of his too-short life and career. He was frequently photographed playing Gibson Flying V and SG guitars, played through many Fender, Sunn, Supro and Sound City amplifiers, and must have tried who knows how many different types of pedals (of the relatively limited number of makes and models available in the day). But his most revered setup is this: Fender Stratocaster into a Vox Wah-Wah, Octavia, and Fuzz Face (and later a Uni-Vibe) into 100W Marshall JMP100 Super Lead amplifier.

Selecting The Strat

We have already examined the Fender Stratocaster as it pertained to our R&B rig in Setup 3. Many of the versions used by Hendrix had evolved some from the 1950s and early 1960s examples that we concentrated on there, and he was more frequently photographed playing large-headstock CBS models than the small-headstock pre-CBS models that have become the more collectable of the breed. He definitely did play examples of the latter at the front end of his career especially, and – cue onslaught of hate mail and derisive rebuttal – I would argue that the pre/post-CBS issue is all much of a muchness. While this book is largely about recognizing the differences that extreme subtleties of design and componentry can play in shaping classic signature sounds, it is also important to acknowledge that there is always a certain pool of variables that is constantly swirling and impossible to plum to its final depths. If you wanted to stick NASA-grade test equipment on his rig and analyze it to the nth degree (an absurd thought, but stick with me a moment...) you would find that Jimi Hendrix sounded slightly different on any two nights in a row on the same tour, as did Jimmy Page, or Buddy Guy, or Eddie Van Halen, or Stevie Ray Vaughan, or Eric Johnson... Well, maybe not Eric Johnson. But he always sounded like Jimi Hendrix. Entirely like Jimi Hendrix, if you get my drift, even if he used the white Strat instead of the black one on 'Machine Gun' because the latter broke a string on the previous number, or stepped sideways on his Octavia and nudged its setting out of whack for the 'Purple Haze' solo, or whatever.

That said, there certainly were some differences in the build of the Stratocasters of the later 1960s that

Some of the main ingredients of the Jimi Hendrix rig: a 1960s Fender Stratocaster (pre-CBS, in this case), Vox Wah-Wah, Dallas-Arbiter Fuzz Face, and that monstrous Marshall stack. The Sunn amplifiers ad (inset) would have you believe it was otherwise, as it was for a brief period of time.

started subtly to change their sound and performance. In the early *Are You Experienced* days, Hendrix was frequently seen with a sunburst small-headstock pre-CBS Stratocaster with rosewood fingerboard. Later he more often used large-headstock late-1960s models. I have heard it said that this was a conscious preference, and that Hendrix selected the later Strats because the increased wood at the headstock yielded greater sustain, but I always felt that this was over-thinking the matter. For one thing, this theory doesn't account for wood densities, which make poppycock of the whole thing: a wide head with light, porous maple would have a lesser mass than a small head with heavy, dense maple, and would therefore flip-flop the entire supposition. And how many vintage Fender fanatics have come to understand anyway that the lighter (ie, low density) bodies often have greater resonance, warmth and sustain?

Vintage Fender fanatics understand that lighter bodies have more resonance, warmth and sustain

It seems worth turning to a greater authority, though, to help put the lid on the issue. Roger Mayer, the noted Hendrix effects guru and frequent sidekick, who had the pleasure of going on some of those 'need to find a Strat, quick!' shopping trips, had the job of assessing and setting up many a Hendrix Strat for stage or studio. I asked him about the headstock size/sustain ratio theory.

"No, Jimi wouldn't have considered that," Mayer told me. "All the guitars that we used were bought out of necessity; there weren't that many Stratocasters around in those days, and they were very expensive. Also, in the 1960s nobody paid much attention to whether pre-CBS Fenders were any better than CBS Fenders. They were all about the same, and often none of them were very good, to tell you the truth. I can't see a slightly bigger headstock making any difference anyway."

One thing that might make a slight difference in 'the Hendrix Strat' – and Mayer supports this thinking, too – is that because of the flip-flopping of the headstock, the low-E string would be wound around the tuning post furthest from the nut. Thanks to the string tree (now retaining the E and A rather than high B and E) this lowest string would still have suitable downward pressure in the nut to keep it stable, but with its tuner-post being anchored at the end of a greater expanse of wood, its vibrational energy would have a greater mass of wood through which to resonate, and therefore a slightly fuller, more muscular tone. Slightly. And that's always the key word. Even if the effect is there, you still want to carefully weigh its significance before you run out and purchase a left-handed neck to bolt onto your right-handed guitar to make it 'sound like Jimi's.' Before making any radical selections in your own 'rig emulation' bid, it's always worth reminding yourself that Jimi Hendrix borrowed Noel Redding's Fender Telecaster to record 'Hey Joe' and 'Purple Haze;' it's a sobering revelation for those who always quoted the tracks as classic examples of great Stratocaster tone.

Other variations between types of Strats used by Hendrix certainly make a sonic difference, too, but as he used them both through the course of his career, which are you going to choose? The earlier pre-CBS Strats and some of the CBS models he played in 1967 and 1968 had rosewood fingerboards, but after that period Hendrix displayed a preference for maple 'board Strats. As we have discussed, the latter lends a significantly tighter, snappier edge to the guitar's overall sound, while the former offers a degree of warmth, roundness and sizzle. You can clearly hear that toothsome rosewood 'blur' in the slightly more raw early sounds, while Hendrix's later work often exhibits a punchier, overall 'bigger' attack… or at least we can convince ourselves that we think it does. Again, the tonal recipe proves itself in some places, but pushing the analysis to extremes becomes its own absurdity. Nevertheless, the fingerboard woods will make a difference in both sound and feel that most keen-eared guitarists who pick the two up can detect after some listening, and depending on how many other influences there are upon your tone (amp type and settings, effects, sheer volume and distortion), it can be enough to play a significant part in your guitar selection.

Another much-talked-about 'flip-flopping a right-hander' alteration was the reversing of the center two of the Strat pickup's staggered pole pieces, resulting in the higher pole now sitting under the wound D-string rather than the G-string. But the effect of this would be even more minimal, possibly undetectable.

If anything, the change would help to slightly balance out the response of these two strings, as Fender originally raised the G-string pole piece to compensate for the lower output of a wound G-string in comparison with the plain B. As the G-strings in lighter sets were no longer wound at this time, the compensation was better placed at the D-string anyway. Even so, these are already two of the higher pole pieces on a Strat pickup of the day, and the difference between them is minimal (a difference easily negated by the difference in pole-to-string gaps between a fretted and open string, for example, or a string fretted at very different places on the 'board). Thanks again to the informative Roger Mayer, we know that Hendrix's string gauges ran .010, .013, .015, .026 (wound), .036 and .038, (Fender 150 Series Rock'n'Roll Lights). The use of a .015 G-string versus a .017 was a very conscious decision, and went further than this pole piece reversal toward balancing out the volume of the individual strings, and keeping the G from leaping out of the sonic picture. In any case, you reverse the guitar, you reverse the pickups too. It was never a conscious decision to keep them that way, and far too much trouble to put them back 'the right way around,' requiring the removal of body wood at the back of the pickup routings and extending the lead wires. Forget it.

Weaker Pickups, Bigger Amps

Greater standardizing of the mechanical winding procedures used to manufacture Fender pickups meant a decrease in output strength in the late 1960s over the specs of the 1950s and early 1960s, and this would be of far more significance than headstock sizes and slight pole piece reversals. The guitars Hendrix was playing most often from 1968 onward would have had even weaker pickups than those of the previous 15 years – and as we have seen, they were never a high-output pickup to begin with – but this worked toward Hendrix's sonic ends to some extent, whether a conscious selection on his part or not. A weaker pickup of that type would have a brighter, more high-harmonics-rich sound, and would also be slower to drive a tube amp into distortion. The combination of a cranked Marshall JMP100 and a Fuzz Face already offered

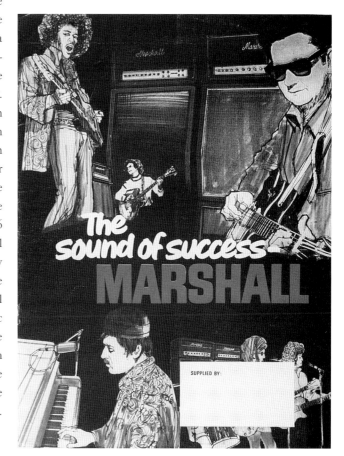

Stars of the day promote their amplification of choice on this stylishly illustrated Marshall catalog cover.

about as much distortion as most players of the day were likely to want, so anything that helped get you toward the opposite end of that spectrum when desired could be extremely useful. Injected into Hendrix's setup, these thin, bright pickups gave loads of cut and sting to the Marshall's roar, yielding a really slicing tone. On top of that, the combination made for an extremely touch-sensitive rig – one allowing you to back off your pick or fingertip attack to easily sweeten up the sound without even having to wind down the guitar volume dramatically (more so than with a Les Paul, for example, which remains pretty fat until you drop the guitar pot right back), and to elicit a loud, firm tone with a fullness but no excess of distortion when desired. Somehow the single-coil pickup into, say, a fuzz box, wah-wah, and then a really pushed 100W sounds a little more live-wired and unhinged than the smooth liquid warmth of a humbucker; there's more of a crackling electricity to the sound, but you can easily warm it up a little by rolling off the guitar's volume and tone controls as desired. The tonal palette here is broad, and Hendrix dipped into the entire spectrum.

Other than the changes detailed, the Stratocasters of the late-mid and late 1960s weren't so very different from those of the early part of the decade. Neck shapes were somewhat different, often a little fatter than the ultra-thin profiles of 1959-62 but nowhere near as clubby as some 1950s necks, but they always varied noticeably from Strat to Strat of the same year even. The quality of body woods was starting to deteriorate slightly, with CBS notoriously churning out the products with both eyes on the bottom line, but they weren't yet the totally indifferent deadweights that we would so often come to see in the 1970s. More dramatic changes in the model would follow in the next decade: the move from pressed steel to die cast bridge saddles, the elimination of the staggered pole pieces, polyurethane finishes, and the notorious bullet headstock that accompanied the three-bolt 'Micro-Tilt' neck attachment. In 1968 or so a Strat was still a Strat, according to many Fender fans, but by part way through the 1970s it was something quite different.

More than 30 years after the guitarist's death, the Strat's associations with Jimi Hendrix are still one of the model's greatest selling factors.

Just as we have previously covered an earlier generation of Stratocaster in this book, we have also already analyzed one of Marshall's flagship guitar amps. But many great gear makers have moved from classic to classic, and this British amplifier manufacturer is one of them. While the JTM45 half-stack and its partner the model 1962 – or 'Bluesbreaker' – combo are gorgeous pieces of gear by any standards, they really aren't definitively 'Marshall.' When players talk about 'the Marshall sound' they essentially mean the sound of a Plexi of late 1966 to 1969, and while this legendary amp-maker's models evolved further through the years, that seminal tone template remains at the core of what most Marshall players seek. It's a sound so ingrained in rock's sonic lexicon that most of us can hear it in our sleep (or is that just tinnitus?).

The Marshall legend may have been conceived in 1962 when Jim Marshall and Ken Bran sat down to copy the 5F6A Fender Bassman (as thoroughly outlined in Setup 3), but it was a protracted gestation period, and the true Marshall sound wasn't born until some four years later, when the JTM45 evolved into the JTM50 – famously known ever after simply as 'the Plexi.' Make no mistake: its predecessor was a great amplifier. The JTM45 models of the company's first four years are juicy, raw, soulful performers. The fact is, though, they are very much like the bigger late-1950s tweed Fenders, too, and therefore not quite a unique sounding product like the models that would follow.

Jimi Hendrix
plays

British Amp, British Tube

Come the mid 1960s, however, the KT66 tubes used in the JTM45 models were in short supply and expensive to boot. The cost of importing US-made 5881s or 6L6s – which the amp was born with in 1962 – made no better business sense. The relatively newer, and sturdy and powerful, EL34 output tubes got the nod, and Marshall redesigned its amps to take these taller, slimmer bottles. Along with the output-tube swap they dropped the GZ34 tube rectifier – perhaps partly because solid-state silicon diodes simply promised to be more reliable, and partly because these new EL34s could take the far higher voltages that diodes were capable of supplying – and redesigned the power supply stage of the amplifier accordingly. In the broad sense, the amplifier really hadn't evolved far. Examine the circuits of a tweed Bassman from 1959 and a Plexi from around the middle of that amp's heyday, say 1968, and you'll see that the preamp design, the positioning and values of the tone controls, and 90 per cent of the signal capacitors are all exactly the same. The only truly noticeable differences are the aforementioned change to EL34s, the solid-state rectification, and much higher filtering in the power supply. But what a difference in sound! The rectification and filtering changes firm up the low-end and tighten the overall response respectively, for a muscular punch with plenty of thump in the bottom, while the output tube swap brings in a real crispy-cream tonality – lots of crackle in the highs, grinding lower mids, and a smoother onset of breakup throughout the frequency spectrum. (Check out CD tracks 8 and 34 in quick succession to hear the difference displayed by these changes – they give you a very similar Strat played through a tweed Bassman and Marshall Plexi respectively.)

Plexis did also contain another basic but significant constructional change inside the amp head: the chassis were now made from steel rather than aluminum, and were therefore sturdier and could better endure the rigors of touring. The type of metal from which a chassis is made can also effect the electromagnetic fields around certain components, the transformers in particular, so this might indeed subtly affect an amp's sound in some cases. You'd be hard-pressed to pin any sonic differences down to this factor even in a direct A/B test (if such a thing were even possible to set up: "quick, now remount everything onto the aluminum chassis!"), but it is another subtle change in these amps' sonic evolution.

Things you can't see without putting some test equipment on the amp include somewhat higher DC voltages on the tubes – not a lot higher, but enough to make a difference. The rule of thumb goes 'higher voltages = higher output levels,' (although other factors do contribute) and while most JMP Plexis' voltages are only up to around 500v DC from the Bassman/JTM45's 430v DC, this makes a big difference given the power-conversion efficiency of the EL34s of the mid 1960s. On the JTM45, the '45' was just a model number. While many players and dealers alike consider it a statement of a '45W' output rating, the average JTM45 only puts out about 30W-35W. The name given the JMP50 was closer to the truth, but in fact erred in the other direction; most of the dual-EL34 heads actually put out close to 60-70W in really good condition, while so-called 100-watters can top out at nearly 150W.

Along with the changes, some other factors left well enough alone are equally significant in the Marshall sound. Whereas Fender had gone to new preamp and EQ circuits for its brownface and blackface amps of the early and mid 1960s in a bid to EQ out more clean headroom, Marshall had retained the extremely tactile, touch-sensitive 'cathode follower' tone stack, beloved of countless rock and blues players. They also kept the Presence control, which is useful for dialing in a little more cut and bite in the highs but without inducing the kind of trebly harshness of many 'bright' switches. Add together the few stages that changed and the few that stayed the same, and you've got a magical combination of a juicy, touch-sensitive playing machine with crackling, cutting highs, great low-end oomph, and a gorgeous, open-throated growl when you hit it hard.

Plexi Transitions

You can see by now that the term 'Plexi' is itself something of a misnomer. During 1965 Marshall began putting these new gold-backed control panels on the JTM45 models, which still carried KT66 output tubes and a GZ34 rectifier, and these sound nothing like what most rockers are looking for in 'a Plexi'. Then in 1966 the transition arrived only in pieces, as Marshall designers tinkered with the need for different tubes, and more powerful amplifiers. Nevertheless, the name helps to define amps that were fairly (though not completely!) uniform in design and construction through that brief 1967-69 period. It's interesting to note, too, that Marshall used the model designation 1987 for its flagship lead guitar amps manufactured between 1965 and 1981, even though the better-known front-panel designations evolved from JTM45 to JTM50 to JMP50, and so forth. In any case, the Plexi hadn't really settled into its definitive form until 1967, when the EL34s, solid-state rectification, steel (versus aluminum) chassis, Plexiglas control panel and JMP model designations all came together to sum up this classic.

Other internal changes through the years of the JTM45/Plexi/Metal-panel transitions are spoken of with hushed reverence by both players and collectors, but are as often the result of accident as of any conscious evolution of design. Marshall's output transformers did certainly change over the years, to cite one component example, but this seems to have been as much down to availability of supplies and a certain hit-and-miss trial of new combinations of components as to any hard workshop R&D of the sort that, say, Fender's designers took part in through the 1950s and early 1960s. As with all pieces of musical hardware, any slight change in construction can make a difference, whether intentional or not. Marshall Plexis aren't the first classic piece of kit to have come together partly through a series of happy accidents (and partly, to give credit where due, through plenty of considered design and quality manufacture). If there had arrived a glut of cheap but quality US-made 5881s and 6L6s, or if some big European or British market

Marshall Plexis aren't the first classic piece of kit to have come together partly through happy accidents

had developed a demand for increased production of KT66s, Marshall might never have moved to the EL34 that now largely defines its trademark sound. Then again, maybe it would have.

You hear some talk about Jimi Hendrix having swapped his Marshalls' output tubes to US-made 6550s, but this is really only a factor of the very last portion of his career. He apparently preferred his Plexis to carry these tighter, cleaner sounding tubes during US tours or recording, but he was also using some Fender and Sunn amps at these times, and a whole impenetrable range of amps and sound chains in the studio besides, so it doesn't seem to be an avenue worth pursuing too strenuously. These tubes would have been extremely expensive and hard to come by in England during the time he was launching his career there, and the amps would have required modification to use them. In any case, extremely good sources who had their hands on these very amps and tubes back in the day tell me his Marshalls definitely retained their EL34s for the classic English recordings and live dates, and that the same were often taken to the US for those tours (though certainly many were rented for American tours in throughout the years, too), so the EL34 version of 'the Marshall sound' seems like the best benchmark.

Within the Plexi years themselves, most other ingredients being equal, Marshall fanatics get most excited about whether an early amp's power transformer is a 'stand up' or 'lie down' mounting – and there are some voltage supply differences between the two. Prototype and early 100W JTM100 models with dual 50W OTs rather than the single 100W OT that would become the norm in the JMP era also generate a lot of excitement. Most reports indicate that all such variations were really just a matter of supply rather than of conscious design; Pete Townshend of The Who was pressing Jim Marshall for a louder amp, no 100W iron was readily available, so the new monster got two 50W OTs. A collectable amp indeed, but maybe not the most sensible design from a player's perspective. In any case, throughout these years component selection usually depended in equal parts on what was needed and what was available, as with most amp-makers, both then and now.

In recent years, the model 1987 JMP50 has become the most desirable of the Plexis. Few guitarists have the opportunity to make the most of the 100W-plus maelstrom of the JMP100, and the 50W Plexi has therefore become the more desirable of these Marshalls, able as it is to achieve that lush, more-ish rock splendor at slightly less foundation-demolishing volumes. This extends even to the surprising inverse relationship of 50-watters generally fetching more than 100-watters on the vintage market – if you can find them at all. In the late 1960s, however, when stone-age PA systems labored to fill cavernous venues for the seriously loud business of rock, the 100W Plexis were the stacks of the stars. Standing atop a straight-front

Even the string-maker is looking for a promotional piece of the mythos.

1960B 4x12″ 'bottom cab' and angled-front 1960A 'top cab', one of these 4xEL34 beasts moved some serious air, and when cranked toward max still offered all the gorgeous touch sensitivity and creamy playability of the smaller half-stacks. Jimi Hendrix evolved from his early use of JTM100s to JMP100 stacks; and for his work with Cream, Eric Clapton moved to the same from the 'Bluesbreaker' combo of his John Mayall days. Genuine Plexis of any type are hard to come by these days, but players who are able to make use of a JMP100 are in luck in a sense. Most searches of the vintage dealers both in the USA and the UK will turn up five 100-watters for every JMP50. The list of guitar stars who have used JMP50s to take their tone to the top over the past 35 years is really too long to mention, and I guess that is where all the good amps have gone.

For Hendrix, the 100-watter was a necessity. His Stratocaster run into a JMP100 and a pair of 4x12″s offered a vocal, flute-like, rich clean tone with the guitar's Volume control wound down, and no end of growl and sting with it right up to full, with plenty of shades of crunch and bite in between. Step on a Fuzz Face, and he was full-force – an enormous sound at his fingertips. He was such a dynamic player, too, with great subtleties of attack and wide-ranging touch, that a 50-watter just wouldn't have had the headroom to broadcast his message live. Smaller amps in smaller rooms, or in the recording studio, offer the opportunity to drive those output tubes into the sweet spot without blowing away the audience, or the mikes and meters. In too big a room, though, the player is often forced to thrash away full-steam in order to keep the levels pumping, and isn't able to make best use of dynamics and subtle touch-sensitivities in a good tube amp. Today's big touring artists have the advantage of state of the art PA rigs, and can therefore indulge in easily driven 50W or even smaller amps to broadcast that sweet spot at arena-filling volumes but without taking their bandmates' heads off in the process. Back in the late 1960s, however, the guitar stack was relied upon to bellow out that gut-thumping wail that fans expected in a live rock show, and Hendrix knew how to play the big rig better than most.

Speakers and the cabinet they are housed in play a big part in forming the sonic signature of any amplifier, and these were evolving throughout the mid to late 1960s right along with the electronics of the amps. Marshall had been using Celestion G12M 'Greenbacks' before the Plexis' arrival, but around this time the drivers were upgraded from 20W to 25W units, and were approaching the sound for which they have ever remained renowned. The closed-back plywood cabs themselves changed through the course of 1966, too, their dimensions slimming down somewhat, while their construction featured stronger finger joints at the corners. Towards the late 1960s, Marshall also employed sturdier 30W Celestion G12H drivers in many cabs. The 'H' in the name stands for 'heavy magnet;' a rule of thumb for speakers says the heavier the magnet, the better the low-end response, and although these were first introduced to help handle bass reproduction, plenty of guitarists came to prefer their power and girth, including Hendrix himself.

Loaded with G12Hs, each 4x12″ in a full stack was capable of handling a 120W input rather than the 80W or 100W of early and later Greenbacks respectively. This would also help give such a stack with a JMP100 on top a little more headroom than the norm, and coupled with the drivers' firmer low end (Greenbacks tend to go muddy in the low frequencies pretty quickly) and higher efficiency, would make for a thumping rig with lots of punch, even with a single-coiled Strat plugged into it rather than a Les Paul or SG or similar. Celestion makes a very accurate reissue of the G12H-30 today, and it's an excellent sounding speaker, with a lot of the sweetness of the hallowed Alnico Blue – but at a lower price, and with better power-handling and a firmer, bolder low end.

Cosmetics changed very slightly throughout the years of the Plexi, but not so much as they had through the first few years of the JTM45's lifetime. Certainly the basic-black look of the Marshall amp may appear more uniform throughout the company's history than the varying models of other big makers, but details such as the move from the gold-embossed plastic logos on the JTM50s to the small white plastic script logos, the arrival of the JMP designation along with the gold-backed Plexiglas control panels in 1967, the switch to aluminum control panels in 1969, and the uniformity of wide-body head cabs by around 1970 are easily distinguished by any Marshall aficionado. Given that these amps have been popularly defined ever after by the material used for their control panels, the change to brushed, gold-anodized aluminum in 1969 has become a major deal to collectors, but it was really just another minor alteration of materials in the broad sense. In itself, it would trigger no sonic changes whatsoever, but while the amp's circuit remained the same through the early metal-panel years, the inevitable variances in component supplies and somewhat higher voltages found in many examples meant that many units off the assembly line soon began to sound slightly different from those of just months before. Many aggressive rock players will even tell you they prefer the aluminum-panel JMP50s for their growl and attack, but the Plexi remains easily a rung above it on the vintage-value ladder for most collectors. Through the course of the 1970s, however, the construction and design of Marshall's flagship guitar amps did evolve ever further from the JMP50 template, and the available models became very different pieces of rock hardware indeed. For most diehard fans of Marshall's storming first decade, the arrival of printed circuit board (PCB) construction around 1974 or of the Master Volume designs in 1975 mark the true end of the vintage era.

As they were only manufactured for less than three years, between 1967 and 1969, any true original Plexi in decent condition is going to cost you some cash, but at least there are a range of ways to get there. The metal-panel amps of the early 1970s are really very similar sounding and go for somewhat less money, but they are still getting bloody expensive by workingman standards. A handful of Marshall reissues – notably the great examples from 1988 and 1991-93 – offer a plausible glimpse at that tone, while many 'boutique' builders in both the UK and the USA do very good contemporary Plexi-based models that might be less of a risk to take on the road. To top these, a Plexi model is included in Marshall's own range of hand-wired reissues which has just arrived on the market at the time of writing.

Of course, as I mentioned toward the start of this chapter, as well as straying from the Marshall path occasionally, Hendrix also strayed from the Fender path at times, to use – most famously – Gibson Flying-Vs and SGs. He played a range of tunes on these later in his career, but most often turned to the Gibsons for heavy blues numbers. With their set necks and all-mahogany or korina

Fender's Stratocaster had already achieved legendary status in the first 12 years of its existence. Then Hendrix picked one up...

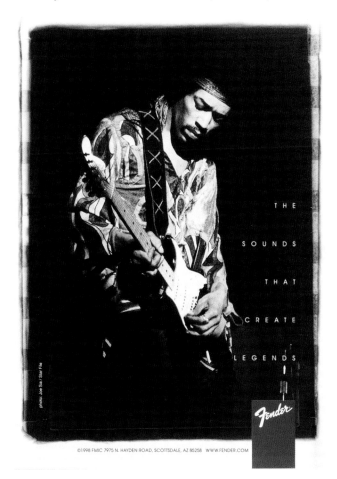

construction, plus fat, bold humbucking pickups, these were warm, thick-voiced guitars, and would drive his Marshalls even harder, or any amps, for that matter. With the Gibson guitars at the input, Hendrix's rig points us more toward the classic stadium rock sound of the 1970s: a Les Paul or SG into a metal-panel Marshall stack. Eric Clapton and Jimmy Page had already led the way down this road, and countless heavy rockers followed them along it over the next decade and more.

Rather than carrying on with this humbucker-loaded Gibson sound in the Hendrix framework, our CD samples for this chapter conclude with a couple of tracks that are more in the style that some big rock players were exuding by the mid 1970s or so. You can easily hear that the SG Custom through a metal-panel Marshall 1987 Lead amplifier has elements of Hendrix's Strat/Plexi tone, but with a more all-encompassing crunch and crackle. You could argue there is less to be plumbed here by way of dynamics, but countless players have found it an enthralling and more powerful lead guitar sound than the Fender guitar and earlier Marshall were capable of.

Fat Fuzz And Wicked Wah-Wah

Then again, for plenty more still, that Strat/Plexi combination will always remain the setup to beat. Although no player is entirely going to reproduce Jimi Hendrix's playing technique – and the 'finger tone' that some people like to acknowledge for being as individual as fingerprints – the Stratocaster and JMP100 stack are going to get you a long way to doing your own thing with a shadow of his awesome sound. The effects units that he turned to for added spice might help to take you even further.

I always feel that part of what helps to define Hendrix's greatness is the fact that he was a pioneer in the use of effects pedals – strings of multiple units interacting together, in particular – but never sounded like 'an effects-heavy' guitarist. We think of his great musicianship, style, attack, and the sonics he used are really just subtle doses of light and shade. He played his effects, rather than letting the effects play him, and they were never used for novelty's sake. The Dallas-Arbiter Fuzz Face, Vox Wah-Wah, Roger Mayer Octavia, and Univox Uni-Vibe are hailed by Hendrix copyists as essential ingredients for 'sounding like Jimi' – but I think a subtle approach to tapping their capabilities does the most justice to both the Jimi Rig, and to these components' use for other genres of music.

The Fuzz Face was preceded by Maestro's Fuzz-Tone and a few lesser variations on the theme, but is arguably the most hallowed of all vintage fuzz boxes. Hendrix found his first example of the smiling, round pedal not long after it first arrived in the Arbiter company's Sound City music shop in London in 1966, and quickly put it to stunning use. Early Faces were extremely variable in sound and quality, and Hendrix and other players of the day learned early on that they needed to play all they could get their hands on to sort out the few really sweet ones. Even so, electronics wizard Roger Mayer would frequently service and modify these units to try to get the best out of them, so it doesn't seem like they remained entirely stock for long.

These pedals' lack of uniformity stems from the inherent variability of the germanium transistors that were at the heart of the simple circuit. These little metal-clad transistors, which were a popular choice before silicon components became widely available or cost-effective, had enormously wide tolerances of specification by today's standards. Gain levels varied widely even between pieces from the same batch, and the Fuzz Face carried two of them, usually either NTK275 or AC128 types. Back in the day, these don't appear to have been very carefully matched or selected, so two transistors of entirely random gain levels could land in these vital positions on the circuit board – and the sound of two Fuzz Faces side by side on the guitar store shelf could therefore vary enormously because of this. For this reason, most of the better makers who still use germanium transistors in certain vintage-style fuzz circuits carefully select and match them for ideal gain levels.

Germanium transistors are somewhat softer and smoother sounding than their silicon partners, with a playing edge that can feel a little more compressed and tactile. A good Fuzz Face can sound crisp yet smooth, with a sound that fattens your signal enormously but without swamping it in an opaque haze. Classic units carry only Volume and Fuzz controls; the latter is self explanatory, though in addition to upping the filth content, winding it towards max also serves to increase sustain. Along with their own sonic properties, the pedals are also great for driving big tube amps into distortion with the Volume control somewhat advanced. Bad Fuzz Faces often sound muddy, woolly, and sometimes just wimpy of body, maybe with plenty of dirt but no edge and definition.

Unlike plenty of other extreme fuzz pedals, a good Fuzz Face is a very playable effect – its distortion levels can be controlled at the guitar's Volume, and it responds beautifully to playing dynamics. Hendrix knew how to make the most of this, and rather than slam his Face into a Marshall JMP100 full-force all the time, he brought the fuzz in and out as needed, and even when switched in used his own touch and the pedal's drive levels to further enhance his dynamics rather than to swamp them. Generally a vintage fuzz of this type works best when placed first in the effects chain, but that isn't always possible; wah-wah, in particular, really needs to take that position to do its best EQ-filtering work (although other positions will offer up some interesting effects, if not 'classic wah' as it was intended). This was the case with Hendrix's lineup, but the fact that a Vox Wah-Wah took place of pride in the string, usually followed by an Octavia, didn't seem to hamper his Fuzz Face's effectiveness any. Hendrix also used a number of fuzzes custom-built by Roger Mayer, the main type eventually dubbed the 'Axis Fuzz,' but in the early days it was mainly the 'Faces.

Both Jimi Henderix and Eric Clapton achieved their expressive, vocal wah-wah sounds with a Vox unit.

In addition to modding other makers' effects used and later contributing the aforementioned custom fuzzes, Mayer also designed and built one very famous Hendrix-associated unit himself: the Octavia. Originally only available in as few as half a dozen custom-made units for Hendrix and a few other pros of the time who requested one, this relatively simple but radical effect was first prominently heard in the lead riffs of Hendrix's 'Purple Haze,' and soon after featured on much of the guitarist's work. The Octavia creates a fuzzy artificial octave-up effect by virtue of a circuit that is extremely clever in its simplicity. It is crude and imposing in some senses, and takes even more playing with than most guitar effects to really get the hang of, but can make a huge impact – and fatten up a sound enormously – when used well. These pedals can only track one note at a time, so even double-stops elicit

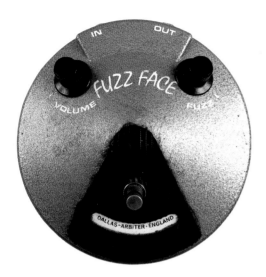

The Dallas-Arbiter Fuzz Face churns out a fat, tactile tone that makes it an all-time great among fuzz boxes.

a dissonant clank. And they are much happier with higher than lower frequencies, but simultaneously prefer the purer, less harmonically-saturated signal from a neck pickup to that from a bridge pickup. Precisely played single-note riffs halfway up the neck or beyond with a Strat's neck pickup selected – and, ideally, a little treble rolled off – elicit the best response.

Hendrix achieved real mastery of this, as have a few others, and used it to produce a spacey but convincing octave-soloing sound that was swift and funky. Used well, it's a real head turner; used poorly, it can be cumbersome and clunky. The original Octavia never hit the market as a production effect, but was copied by the Tycobrahe company for a number of years, and has since arrived in a variety of forms from other makers, including Roger Mayer himself, who returned to guitar effects building in the early 1980s after more than a decade of designing and manufacturing high-end pro audio processors for recording studios.

The same Jennings Musical Industries that manufactured Vox amplifiers made some early wah-wahs in the UK, then farmed out the work to Jen in Italy, and these were the units that Hendrix, Cream-era Eric Clapton and some other major late-1960s artists used for their singing, vocal-like tones. A wah-wah is an extremely expressive pedal, but takes a lot of practice to make the most of. Rather than just rocking away in the more stereotypical disco-rhythm or cop-show soundtrack 'whacka-whacka' style that was heard so much by the middle of the following decade, Hendrix worked the powerful subtleties of the wah-wah to elicit everything from singing to talking to weeping sounds from his rig, along with plenty of effects that aren't even immediately identifiable as 'wah,' but bend and shift the tonality of the instrument with gentle, rippling frequency transitions.

Workings Of The Wah-Wah

A wah-wah pedal contains a treadle-controlled potentiometer that governs the frequency sweep of a

The Univox Uni-Vibe was designed to reproduce Leslie cab sounds for electric organs, but Hendrix took the effect to new heights.

simple tone filtering circuit. Clever players had for years been achieving some basic wah-like sounds by pumping the Tone controls on their guitars, but the battery-powered pedal form of this effect is much more powerful. By boosting a specific frequency band (creating a 'peak') within the guitar's frequency spectrum, then sweeping this relatively narrow band up and down across that spectrum, the wah-wah causes certain notes in a riff to leap forward with a vocal-like 'wah' – as the name implies – rather than simply rolling the high frequencies in and out of the signal, as turning any ordinary tone control on a guitar or amp will do. The vintage Vox units are beloved for their wailing approximation of a human vocal tone, while the classic Cry Baby's sweet, fluid sounds are also much loved. Either works best in front of other effects, and fuzz in particular, because it wants to filter the raw frequency spectrum straight from the guitar's pickups, which can then be fuzzed, swirled, echoed or whatever, rather than taking a fuzzed signal and sweeping this boosted frequency band up and down it, which is a whole other mess entirely.

In addition to the intentional effect of its filtering circuit, vintage wah-wah pedals had the unintentional effect of sapping some high end from the guitar signal even when out of circuit ('tone sucking,' as most refer to it today). Such performance has come to be seen as detrimental to your sound, and often was so in the 1960s as well, but guitarists like Jimi Hendrix used even this to their advantage. These wah-wahs were one way of taming the fierce highs of the High-Treble channel on a Marshall Plexi, and making it easier to achieve warm, plummy, clean tones, even with a Strat plugged into the rig. Of course Hendrix's wah-wahs were also frequently modified by Roger Mayer, too, to enhance their frequency range according to the key of the song and so forth, and in the studio in particular pre-gain and bypass stages and parallel-paths to the amps and mixer would often be used to get around any tone-sucking issues.

As creative and adventurous a guitarist as he was, Hendrix turned to many other effects in the studio, but the only other black box in his 'every day' pedal chain from 1969 on was the Univox Uni-Vibe. Thanks to its Hendrix associations, and its later use by the likes of Robin Trower and Stevie Ray Vaughan, the Uni-Vibe has been 'cloned' by a number of boutique makers in recent years. But the original hailed from the Shin Ei company of Japan, and was designed as a Leslie cabinet-style rotating speaker simulator for organ. It achieves this in ways that are relatively simple, but because of the discrete, totally solid-state analog circuitry, it also involves a pretty complex-looking design for its day. This is another piece of vintage kit in which a few happy accidents come together to produce magical tones that we can assume are even beyond the realm of anything the original designers and manufacturers envisaged, but which have been beloved of guitarists ever since the units hit the shelves.

The Uni-Vibe actually functions as a four-stage phaser, and its swirling, liquid tones come courtesy of the four rather crude lamp-and-photo cell pairings at the heart of its circuit. It is often a noisy effect, and a complex thing to manufacture compared to the average fuzz or wah-wah, but a listen to Hendrix's 'Voodoo Chile,' 'The Wind Cries Mary,' 'The Star Spangled Banner' from Woodstock or 'Machine Gun' (especially the live performance from the Fillmore) will show you the range of textures of which this unit is capable. Plenty of 'boutique' effects makers have told me they just can't

You can go a long way toward crafting your own approach by learning what's at the heart of the stunning sounds of a guitarist like Hendrix

reproduce that sound with anything other than the bulbs and light cells, but some do improve upon the unit's range and noise by updating other sections of the circuit, and good sounding versions are currently available from Fulltone, Roger Mayer, Voodoo Lab, Sweet Sound, Prescription and others.

Hendrix's guitars and amps were pretty straight, although kept in good playing condition, and of course he was playing a right-handed guitar restrung and held upside-down for left-handed playing, with all the subtle alterations that introduced. But his effects were frequently modified and, for recording in particular, even segmented out to provide many more sonic variables than the stock units would have allowed. Knowing this, it's clear that you are unlikely to be playing through exactly the same circuits that Jimi played through back in the day, even if you can track down – and pay for – units of the same make and model he used. All of which only shows the relative absurdity of trying to mimic both the style and setup of any great artist. The variables in any outstanding performance range far beyond the equipment and outwardly detectable basics of style and technique; but you can go a long way toward crafting your own outstanding sound and playing approach by learning what's at the heart of the stunning sounds of a guitarist like Jimi Hendrix, then applying them toward doing your own thing.

Roy Buchanan goes for broke on an early 1970s Telecaster.

SETUP 9
COUNTRY TWANG

E ven with eyes closed most readers could guess my country guitar of choice for this chapter. As we saw in Setup 2: Rock'n'Roll, many electric players evolved from the pre-solidbody years of country into the early years of rock'n'roll using big hollowbodied Gibsons and Epiphones and, later, Gretsches. But ever since Leo Fender screwed together his legendary slab-bodied creation and launched it on the western swing band and session scene of southern California, the Broadcaster – soon Telecaster – has been King of Country, and played by more stars of the genre than any other guitar. Although the model changed in a number of minor ways through even its pre-CBS years, and in further more dramatic ways beyond them, Leo got a hell of a lot of things right straight off the bat; it's the instrument that put the twang into country, and for plenty of guitarists, this first-ever mass production solidbody guitar is the only tonal tool that needs to live in the toolbox.

Our country amp arrived 14 years after its six-string partner debuted, but in the years since then the Fender Twin Reverb has proved itself the big-gig twangster of choice, and alternatives used before its arrival have mostly fallen in its wake since 1964. But I'm going to add an unprecedented twist to this chapter, and make the amp choice a duo: both a blackface Fender Twin Reverb and blackface Deluxe Reverb. The Twin – as seen in the main photo – will make up the header rig as our picker'n'grinner would use it on stage, while for studio dates he would naturally turn to the zippier, more easily manageable Deluxe, as heard on the CD. What a pair! What a trio! We might like occasionally to add the compressor pedal that became nearly universal in the studio within a few years, but otherwise these amps' reverb and tremolo are about all the effects most country players were likely to need on a regular basis... given we are talking about the days when country was still country, and not the hyper-produced Stetson-pop that so much of the Nashville product has evolved into.

If the lowly guitarist was going to get ahead, he needed an instrument that would let him roll out enough volume to be heard above the band

Clarence Leo Fender was a trained accountant turned radio repairman and general electronics tinkerer who first entered the musical instruments business in partnership with fiddle and lap-steel player Doc Kaufman in 1945. Adopting the K&F name, they worked initially out of the the Fender Radio Service store that Leo had opened in the LA suburb of Fullerton in 1939, and that southern California location remained synonymous with Fender guitars throughout their founder's association with the company. With Kaufman's departure in 1946 Fender started trading under his own name – first as Fender Manufacturing, then as Fender Electric Instrument Co in 1947 – but carried on with the stock-in-trade that had launched K&F, the lap-steel guitars and amplifiers that then still constituted the forefront of the fledgling electric guitar movement. While Fender lap-steels earned a pretty good local reputation in the early years, Leo's experience selling and repairing radios, and occasionally custom-building amps and PA systems for LA musicians earlier in the decade, clearly gave him an edge in the amp business. Players of the newfangled 'electro Spanish' guitars were also using sturdy, efficient Fender amplifiers before the company even made such a six-string of its own. When it finally did, though, it would change the face of the guitar, and of popular music, for all time.

It's hard to imagine now, but in the 1940s hollowbody electrics were still limping along as the poor relation to Hawaiian and lap-steel guitars. Acoustics were popular with everyone from singing cowboys to starry-eyed collegiate troubadours, but many musicians felt the guitar would never cut it in the band environment. Right up until Leo Fender's masterstroke of 1950, it still looked debatable whether or not it

A duo from twang heaven: a 1952 'blackguard' Fender Telecaster and 1965 Fender Twin Reverb amplifier with dual JBL speakers. This clean-but-mean pair virtually defines the Nashville guitar sound, but you'd want a personal roadie to load out that combo for you.

Note how the original Broadcaster name is blacked out in this catalog, with "Telecaster" stamped above it.

was cut out to do so. Hollowbody electrics had afforded struggling guitarists their first glimpse of the spotlight, but they were still big, boomy and muddy sounding through the amps of the day and, perhaps most restricting of all, prone to runaway feedback of the most unmusical variety. What's more they were a lot of effort to play and make the most of when amplified. If the lowly guitarist was going to get ahead, he needed an instrument that would let him roll out enough volume – and with a sharp enough tone – to be heard above the band in the big venues that dance orchestras and western swing bands were filling.

When this revolutionary new instrument took hold, it would not merely be heard above the band, it would prove a ticket for countless horn sections to hit the road. With the power of the solidbodied electric (and to be fair, the ever-improving electric hollowbodies, too), a pair of guitars, a standup bass and a drum kit could wallop out enough sound to fill a large dance hall on a Saturday night. The four-piece guitar band is something we take for granted now, so it is all too easy to ignore the cultural impact of this. Sure, hollowbody alternatives were fairing better all the time too, but it took the bright, punchy, virtually feedback-free Telecaster to point the way and, more to the point, show us that the electric guitar really was a breed unto itself. To many professional musicians of 1950 the debut Fender electro-Spanish model was a laughing stock, a mere novelty at best, and it can be difficult today to step back and see what an amazing piece of lateral thinking the design was in its day. For the Telecaster, Fender broke down the component parts of the guitar and rebuilt the instrument from the ground up, with its amplified purpose solely in mind. The results may have appeared crude, but the instrument achieved all expectations its designers had set out for it. In this roughly hewn maple and ash plank, the struggling instrument's shackles were finally shed.

In addition to the radical sonic performance of the new instrument, Leo Fender's screw-together assembly method was another boon to the working musician, allowing easy repair and adjustment, and total replacement of even major components like the neck or the body if necessary. What would this work cost you on a Les Paul? On a Tele, just the cost of the part. This erector-set philosophy extended beyond the then-radical four-screw neck/body join to the basic stamped metal bridge and control plate, the flat screw-down pickguard, and the... well, that's about all the hardware there is, really, other than the Kluson tuners and knurled brass knobs. This was a stripped-down design to the max – literally every piece was screwed or bolted together, with nothing glued – and it showed the way forward for low-maintenance designs that would become the norm for rock guitars.

That's 'Caster' With A 'K'

Fender went into development of its new instrument in 1949 and put it on the market in 1950, pretty quick work for such a revolutionary new product. The first few prototypes were dubbed Esquire, but the company settled on the Broadcaster name before going to market, using the former moniker for the single-pickup models that would soon follow. In 1951 the Gretsch company pointed out the similarity to the 'Broadkaster' name used on its popular drum kits, and Fender agreed to drop it. Model-less 'Nocasters' were turned out for a few months while team members scratched their heads and puzzled over a new name, but by late 1951 Telecaster was emblazoned on the headstock – a prophetic nod to the guitar's foreseen impact on the modern age, and one it has retained ever since.

By the time Broadcasters were rolling into the guitar stores, they had settled into a finished form that is still recognizable in Telecasters today, and which has undergone very few outwardly major alterations in the guitar's 55-year history. Very few pieces of technology are put together so well right from the start that they not only survive their first decade as a market leader, but remain as relevant and revered – in essentially unchanged form – more than half a century later. Consider that Fender achieved this in a design that had no precedent of its type in production in the guitar world, and the feat is all the more amazing. (Yes, limited numbers of Rickenbacker, Bigsby, ViviTone, Audiovox and a few other solidbodies were made before the Broadcaster – and Fender was certainly aware of the Rickenbackers in particular – but these guitars were constructionally different, and you certainly couldn't say they ever sold in numbers that provided any real test of the potential market, or even much constructive feedback from players.)

Come late 1952 and 1953, dealers who had first scoffed at the new Fender solidbody and called it a 'canoe paddle' and a 'snow shovel' found themselves stocking the Telecaster, which had not only failed to vanish, but was growing in popularity on the heels of endorsements from picking virtuoso Jimmy Bryant and country swing artist Bill Carson. The blonde plank was showing up in the hands of more and more country artists, and those of a few blues stars and jazz players as well. Before the Telecaster's arrival there was nothing especially 'twangy' about country music, certainly not at the hands of its smooth virtuosos like Chet Atkins, Merle Travis or Hank Garland. After Fender introduced its solidbody, however, both 'T-words' came to define the country and western guitar solo as pickers took up the Tele in droves.

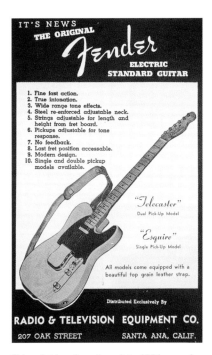

This print brochure from late 1951 or early 1952 shows that the Telecaster name is now officially established for the two-pickup model.

Many of these musicians did convert to the fancier and more versatile Stratocaster when it arrived in 1954 – developed with significant input from Carson, with whom Fender had fostered a close association – but many of the country players among them returned again to the more austere Tele. It did everything they needed from an electric guitar with less fuss and fiddling, had a more solid and piercing tone, and of course had that extra span of clear air between the bridge and neck pickups for fingerpickers to really dig into, a function that some musicians always found the Strat's middle pickup interfered with. The Tele had been tested, by Fender's own top dog, no less, and proved its strength. Since then, thousands of country artists have needed to look nowhere else.

Between what we would call the prototypes and the eventual, settled-in production models, Fender marketed a few variations of its debut solidbody with the Esquire name. Single-pickup models had black bodies made from laminated pine that were a little thinner than the standard to come, and maple necks that looked as we would expect, but carried no truss-rod. A few two-pickup Esquires with truss-rod equipped necks followed, but by October of 1950 the Broadcaster that settled in as the standard model had most of the features that have become beloved of Tele fans: 1 ¾" thick ash body made usually from two pieces of wood glued together side-by-side, one-piece maple neck/fingerboard with 21 frets and truss-rod adjustment at the body end, two pickups – a powerful uncovered bridge unit with flat pole pieces and tin base plate, and a smaller covered neck unit – black pickguard often referred to as 'bakelite' but actually made from a lacquered fiber material similar to that used for the circuit boards of Fender amplifiers, chromed knurled brass knobs, three-way switch, chromed stamped steel bridge and control plates, and steel bridge saddles.

Meaty Twang, Odd Switching

The bridge pickups on these early Broadcasters were powerful affairs, with resistance measurements often reading in the upper 7K and sometimes into 8K, so their sound was correspondingly fat and meaty. These early guitars also had an odd wiring arrangement that offered no actual tone control, but a Volume and Blend control instead. The selector's forward position selected a 'deep bass' sound from the neck pickup (achieved with a simple network of capacitors), the middle position selected the straight neck pickup, and the rearward position selected the bridge pickup with the neck unit blended in as desired. By 1952, the year in which the gorgeous Telecaster in our main photo arrived, this had changed to the still seemingly archaic wiring that Fender maintained until the mid 1960s. This offered: switch forward, neck pickup with preset bassy sound; switch center, neck pickup with Tone control; switch back, bridge pickup without Tone control. As you can see, there was no both-pickups-on sound from these guitars, and limited use was made of the Tone control (plus, that 'bassy' sound was of pretty limited use in itself); unsurprisingly, quite a few players rewired their Teles for the more versatile sounds that have become the modern standard. Routing these bridge pickups straight to the output after the Volume control, however, without the added resistance of a Tone control, lets them retain just that little extra bit of signal strength that helps to make many early Telecasters real screamers.

'Blackguard' Telecasters, named for the pickguards that used this black fiber material up until the summer of 1954 when white plastic replaced it, have bridge pickups that are usually a little less powerful than those on the Broadcasters, but still hotter than much of what would follow. By now these unit's base plates (often referred to as 'grounding plates' although they did much more than ground them) were cut from thin brass sheet rather than the previous tin or sometimes copper. In addition to providing the pickup's ground connection, this plate which is shaped to the base of the pickup and held in place by the mounting screws that are threaded through it, actually changes the pickup's response slightly, raising its output by up to about 10 per cent and sharpening its attack. Because it does so without increasing coil windings or magnet strength it helps to make for a powerful pickup that is still sharp, clear and toneful. A number of clever replacement pickup makers have recently used this same technique to give a boost to their own designs, even many intended for use in other guitar types, such as Stratocasters.

The way in which the Tele's bridge pickup is mounted in the bridge plate also greatly affects its sound. A Tele's configuration of having holes drilled from the back to the front of the body with strings secured in metal ferrules at the back and passing through holes in the bridge plate has always been among the most solid and stable forms of string anchoring in the history of the solidbody. As the strings pass at sharp

break-angles from these bridge-plate holes they exert excellent downward pressure on the saddles (which by 1952 were flat-bottomed brass rather than the original and later steel), and this in turn imparts a lot of vibrational energy into the bridge plate itself, which is not secured to the body wood by any screws at its forward edge and therefore vibrates somewhat with the energy of the strings. The result can be some mechanically induced feedback in microphonic pickups, but as surprisingly few of these exhibit chronic signs of this problem (and when they do, can be cured with a simple wax potting job), the sonic effect usually translates as a spiky, sharp, ringing tonality with loads of bite and the ability to cut through the muddiest band. In short, the archetypal Tele twang, which on an early example of the model is usually a much beefier, fatter sound than that of the Strat's bridge pickup, with more midrange honk and a greater ability to drive a tube amp into breakup. The use of three bridge saddles, a pair of strings to each, requires compromises in intonation, but offers another solid point for transference of the strings' vibrational energy into the bridge, into the body, and through the pickup.

Rick Nelson and James Burton play

When Fender switched briefly to anchoring the strings in holes drilled through the rearward lip of the bridge plate in 1958 and early 1959, the guitar's sound suffered slightly in solidity, sustain and resonance. Musicians let the company know about it, and the through-body stringing was resumed. Despite its simplicity, there are many factors that contribute to a Tele's classic sound, but a good many of them are wrapped up right here in this string anchoring/bridge plate/pickup mounting configuration.

Telecaster Tone Secrets

Tele neck pickups are a little less magical and mysterious, and somewhat underappreciated, but can still be very good sounding units, and are impressive pieces of compact pickup design. Each of the Telecaster's two different pickups originally came from different Fender lap-steel designs, and examples of each can be seen on vintage 'steels. Despite their size, these neck pickups usually have equal or slightly higher resistance readings than their partner bridge pickups, and specs remained at 7K to 7.5K or so even into the early 1960s, when Tele bridge pickups were starting to get weaker than their 1950s counterparts. Some jazz players have long favored the way these little chromed-metal covered single coils can elicit warm, rounded tones from a solidbody, but in other genres they usually aren't turned to as much as the bridge pickup, which is where most players consider the bulk of the Tele tone to be happening. That boost that the bridge pickup's base plate gives its response helps to counter the minor imbalance in resistance between these two pickups, and despite the higher reading from the neck units, they rarely sound boomier – and sometimes sound even noticeably weaker – then their counterparts.

The Tele's early appeal with musicians bold enough to give one a try usually stemmed from two quarters: its sharp, cutting, sustaining sound, and its easy playability. Right from the start, Fender necks were a thing apart from the crowd, from the elegant ripples of the minimalist headstock right down to the four-screw attachment format. Early Telecasters are renowned for having fat, clubby necks, but they weren't always overly girthsome, and certainly felt a lot sleeker and faster in the hand than plenty of other makers' necks of the early 1950s. Our featured 1952 Tele has a nicely rounded 'D' profile that is very comfortable in the hand and not overly chunky at all. Overall, though, they were generally bigger necks in the 1950s than in later decades, and these are famed for both their shape and their tone, that added thickness of maple contributing further body and sharp-edged resonance to the overall sound. With any of those that are short of being real baseball bats, that 7 ¼″ fingerboard radius adds to the impression of roundness and in-the-hand ergonomics, too, and gives these instruments an extremely playable feel. To top it all, the lack of a large heel as required in the dovetailed/glued attachment format of other makers provided what would have seemed like excellent upper-fret access in its day, right up to the 21st fret – which, though measly by today's standards, was already one or two more than many hollowbody archtop electrics with cutaways were providing.

The feel of all vintage Fender necks varied considerably depending upon who had hand-finished the shaping work (and perhaps what kind of mood they were in), while the profiles evolved constantly. These 'D' profiles peaked in a sharp 'V' around 1957 – the famous 'boat necks' that some players love, and others just can't get on with – which in turn began to flatten out considerably into the very thin 'C' necks seen at the turn of the decade. All have some appeal, and most shapes have major fans, short of the indifferent

Along with getting the body shape wrong, CBS-owned Fender somehow decided to predate the Telecaster's arrival (even as the Broadcaster) by a full two years. The 'Telecaster' on the left could never have existed in 1948.

efforts on some of the 1970s guitars (although you find many great Teles from that decade, too).

More than simply easing manufacture and repair, the four-screw neck attachment has its own sonic signature. It yields a snappier tonality, with somewhat scooped mids, but the latter is partly made up for by the fat, honking response of the early Tele lead pickup. Also, surprising to some, this configuration doesn't always provide less sustain than with glued-in or through-neck designs, and many Telecasters are amazingly resonant, ringing instruments. The great woods used in the 1950s and part of the 1960s contributes to this; ash stocks grown in the south of the United States, referred to as 'swamp ash' because, well, the trees grew in swamps, were still affordable – which, to be honest, was Fender's first and foremost consideration – and provided a body material that was both light and strong. These trees' watery environs contributed to a more porous growth that yielded a lighter wood once the timber was dried and aged, and a fortunate side effect of this was a warmth and resonance beyond that of some harder and more tone-deadening denser ash varieties. Of course the light weight of many of these 1950s Fenders is also a plus; these 6 to 7 lb featherweights came to be truly appreciated two decades later up against the 9.5 to 10 lb leadbodies Fender was often turning out in the 1970s, and along with the relief of strapping one of these on for three sets a night, players noticed that they rang and sustained beautifully, rather than piddling out as a 'light' guitar might be expected to do (this in an age when the real deadweights were often considered the kings of sustain).

We have already analyzed the Stratocaster in this book. But of course the Tele came first, and set the pace for the headstock-end of the Fender neck, with its desirable straight run from nut slot to tuner and natural break angle from slot-bottom down to tuner post, both boons to tuning stability and string anchoring at the nut. Despite their frequent replacement with Schallers, the vintage Kluson tuners are perfectly functional when kept in good condition, and their lightness is another bonus.

The traditional 25 ½″ Fender scale length has also been visited before, but it's another major factor contributing to the Telecaster's sparkling, harmonically saturated response, which in truth is richer and more lush than the thin, bright twang that many people with little hands-on Tele time expect it to be (a reputation not adequately countered by many examples from the 1970s and 1980s). Overall, the classic Tele sound has boatloads of grind and punch, with lots of trebly twang, sure, but more than that alone – a brightness surrounded in a gnarly, honking growl, more like. While you hear classic country Tele tone at the hands of James Burton, Roy Buchanan or earlier Albert Lee, its power and sustain have also lent it to many rock outings with surprising muscle and drive: Jimmy Page's 'Stairway To Heaven' solo and other heavy moments on the first two Led Zeppelin albums, for example, or Jimi Hendrix's 'Purple Haze' and 'Hey Joe,' and plenty of what Keith Richards has done with The Rolling Stones. In the blues department, Mike Bloomfield and Muddy Waters display the range of this instrument's ability to growl and sing, and both Eric Clapton and Jeff Beck used one for some meaty R&B riffage with the Yardbirds.

That said, and for all the silky comfort of many Fender necks, Telecasters were always somewhat crude instruments, and sometimes felt like more work to master than the relative ease of a well setup Gibson Les Paul or ES-335, for example. The longer scale length takes a little more finger muscle to deal with,

For all the silky comfort of many Fender necks, Telecasters were somewhat crude instruments

and these guitars are harder to bend, too, with noticeably more roundness in the fingerboard radius to push against, and slightly higher, thinner frets. This tight fingerboard radius also means a matching curve to the strings in the proper setup, so some players find their fingers don't hop around the 'board quite as nimbly. The traditional Tele setup often leaves a little more air between string and fret, too, for a higher and heavier action than many Gibson-wielding rockers go for, but many players love the extra effort that Telecaster playing can require, and even feel the slight struggle keeps them more in tune with the instrument. And for all of this, most Teles in good shape, in the hands of a good tech, can be put into pretty silky playing condition when required. On top of this, the Tele's wider string spacing at the nut and particularly at the bridge make it great for fingerpickers to get a grip on, and purveyors of intricate chord work or flowing jangle styles often find it a model that really suits them as well, whereas most Gibsons can feel a little cramped.

The crudity of the Telecaster's look is partly what inspired a sleeker, more modern design for the Stratocaster – more Detroit tailfins and chromed grilles than the hinged hood and spoke wheels of the Model T-like Tele – but it's an archetypal look, and plenty of players love it. The contrasting monochrome 'blackguard' Tele models before mid 1954 are considered the ultimate classics, and many guitarists will tell you a proper Telecaster has to have a maple fingerboard, too. Many of the rosewood models of 1959-1965 are fantastic guitars, and sound just as much a Telecaster as a lot of more highly prized 1950s examples. In some respects you could argue that the 1960s Teles were the more archetypal country guitars, as this was more the heyday of the Nashville session scene, and these models had that slightly thinner, twangier sound besides. But the maple-neck 'blackguard' Telecaster is where it all got started, and these are just too cool to pass up .

Other constructional changes were equally significant – or insignificant, depending upon your stance

– and included the move to smooth steel then threaded steel saddles, a decrease in pickup strength in the early 1960s and again in the late 1960s, lasting through much of the 1970s, and other minor alterations. One major change included the fact that Fender got the Tele body shape wrong in the early 1970s thanks to a new router setup that couldn't manage the curves of the bass-side bout, particularly where it joined the neck. At that point, the Tele really wasn't a Tele anymore. Various reissues have since recaptured much of the magic of the vintage Telecaster, beginning with the '52 Reissue of 1982, and running right up to the present-day Fender Custom Shop versions of the instrument, not forgetting the more affordable vintage-style Japanese and American Series models. The early made-in-Japan Fender Squier Telecasters have also earned a lot of respect, and are even becoming collectable in a more modest sense. Telewrangler Chuck Prophet, formerly of country rockers Green On Red, is a longtime fan of these affordable variations on the classic theme.

As country guitar moved steadily away from what we might now perceive as the warm and jazzy tones of much of the 1940s and early 1950s western swing playing and toward the clean, bright twang that has defined the genre for more than four decades now, so Fender was on a quest for a tighter, brighter, sharper sound from its amplifiers. While the tweed models of the 1950s are all-time rock'n'roll and blues classics, they always broke up too quickly for some tastes. Players in need of an ultra-clean performance at big volumes wanted amps you could push right up towards max without a hint of dirt creeping into the signal. Meanwhile, reverb was becoming an ever more popular effect, and tremolo had already made

A pair each of custom color Telecasters and Esquires.

its mark as a country-certified sound. Wrap up these goals in a powerful, professional package, and you'd call it the Fender Twin Reverb.

With the brownface models of 1960 Fender was already making a bid for more headroom, and this rethink was consolidated with the blackface models of late 1963. One of the first places its designers went to achieve it was the preamp, and they worked along from there to change every stage of the amps. The circuitry governing the first couple of gain stages was changed significantly in order to make use of the more plentiful but higher-gain 12AX7 tubes in place of the gentler 12AY7s in the tweed amps' first gain stages, but to do so without introducing any extra distortion from this more powerful bottle. The new configuration completely changed the topology of this first stage of the amp, put the volume control after the tone stack rather than before it, and raised the voltages on the preamp tubes from around 150 VDC to 240 VDC, which – as used by Fender – had the effect of making this stage tighter and more 'hi-fi' rather than hotter, as the notion of higher voltages might imply.

Fender's engineers also dropped the juicy, touch-sensitive cathode-follower tone stack that we examined in Setup 3: R&B – which placed the EQ section after the cathode output of the second preamp tube in the larger tweed amps – and replaced it with a tone stack rigged between the plate (anode) output of the first half of the channel's dual triode preamp tube and the grid (input) of the second half of the tube. While doing so, the tone capacitor values of the Bass and Middle controls were also changed from a pair of .022μF caps to .1μF and .047μF respectively.

All of this made a considerable difference in the voice of the amplifier, the cap change in particular being described by some as 'constricting' the tone, but the effect was part of an overall overhaul with specific end results in mind. The new EQ configuration stamped a little less of its own character on the tone, and along the way was less prone to overdriving the following stages. Also, the amps now had an independent tone section for each channel – either Treble, Bass and Middle or just Treble and Bass, depending on the model – and each channel used a different preamp tube, rather than sharing one for the first and second gain stages, so independent voices could be set up for each, a factor that might have driven the evolution almost as much as the quest for louder/cleaner performance.

The next stage to pick up the signal after the preamp/tone section is the phase inverter (PI), and Fender dealt out significant changes here, too. The efficient, high-end 'long-tailed pair' topology that had been seen on bigger tweed amps of the late 1950s was employed almost throughout the range, but the circuit was changed slightly to revolve around a lower-gain 12AT7 that would drive the output tubes a little more gently at given signal levels. As such, this PI offered very little distortion of its own and passed a clean, crisp signal to the output stage. Little was changed between the PI and the output tubes and the output tubes and the output transformer (OT), but designs of the latter were certainly upgraded to suit the end goal.

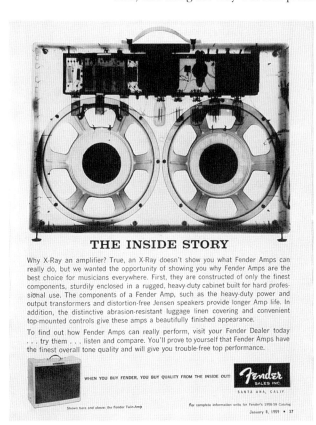

THE INSIDE STORY

Why X-Ray an amplifier? True, an X-Ray doesn't show you what Fender Amps can really do, but we wanted the opportunity of showing you why Fender Amps are the best choice for musicians everywhere. First, they are constructed of only the finest components, sturdily enclosed in a rugged, heavy-duty cabinet built for hard professional use. The components of a Fender Amp, such as the heavy-duty power and output transformers and distortion-free Jensen speakers provide longer Amp life. In addition, the distinctive abrasion-resistant luggage linen covering and convenient top-mounted controls give these amps a beautifully finished appearance.

To find out how Fender Amps can really perform, visit your Fender Dealer today . . . try them . . . listen and compare. You'll prove to yourself that Fender Amps have the finest overall tone quality and will give you trouble-free top performance.

WHEN YOU BUY FENDER, YOU BUY QUALITY FROM THE INSIDE OUT! *Fender* SALES INC.

SANTA ANA, CALIF.

Shown here and above: the Fender Twin-Amp   For complete information write for Fender's 1958-59 Catalog

January 8, 1959 • 37

A high-powered tweed Twin reveals all in this clever X-ray ad.

The biasing arrangement of the fixed-bias class AB amps was also changed, giving a proper bias adjustment control on more amps in the range rather than the fairly crude auto-biasing circuit that many of the fixed-bias tweed and brownface amps carried. (Remember, these terms are potentially confusing: fixed-bias amps govern their output tubes with a circuit that often allows an adjustable level to be set, whereas cathode-biased amps carry a preset, nonadjustable bias resistor tied to the cathodes of the output tubes.) The ability to bias these output tubes at their optimum level – rather than relying on the hit-and-miss, plug-in-and-play formats of many previous designs – was yet another bid toward greater efficiency and, therefore, improved headroom.

In the power section, higher filtering aimed to keep these amps clean from 60 Hz hum and firm in the low end, and solid state rectification gave the bigger models higher sag-free voltages to play with. Presence controls were dropped for a simple Bright switch that passed some of the high frequencies on around the volume control when switched in, and the negative-feedback loop was subsequently increased slightly.

High Fidelity, Low Distortion

Overall, Fender was aiming to manufacture a more high-fidelity guitar amplifier, and all of these alterations worked toward that common goal. These moves carried on into the silverface years, when a lot of guitarists felt they had gone too far with the 'distortion clamping' changes and had begun to rob many designs of their touch and tone. Roll the designs back to the blackface amps of approximately 1964-67, and you've got many players' ideal for a shimmering, full-voiced clean tube amp with just a little bite when you crank it up and play hard. Not only are these models mostly more powerful than their tweed predecessors, with the aimed-for higher headroom, but they possess a very different feel and sonic signature entirely. Whereas a creamy smoothness and midrange grind might define many cranked big tweeds, the larger blackfaces, when played beyond 5 on the dial, exhibit tight, thumping lows, spiky highs (verging on the decapitating in some cases), and a certain hollowness in the middle – a scooped voice that works toward a broad soundstage without any obvious humps in the frequency spectrum. Not that these are entirely tame animals, either, and when really cranked they carry a stinging edge that is quite different to the tweeds' gritty roar. In just a few years Fender had pushed its designs to an entirely new dimension, and the modern guitar amp was with us both in sound and form.

Of course the things most players would have noticed first were the Reverb and Vibrato, effects that had arrived sooner on other makes but would arguably reach their zenith on these mid-1960s Fenders. For the latter, Fender boiled down the complex circuits of the brownface amps, which often required up to

The onboard reverb is a great sounding version of the effect for country, rock, and jazz

two and half tubes to create the effect, to an extremely efficient and good-sounding circuit based around a single 12AX7 tube and a photoresistor. These circuits have a good range of speeds available, and can go from subtle ripple to a choppy, gated on/off effect. A sound somewhere in between became one of the essential spices of the low-string country signature riff, giving an atmospheric bounce to countless G-runs and chorus turnarounds. (Although Fender used the term 'Vibrato' on the amp panels, this was actually a pure tremolo effect rather than the pitch-fluctuating wobble of true vibrato. Conversely, the company also called its guitars' vibrato arms 'tremolo arms.')

The reverb circuit in Fender amps is very different from that in the company's three-knob outboard Reverb Unit of the early 1960s. The latter has more depth and 'sproing' and is undoubtedly the sound of surf – and maybe a rockabilly-preferred tone as well – but many players prefer the smooth, round sound of the amp-based effect as typified on these blackface models. The amp-based version is just as much a 'real tube-driven spring reverb circuit' in that it carries a small OT to drive a portion of the signal through a long-spring pan, but instead of the Reverb Unit's large 6K6 output tube, 12AT7 and 7025 (a 12AX7 type) it uses just the latter pair, one as driver and one as recovery tube. If anything, this effect is a little smoother and less dramatic than the outboard version, though it has just a single knob for depth rather than the predecessor's Mixer, Dwell and Tone controls. In any case, it's a great sounding version of the effect for country, rock, and jazz, and together with the onboard Vibrato helped to make these deluxe mid-1960s Fenders impressive and full-featured sound machines.

In the form of the Twin Reverb, all of these circuit changes added up to one of the loudest and best performing combo-format amplifiers available to the professional musician. Four 6L6 output tubes were run at somewhat higher voltages than in the tweed amps to pump approximately 85W from its hefty OT into two 12″ speakers housed in an open-back cabinet. Standard speakers were Jensen C12N or Oxford 12T6, both ceramic designs, the former usually the more desirable. These are both firm, full-bodied speakers with pretty good retention of low frequencies up to high volumes and potentially piercing highs. Fender offered JBL D120F speakers as a factory upgrade, and these make for a louder, more full-throated and heavier amplifier. (Seriously, these Twin Reverbs are always heavy combos, but with a pair of monster-magnet JBLs they become real backbreakers.) Cabs were still made from fingerjointed solid pine boards, but speaker baffles had changed to particle board in 1962, and were also more firmly fixed than the tweed and early brownface baffles. A minor point, you might think, but the tighter, less resonant baffle makes for a punchier amp all around, and definitely contributes to the evolving voice of these models.

From Killer Clean To Cutesy Crunch

Stick a good Telecaster into one of these monstrous Twin Reverbs – especially one with a pair of JBLs like that in our main photo – and you have got a bright, tight twang machine for sure. There's a ton of bold, taut snap and sparkle from the bridge pickup, with excellent grunt for lower riffs too. This really is the epitome of clean, country style... but don't think there isn't some grind and crunch here if you really want it. To get these babies sliding into breakup you have to roll them up higher than most other Fender amp designs of the day, and by the time the serious crunch kicks in you are at near-deafening sound pressure levels in anything but a very big room. It's a thrilling ride, no doubt, but few smaller studios, bar gigs or clubs can handle it. But hey, that's why we're plugging in our blackface Fender Deluxe Reverb instead for recording work and more intimate venues.

No Nashville pro would have expected always to use the same amp for both his major concert and recording dates, and a 22W Deluxe Reverb would alternately give him much of the tonality of a pushed Twin but at considerably lower volume levels. A smaller amp lets the player dial in the sweet spot at levels manageable both by the human ear and sensitive recording mikes, which makes the combination at the same time a more playable and more toneful setup than trying to rein in an 85W Twin, which will sound thin and numb at the same apparent loudness as a semi-cranked Deluxe. On about 3 out of 10 on the Volume control, a DR will remain shimmeringly clean with a good, beefy maple-neck Tele injected, and volume levels will be enough to gig a small club with a fairly restrained band, or record even in a home studio without getting the neighbors too angry. Wind it up to just 4.5 or 5, though, and these 1x12″ combos start to go gnarly pretty quickly, while at 7 or beyond they can really start to roar... in their own diminutive way.

For all that it looks like a mini Twin, though, the Deluxe is a somewhat different beast, due mainly to the way its smaller 6V6GT output tubes respond to the blackface preamp topology, and to other variables besides. The Deluxe's preamp tubes are back down to the 170 DC to 180 DC voltages that approach the lower levels that helped to make the tweeds so touch sensitive, while the voltages on the 6V6GTs are up close to 420 DC, way beyond the 350 VDC that some tube-makers specified as the maximum for these components, even back in the days of the great US-made types of the 1950s and 1960s. The latter was done to wring a little more volume and, yes, headroom out of these amps, but the result is a hot wailer of a combo when wound up that's nevertheless very different sounding than a cranked narrow-panel tweed Deluxe of just three years before. Coupled with the different voltage levels the preamp is receiving, this makes for a juicy, tactile feel with plenty of dynamics and an easy output tube distortion that encompasses everything from easy crunch to highly compressed, saturated distortion when floored. Side by side, the Twin and Deluxe Reverbs make a great pair – gorgeously contrasting and complementary, yet with a lot of the same core tonalities that define the blackface Fenders.

By late 1963, and certainly 1964, Fender had realised that the true color of rock'n'roll was black. View these blackface amps of 1963-67 with 40 years of hindsight in your pocket and their styling appears extremely forward-looking. Although recent years have seen a return of retro cosmetics in a range of colors and coverings from tweed to tan, blonde and brightly colored Tolex, these all looked decidedly 'livingroom furniture' in 1965 when parked next to a glossy black Fender Twin Reverb with silver-thread grille cloth and businesslike blackface control panel. They were among the most professional and 'serious' looking amps of their day, barring perhaps the styling evolution of Marshall heads by 1966, and arguably had more lasting design virtue than the silverface update that would follow them. These are some of the best built Fender amps of all time, too, as the company had really honed its game through the tweed and brownface years, and wasn't putting all efforts into mass production and the bottom line, as in the silverface years and after. These Fender amplifiers were built to last, were easy to repair when they did need work, and contained components of a higher grade than those generally available soon after. Sure, the company bought in bulk and with an eye on the profit margin, no doubt, but opening up a stock blackface amp today can make many a hardened modern-day tech weep with delight.

While the two certified countrified effects were already onboard these amps, plenty of pickers naturally availed themselves of other sonic treats in the studio, and compression became a favorite for wringing a little more smoothness and sustain out of the rig. As this effect became available in compact pedal form, units like the MXR Dyna Comp and Dan Armstrong Orange Squeezer could be found near the top of every session man's bag of tricks.

A compressor pedal is designed to function as a compact version of the larger studio processors, leveling devices which smooth the attack and decay of a signal by softening the front edge of the note and amplifying its tail. Most compressors also offer some boost, which can be used as pure, clean gain boost with the

History repeats itself, again, in another Fender amp reissue.

compressor functions turned down. Compression is often as much a feel thing as a tonal consideration, used for that extra dynamic edge, touch sensitivity and softness of attack – not to mention sustain – that it gives any playing style. But the popular models of the 1970s usually also added a certain thickness and warmth to the signal that can be subtly addictive; many players who get hooked on them find it difficult to play without the pedal engaged.

The sonic results of all this have a lot of applications in the field of country guitar; they help to smooth out the spikiness of jagged chicken-pickin,' add a silky softness to flat-picked solo lines, and give shimmer and ring to jangly arpeggio chords. Tele to compressor to Deluxe Reverb – I'd hate to try to count up the session dates that relied on that rig, even out of the realm of country, and the sound endures today.

The namesake of The Jon Spencer Blues Explosion rams trash guitar through junkyard amp.

SETUP 10
AMERICAN GARAGE

This hardware hails from the late 1950s to early 1960s, but the vibe is timeless. It's the sound of kids in ripped jeans and t-shirts cranking up budget gear from catalog houses, department stores and pawn shops, and making one almighty hellfire racket out in the garage. This is where the spark of rebellion ignites the birth of rock'n'roll over and over again for eternity, where the sweet filthy edges of the sound are continually rediscovered, where starry-eyed young guitarists still exclaim, "Hey, check out what this old thing sounds like if I put it on 10!" And where the neighbors continually threaten to call the police unless you turn down that damn racket. It might be just a $59 guitar into a $72 amp, but it sounds like God in a two-car detached bay with your drummer and bassist pounding away behind you, the door raised to let in a wisp of the August evening breeze, and a couple of girls from down the block hanging in the driveway and checking out the show.

Plenty of guitar makes fall into this category, and they are the models that any longtime player over the age of 40 probably started out on back in the late 1950s, 1960s or early 1970s. Back then, they just didn't do a good Fender or Gibson copy for $179, like you can get today. The beginners' axes available were roughhewn, crude of sound and design, and often Picasso-esque in look, but plenty of players used them as stepping stones to better guitars and major careers. That said, quite a few of them were really good-sounding, good-playing pieces, too, and once set up correctly could really do an aspiring rock star justice. We're talking guitars from Harmony, Teisco, Kay, plenty of rebadged models made by Valco, and odd-

The underpowered output and resonance-free tone of a low-budget beauty can be just the thing

named or nameless Japanese imports… but more than anything else, the mighty Danelectro and its Sears & Roebuck derivative, Silvertone. And while the rich kid down the road eventually got a Fender Mustang or Gibson Melody Maker for Christmas, the guy who stuck with the used Dano U-2 eventually learned to play the thing, and even finally got the girl.

When I was growing up and just a couple years into my own guitar addiction, the kid across the street had a Silvertone amp-in-case set, and I used to kind of laugh at the thing, what with my refinished 1964 Fender Jaguar and 100W early-1970s solid-state amp poised for serious rocking. But that little one-pickup Masonite guitar and 3W amp used to sound pretty good coming through his bedroom window at night, juicy and raw, while I struggled in the basement to get even a little bit of sugar out of my big, cold tranny beast (an early Big Muff saved my soul in those days). When I finally checked one out for myself a few years later – after I had come to appreciate the beauty of tubes, for one thing – I was dismayed to think of all the fun I had missed. These things had been hanging around for the cost of a sunny weekend's worth of lawn mowing, and their bigger brothers were within reach for not a lot more. Who could have guessed these amps were such evil, twisted tone monsters, and could sound just so damn cool?

Most players who have been at it for some time have learned to appreciate the beauty of a finely hand-crafted guitar and amp – something in the so-called 'boutique' crowd, for example, that will cost you $2,500 to $4,000 per piece. But those who also learn to appreciate the spice, spit and fury of some of the cheaporama brands that were with us in the first couple decades of rock'n'roll are far richer for it, and primed to have a lot of fun. For all that selected tone woods, hand-carved profiles and custom-wound pickups can serve up the most intense slice of aural ecstasy to be had from a vibrating steel string (with a little help from a silver-soldered, point-to-point wired, NOS-tube-powered upgrade of archaic amplification technology), the underpowered, microphonic output and virtually resonance-free tone of a

Harmony, Teisco and all the rest of them might have had their aspirations, but for garage-rock thrills of the highest order, the Danelectro and Silvertone brands were the classy way to go. This 1958 Silvertone U-3 guitar and Medalist amp are the top dogs of bottom shelf gear pairings.

low-budget beauty can sometimes be just the thing to tickle your sense of sonic splendor. And ramming it all through a low grade tube circuit with flapping speakers in a cardboard cab can just be the icing on the cake.

When we're talking department store-grade rock action, the Silvertone U-3 and Medalist amplifier of around 1958, as seen in our main photo, are definitely from the top of the heap. When bought new, these would have been the pride and joy of a player who knew the trick of going budget-brand but fully loaded; maybe he could have had a Fender Duo Sonic guitar and Princeton amp for something in the same ballpark, but for his hard-saved spending money he took home a top-of-the-range three-pickup wonder and a two-channel 80W 2x12″ combo with tremolo to plug it into. For the guy who picked up the set 15 years later, slightly used but well cared for, the $100 bucks was a total steal in 1973... even if not many people realized it (this time, it was all the new owner could afford). Man, these sweet semi-solid chipboard planks were just hanging around in the 1970s and early 1980s waiting for anyone with spare change from a six-pack to come along and make them their own, and people were practically paying you to take the amplifiers away – fat, filthy blues monsters though they were, if they'd ever been turned up loud enough to prove themselves. They were good bargains first time around, better bargains second and third time around, and they are still great buys today.

Kay amplifiers barely rate a syllable in the annals of tone, but the maker's guitars deserve a decent dose of respect as 'budget vintage' alternatives.

(Along these lines, my own first electric guitar purchase carried an even more upmarket windfall: I was 13 years old in 1975 and a guy had advertised a no-name, single-pickup Japanese solidbody in the classifieds for $35 – not an inconsiderable sum of cash for a kid in those days, compared to the far-more-playable $149 far Eastern Squiers of today. Dad drove me out to the place, we saw the guitar and agreed to buy it, and the seller said, "Oh, hey, I forgot to mention that this old amp comes with it, no charge." He hauled out a dusty mid-1950s Gibson GA-30 and hoisted it into the back seat for us. Two weeks later I dumped that old two-tone suitcase of an amp I'd gotten for free on a school pal for the $35 I'd paid for the guitar, so I was laughing... But the joke was on me, and it was a long time before I got that creamy, thick sound of the cranked brown-and-cream GA-30 out of my head.)

A Silvertone For Mr Sears

The enormous Sears department and catalog store bought in its Silvertone guitars and amps from a range of suppliers over the years, but Danelectro is among the best known, and best respected. From 1954 until the mid 1960s many guitars carrying one of these two names were identical, and the Danelectro-made Sears amps even date from a decade earlier.

Danelectro founder Nathan I. 'Nat' Daniel has a history in the music electronics industry that dates back even further than Leo Fender's. And like Fender he started with amplifiers, beginning in the early 1930s when he made amplifiers for a large department store in New York and, soon after, supplied the early Electar-branded amps for Epiphone. Daniel released his first mass-produced solidbody electric guitar just four years after Fender's first in the marketplace, and sold his Danelectro company to large conglomerate MCA less than two years after Leo Fender's sale to CBS.

In skeleton form, their histories look quite similar, and they were certainly both in place for the birth of rock'n'roll and the groundswell of popularity in the electric guitar in general. But their apparently parallel paths diverge when it comes to the product. Whereas Fender's debut solidbody was at first laughed at, the Telecaster and Stratocaster that followed it pretty quickly proved themselves among the few 'first choice' electrics for professionals, and went on to become two of the most valued vintage guitars of all time. Danelectros were C-list beginners' and students' guitars from the start, and in build-quality and design terms at least they didn't raise their game very far above that level even a few years later when their most deluxe three-pickup models were released. The better examples have definitely attained a certain collectability today, but this pales beside the cachet of vintage Fenders. Save your pennies and you can acquire a very nice 1958 Dano U-3 for $1,000 or a little over (and slightly rough models of all types for less than half that). Care to guess the starting price for an all-original example of Fender's three-pickup model from the same year? Probably pushing 20 times that, by the time this enters print. And that's a far greater price differential than the Fender and Danelectro would have had hanging on the guitar store wall alongside each other in 1958.

Despite the low-end pricing, Nat Daniels was a genuine innovator, too. Danelectro was among the first to pioneer the electric 12-string (originally as the Bellzouki model of 1961). It introduced the six-string bass, and marketed other alternative axes like the 32-fret Guitarlin, the Electric Sitar, and a range of double-neck models. Duane Eddy famously used a Dano six-string bass to elicit his low, rumbling twang on a few tracks, while the company's 12-strings rivaled newcomer Rickenbacker's among pros for a few years.

But innovations aside, many of the 'ordinary' Danelectro/Silvertone guitars sounded way cool, and plenty of pros soon discovered the fact. Jimmy Page, Eric Clapton, Jimi Hendrix and Stevie Ray Vaughan all

The 'U' models and Standards have been favorites of many great bluesers over the years

availed themselves of one or ano.ther model at some point, and you'd better believe it wasn't just for laughs. For anything from metallic slide work, to spiky blues, to chiming jangle, the 'U' models and the Standards that followed were in their element. These guitars have also been favorites of many great bluesers over the years – or, if 'favorites' isn't an accurate description, they were the guitars a lot of these guys used before they received the respect and royalties they deserved, and they used them to make some stunning raw, gutsy sounds.

Strip down our U-3, or its U-1 and U-2 siblings (one and two pickups respectively), or the double-cutaway 'short horn' Standard and Deluxe models that followed from 1958 into the mid 1960s, and it's not surprising that these guitars never attained the values on the vintage market that we see for some of the A-list brands. A center block of poplar – also frequently quoted as pine – holds the guitar together and makes a stable core to bolt the poplar neck to, and the side frames are also cut from poplar boards. Front and back are made from sheets of Masonite hardboard (sometimes called MDF, for 'medium density fiberboard') – none of which you would expect to mellow and age into the resonant brilliance of solid ash, alder or mahogany. Original models did carry Brazilian rosewood fingerboards, however, topped at the head end by a screwed-on aluminum nut and a set of downmarket tuners.

The strings' other end-point consisted of an ultra-simple bridge configuration, constructed of a flat steel plate with notches at its back edge for securing the ball-ends and a thin wedge of rosewood mounted on top to form a saddle section. They were crude but clever devices, and while they didn't allow for any intonation adjustment (though a little height adjustment could be had from the mounting screws), they actually sounded pretty good when in serviceable condition. There's not a whole lot of sustain in these guitars at the best of times, but the rosewood saddle adds a little more round, woody tone to the signal than you'd expect from a Masonite-and-poplar construction. Otherwise the lightness of resonance really helps to up the twang factor that is central to these guitars' character. The materials and the semi-hollow nature of the construction add up to a lightness of weight, too, and that in itself appeals to a lot of players.

Danelectro electronics were a similar blend of simplicity and ingenuity. Guitars of the U-3's era carried the famous 'lipstick-tube' pickups, which were pretty low-powered even for their day, but sounded brilliant and clear, which was a consistent design objective of the 1950s. They were made from alnico bar magnets wrapped with copper wire, and housed in two joined ends of thin metal tube purchased from a lipstick-tube supplier. These units measured only about 4.75K ohms, but were designed for a full, flattering tonality with plenty of lacy highs; in the bridge position they were real sparkle machines, but in the middle or neck position they could even begin to drive a revved tube amp into a little bluesy breakup.

You don't have to be HINDU to play the CORAL® ELECTRIC SITAR

Danelectro CORPORATION
A SUBSIDIARY OF MCA INC.
211 West Sylvania Avenue, Neptune City, New Jersey 07753

Coral PRESTIGE GUITARS AND AMPLIFIERS   *Vincent Bell* SIGNATURE DESIGNS

An unlikely swami goes all-out to get the girl, and the impressive Danelectro Coral Electric Sitar seems to be working its magic.

Bright, High, And Crystal Clear

While many players of the stadium rock and high-gain years dropped their cheapo Danos for their inability to offer the requisite blinding drive levels of the day (Mr Page excepted), plenty of guitarists of the late 1980s and 1990s began to rediscover what others of the 1950s and early 1960s had appreciated. Stick a pickup that was, yes, pretty weak, but bright, clear and well-rounded into a good tube amp at decent volumes, and there's all sorts of fun to be had. With pickups that resolutely refuse to overdrive the early stages of the amp, a crisp, full-frequencied signal is passed along to the output stage, and that's where the sonic gems are unearthed. The combination makes for a live, wiry tone with plenty of dynamics: single notes are appealingly springy and edgy, while hard-hit chords or low-string runs ease into a crackling crunch.

Electronic trickery extended to the nifty concentric controls, with stacked Volume and Tone configuration for each pickup. Two-pickup models carried toggle switch three-way selectors, but U-3 players made their pickup selections by balancing the Volume pots, without the quick-flick aid of any switches. This made things tricky for on-the-fly changes, but kept the guitar's lines clean and uncluttered, and meant you could dial in any combination of one, two or three pickups – and at whatever relative levels you liked – something unachievable on most conventional three-pickup guitars.

Other than a number of ¾ size models, such as the guitars that accompanied the famous Silvertone 'amp in case' set, the notable Dano/Silvertones were made to a 25″ scale-length. Shorter than Fender's 25 ½″ but longer than Gibson's 24 ⅝″, this scale offers a slightly easier feel and fretability than the former, but with a little more harmonic sparkle than the latter. With the lipstick-tube pickups onboard, this adds up to plenty of brightness, but also a little more warmth than you'd get from a longer-scale guitar of a similar design and construction.

Whatever lay beneath that hardboard face, Danelectros and Silvertones were always pretty groovy looking planks. The were available in a range of colors right from the start of the U Series, which included some unusual 'bursts, like the rare Silverburst in our main photo, and had a simple, modern styling that holds its weight in design circles today.

The cheap-and-cheerful amps that frequently partnered these catalog-grade guitars worked a similar crude, no-frills magic, but in a different way. Even today, old tube combos from the likes of Harmony, Kay, Airline, Alamo, Premier, National, Supro – a whole shedload of Valco rebadgers – can make up for their lack of full-voiced brilliance and boutique-grade soundstaging with a certain unhinged fury that works beautifully for certain rootsy, alt-rock, blues, grunge or, well, garage styles. And again, the big Danelectros and Silvertones are really king of the castle.

There's something about so many of these amps that makes you think they are really trying to please you, and playing their glowing guts out despite their considerable limitations. These models generally don't have the air of professionalism of the Fender or Gibson amps of the time – they don't even smell as big-time. But it's as if, even when new, these agricultural-grade constructions of folded tin, paperboard, and radiogram-style electronics knew they were lucky to exist at all in the world of rock'n'roll, and they were just glad to be there.

You occasionally hear talk from vintage-cynical amp techs seeking to debunk the Fender, Marshall and Vox mythology: "Made as cheaply as possible in their day, eye on the bottom line, textbook circuits, so why all the fuss?" And so forth. But hey, if that were true, how did they manage to make these Danos and Airlines and Valcos so much more cheaply? You occasionally get some crossover in components and designs – which, when discovered, gives you a little thrill: "Look, they got their output transformers from Fender's supplier!" On the whole, though, open up a Silvertone Twin 12 model 1485 of the mid 1960s and, despite the four 6L6GCs, tremolo and reverb, it is nothing like a Fender Twin Reverb. Plug in, and it doesn't sound the same either. In some ways, though, you might like it even better.

A Cheaper Grade Of Filth

The same applies to the groovy late-1950s Medalist in our main photo. This Danelectro-made Model 1434 amplifier is the forerunner of the 80W Model 1485 Twin Twelve of the 1960s that has become so popular, with the separate head that tucks in side the 2x12" speaker cab for storage, and of the smaller 40W Model 1484. It has the main features of a tweed Fender Twin – hell, it even has tremolo, which the big Fender lacked, and you could argue that the Silvertone has a more modern styling (black vinyl covering and a gray/silver grille cloth, hmm… we'll see that again in a few years time). But look round the back and all future-now illusions quickly evaporate in the face of the combo's archaic split-chassis design (something Fender had abandoned ten years before), with the preamp circuitry housed beneath the top-mounted control panel, and the power amp down in the bottom of the cabinet.

Like the big Fender, this amp does carry four 6L6GC output tubes, but the test example isn't even as loud as many later – or just better made – 40-watters. The output is probably 55W to 70W max, but this one's original alnico-magnet CTS 12" speakers were pretty seriously shagged (and were not efficient units when new, nor as sweet sounding as a tweed Twin's Jensen P12Ns), and none of the tubes were all-too fresh either, so these factors will partially account for the underwhelming output. Don't get me wrong, though, it's still a pretty loud combo – and hell, it's a sound I could see using on a number of occasions, and I know plenty of guitarists who agree with me. Other Silvertones did use better Jensen speakers, too,

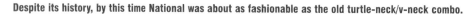

Despite its history, by this time National was about as fashionable as the old turtle-neck/v-neck combo.

notably the 40W and 80W Twin Twelves of the 1960s, and these or other upgraded speakers can make a big improvement to the amp's overall performance.

These big Silvertones are frequently referred to as 'poor man's Fenders,' but that needs a little more debunking. They do use the 12AX7s for preamp duties that Fender had turned to after the lower-gain 12AY7s of the mid to late 1950s, but the Dano designs also often used oddball tubes like the 6CG7 or 6FQ7 in PI positions, and for reverb or tremolo duties too. They carry quite different tone stacks as well, with very different cap values, the chassis and overall workmanship is far flimsier, as is the cabinetry, and none of the outward similarities of format to the larger Fenders makes up for this.

Recorded, the Medalist can still sound huge, with a fat, filthy edge that beats many more refined amps for unhinged rock noises

Nevertheless, crank one up and many people still hear it as 'tweed-like' because of the loose low end and easy saturation. But listen to one side-by-side with the real thing and you'll realize the Dano/Silvertone is a lot looser and easier. The midrange is more rubbery and less aggressive than a good late 1950s Fender, too, and the Silvertone just doesn't have the openness, harmonic depth, or general breadth of frequency range. Overall, the tweed Twin has a fuller, more dynamic soundstage – the Medalist just doesn't sound as big, period.

But you know, I still love the thing. Recorded, too, it can still sound huge, with a fat, filthy edge that beats many more refined amps for unhinged rock noises, but can also sound very 'modern' in the right context. Maybe someone out there remembers just how these things sounded the day they rolled off the assembly line, but more than 45 years later this amp sounds like it has been down the road and back but still wants to blast its heart out. The silvery, chiming treble blended with a loose, wobbly resonance in the low end are the key factors to the sound of this late 1950s Medalist when cranked up. And there's a kind of huffing and puffing effect from the speakers when bottom strings are left open and even barely vibrating, like the thing is having trouble just dealing with the hint of a signal – which really seems to be a damping reaction between the 6L6GCs, OT and speakers that makes it all sound alive. You can hear why so many grungers and contemporary players seeking alternative noises have flipped for amps of this type. Most do use the later 1484 and 1485 models of the early and mid 1960s, and anyone from Mudhoney to the White Stripes to the Jon Spencer Blues Explosion offer great examples of just what these amps can do, live and on record.

Our 1958 Silvertone U-3 makes a great partner with the Medalist, and its bright, snappy tone sends a clean but full-range signal right through to the output stage that results in a wiry, sizzling sound and feel from the amp, for all its farty speakers, tired tubes and mechanical vibrations. Check out the two tracks on the sample CD and see if you agree with my own feelings, but in many ways I prefer the sound of the Medalist with the U-3 to that of it with the admittedly gorgeous 1960 Gibson Les Paul Junior plugged in. The LP Jr certainly induces a more rock-certified distortion, and helps to make the amp sound like something that could pass for legit 1970s heavy rock overdrive; but with the U-3 the sound is that much more sparkling and sprankier, and seems to have a little more dimension to it, too. And in this way, hey, our old Medalist is proving itself capable of a little more tonal virtue than you might expect. Displaying the individual characters of a range of different guitars – rather than just spewing out the same old opaque muck whatever is stuck in your front end – is one of the signs of a great amp. So step up, Silvertone Medalist: you have made the cut.

B.B. King injects Lucille into a big silverface Fender amplifier.

SETUP 11
CHICAGO BLUES

Plug a Gibson guitar into a Gibson amp and you get jazz. Plug a Fender guitar into a Gibson amp and you get country. Plug a Fender guitar into a Fender amp and you get rock'n'roll. But plug a Gibson guitar into a Fender amp and you get the blues – loud, dirty and wailing. Okay, sure, we have already analyzed the gorgeous ribs'n'biscuits R&B pedigree of a Stratocaster into a tweed Bassman, and nobody's going to tell you that rig can't play some serious blues. But for that slightly upmarket brisket and bourbon tone it has got to be a Gibson ES-335 guitar into a Fender Super Reverb amplifier. Make each from around 1964 and you can't go wrong. Then stick 'em into the hands of an Otis Rush or a B.B. King and you ain't going nowhere but right.

For many players in the early 1960s, Gibson archtops were very much guitars to aspire to. Jazz was still the genre preeminently deserved of respect in muso circles, and those wide-bodied f-hole designs just oozed a sort of class that screamed "you've made it." They were never the most ergonomic guitars on which to play real guts-and-glory music, though, where you needed to hug your instrument tight and really dig in, and cranking up to levels where the things could really sing would too often just induce howls of undesirable feedback. Few electric bluesers of the modern age – which we could call the early 1960s to today – got away with large hollowbody models for the main part of their playing. But Gibson's ES-335 had the appointments and the outward look – in short, the class – of a top-shelf Gibson archtop, plus a lot more… and a lot less. It had everything you wanted, while avoiding the traits you were better off without, and in so doing it achieved a near-instant market in precisely that sector that was falling into the cracks between the solidbody and hollowbody electric designs, with plenty of crossover in either direction.

If a Martian landed on Earth today, disembarked his flying saucer, and set about a comprehensive study of the development of the electric guitar (having been sent on the orders of his planet's High Commission to investigate our planet's greatest cultural contribution to the galaxy, you understand), he would probably guess that the semi-acoustic was an evolutionary step between the hollowbody archtop electric and the solidbody. He would be wrong. We all know that solidbodies didn't arrive as an incremental filling-in of the airspace between the traditional acoustic's front and back, as the existence of various semi-solids might imply. Rather the inverse. The semi-solid evolved from the solidbody as a means of either lightening up the load or imparting a whisper of archtop acoustic resonance to the solidbody tone, and more than that besides. Is the design more solid, or more acoustic? In Gibson's case, the ES-335

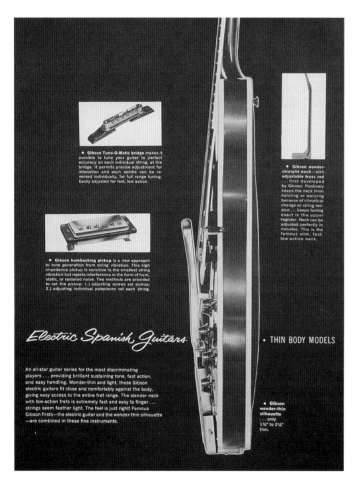

Although relatively few people would remembered why, Gibson's new thin body models still carried the 'electric Spanish' designation, shortened to 'ES'.

served to offer the look and feel of a thinline archtop electric, such as Gibson's own Byrdland, ES-350T, and ES-225T, that had existed since 1955 – and thereby win over potential solidbody players who were still too timid to take on the real thing – with more of the solidity, focused tonal response, and feedback resistance of a solidbody. The thing really was a close-fought scrapple between an ES-350T and a Les Paul, with a symmetrical double-cutaway Mickey Mouse-ears profile thrown in for fun.

As the late 1950s approached, Gibson's Les Paul was proving a moderate success under its own terms. But it had never quite managed to be the rival for Fender's Telecaster and Stratocaster, which had always been a more headfirst plunge into the radical erector-set redesign that forever redefined the solidbody electric vs the hollow varieties. The Les Paul had changed in one way or another in virtually ever year of its short existence since 1952, and was about to undertake its most radical revision to date. Since it wasn't stealing enough of Fender's clients, it needed a partner to win over players tempted by Gretsch, the new Guild thinlines, the many other fat-bodied electric makers, and other rivals. The first ES-335T guitars (the 'T' for 'Thinline;' a year later a 'D' would be added for 'Dual Pickup') rolled out of Gibson's factory in Kalamazoo, Michigan, in April 1958. The guitar found its niche almost instantly, and was arguably more of a success upon its arrival than the sunburst-finished version of the Les Paul that arrived alongside it, given that the ES-335 has survived in the Gibson catalog in essentially unaltered form ever since, while the Les Paul

The neck had the very full, rounded profile that marked the classic late 1950s Gibson feel

'standard' was dropped for a full decade after 1960. In fact, if we can agree on ranking the Stratocaster, Les Paul, and Telecaster at the top of our list of all-time most influential electric guitars in rock and blues, it wouldn't take much to argue for the ES-335's position on the fourth rung down.

In 1958 the ES-335 hit the scene with a 1 ³/₄″ deep 'thinline' body that was 16″ wide across the lower bout, had a solid block of maple running down the center, and a radical rounded double-cutaway design that was the first of its type. It had a top of laminated maple pressed into an arch, and back and sides also of laminated maple. Real f-holes in the body wings were positioned as traditionally for fine archtop acoustics, but because of the forward-shifted neck/body join – which also moved the bridge forward in the ES-335's body – they didn't have the same tonally significant center-on alignment with the bridge. A glimpse through them at first revealed only the empty space of a thinline hollowbody; wriggle a pinky finger inside, however, and you could just touch that solid wood core that ran from neck to end. In addition to its effect on the guitar in so many other ways, this center block construction enabled it to carry a stud-mounted tune-o-matic bridge and wrapover tailpiece rather than the floating two-piece rosewood or rosewood-base/tune-o-matic type and trapeze tailpiece of the fully hollow models to date, a hardware detail which marks another crucial point in this archtop's evolution away from its hollow predecessors.

Up The Neck

A glued-in solid mahogany neck carried a rosewood fingerboard with 22 frets, with virtually unhindered access up to the 20th – where the neck joined the body – and an easy reach to the next two. The fingerboard was unbound on the first examples of 1958, but bound thereafter, which is really more befitting of the rest of the model's dress and design. The ES-335 was built to what had become Gibson's standard scale length of 24 ⁵/₈″ and had a nut width of 1 ¹¹/₁₆″, and the neck had the very full, rounded profile that marked the classic late 1950s Gibson feel before a gradual move to thinner, flatter shapes. As

on our Les Paul from Setup 6 and ES-175 from Setup 7, the ES-335s of this time had a headstock that was raked back at a steep pitch of 17 degrees, which accounted for good downward pressure of strings on nut, but this and the outward splay of the D and G-srings in particular as they break toward the tuner posts can make for some catching in nut slots if these are not kept clear and smooth.

We have yet to talk about the pickups – which we have addressed twice already in this book (funny how a few of the classics keep coming around) – but this is a good place for a quick look at what this combination of solid and laminated woods and airspace is doing for us tonally, before we even plug in the guitar.

As its outward appearance implies, the ES-335 is often spoken of as an equal marriage between hollowbody and solidbody designs, and much of my earlier introduction to the model hoes this same row. But to do the guitar justice it is important to point out the wrong thinking wrapped up in that word 'equal.' You frequently see this guitar's sonic abilities wrapped up in phrases like "the woody warmth of a hollowbody archtop with the sustain and feedback resistance of a solidbody," but this isn't usually the case. The end product of this design is more solid than hollow, since the string anchors at the body end and the pickups are all mounted in the solid center block, with the truly hollow portion of the instrument merely constituting its wings. The strings' vibrational energy is passed at one end through a laminated maple top plate and via the deep-set studs directly into the solid maple block, and at the other end through the bone nut and into the rosewood fingerboard and mahogany neck, and via these back into the maple block. Some of this energy is dispersed out through the portions of the laminated front, back and sides that frame the hollow sections of the guitar, but there is less resonance going on here than the exchange

Only a marginal mount of 'acoustic' resonance is passed into the sound chain

between the solid woods of the neck and center block, and therefore only a marginal amount of 'acoustic' resonance passed into the sound chain.

You can test the purely acoustic factors of the design by trying an ES-335 next to an ES-330 (both unplugged) next time you wander into a guitar store that has both hanging on the wall. The ES-330 is a true hollowbody thinline guitar with a body of the same proportions as the ES-335, although its neck-join occurs at the 17th rather than the 20th fret – which in turn places the bridge at a different position in the body (in fact aligning the center point of the f-holes with the bridge, as in traditional quality designs), another factor that would alter the sound between the two... if not for the more significant fact of the ES-330's lack of a center block. Just tap the top of the ES-330 alongside the bridge and you can ear the

This gorgeous pair from 1965 – a blackface Fender Super Reverb and cherry Gibson ES-335 – represent the stuff of many blues players' dreams, and for good reasons. The Gibson-into-Gibson setup never turned on many bluesers (our player in the inset advertising looks like more of a jazz cat), but into hotter Fender amps those humbuckers could really sting and sing.

acoustic energy of this guitar. It's nothing like that of a deep-bodied ES-175, for example, but it's definitely there. Tap the ES-335 in the same place and you'll note straight away that there's very little top vibration happening. Strum each, and the ES-330 sounds full and round (though admittedly not very loud) up against the ES-335's choked and nasal acoustic response – but depending upon other design variables, you will often get more sustain out of the ES-335, even if you have to press an ear to the body to detect the final seconds of its decay. Aside from the major difference in airspace in the two guitars, a couple of factors account for their very different resonance characteristics. That solid center block really locks down the top and back of the ES-335, so you just don't get the diaphragmatic motion that accounts for acoustic sound in truly hollowbody guitars. What's more, what vibrational energy there is in the wings of the guitar is only passed along to them thirdhand, rather than being the well-coupled secondhand transfer from strings to bridge to top in an acoustic guitar.

The tonal result of all this is that you don't automatically get all that "woody warmth" that is so often spoken of in an ES-335, but rather plenty of snap and sparkle from that maple-on-maple body sandwich. I have played many Les Pauls that have had more of a deep, dark sizzle from the neck pickup than many ES-335s, and there's a tightness and sharpness of focus in some of these semi-acoustics that can surprise many newcomers looking for the said 50/50 solid/hollowbody merger. Some, of course, will have a depth and roundness that hints at an acoustic design, but certainly so will some solidbodies, and the degree of this in the ES-335 depends upon the usual factors of densities of woods used in its construction, pickup variables, setup and so on. In other ways, though, those f-holes and hollow wings can induce some thinline-acoustic-like reactions – particularly in allowing amplified soundwaves to enter the body cavities and induce a little more feedback in many ES-335s than you would expect from purely solid guitars.

The result is that you don't automatically get all that 'woody warmth' that is spoken of in an ES-335, but rather plenty of snap and sparkle from that maple-on-maple body sandwich

ES-335s of 1958 to 1962, of course, carried Gibson's lauded PAF humbucking pickups, and are extremely desirable instruments because of this. These pickups are right at home in the semi-acoustic, and help to provide more of the overall thickness and warmth that some players expect than would, say, a set of P-90s or other single coils. As always, the PAFs contribute to a bold but sweetly musical voice, with plenty of guts when you dig in, but a buttery smoothness when you back off the attack or the volume a little. No surprises in the wiring department for the ES-335, which follows the format of individual Volume and Tone controls plus three-way toggle switch, common to most other two-pickup Gibsons.

A Subtle Transition
Collectors go ape over the dot-neck ES-335s made from the model's introduction until about mid 1962, when the small abalone block position markers were introduced. Certainly the more austere dot position markers have come to be associated with the prime vintage examples, but the fact that the dot period also coincides approximately with that of the PAF pickups has as much to do with this as anything. The outrageously high prices attained by such guitars mean that humble players aren't seen playing original examples all that often, but the second-tier (and still excellent) ES-335s of 1963-64 did find their way into plenty of guitarists' hands. Necks on these were tending toward the thinner Gibson profiles of the mid

1960s – which, it's worth mentioning, plenty of players love – and they carried the 'patent number' pickups that were constructionally identical to the last of the PAFs (see Setup 6: Brit Blues for a more in-depth look at how these pickups changed over the years). Guitars from this brief span also escaped the narrower 1 $^5/_8''$ nut width that Gibson moved to between 1965 and 1968 – just a hair off 1 $^{11}/_{16}''$ you might think, but the change felt constricting to many experienced players' fingers. Overall, the block-neck ES-335 is more representative of the instrument, if less desirable in the pure sense, whether the guitar hails from the 1960s, 1970s or 1980s, although dot-neck reissues have of course become popular options in the last couple of decades.

Gibson ES-335s and their relatives the ES-345 and ES-355 have proved their pedigree on everything from rock'n'roll to jazz to country, but the meat'n'taters of the model sits firmly in the blues and blues-based rock camp. Freddie King, Otis Rush, John Lee Hooker, Alvin Lee, Eric Johnson, Elvin Bishop, Dickie Betts, B.B. King, Eric Clapton and Johnny 'Guitar' Watson have all strapped one on as their main guitar at some point in their careers, and much of their music makes a great place to seek out that sound. For the polarities of the guitar's blues range, you can listen to just two players: B.B. King for smooth, vocal-like Chicago blues riffing and Alvin Lee with Ten Years After for full-throttle British blues-rock.

The ES-345 and ES-355 siblings share the ES-335's construction, with the exception of an ebony fingerboard, wider, bound headstock, and stock Bigsby tailpiece on the ES-355, which was the upmarket, gold-plated model of the bunch. Both vary significantly in the wiring department, however, because of the inclusion of a Varitone rotary switch and stereo output wiring (both optional on the 355, but often present), which split each pickup's signal to a different amplifier. The Varitone offered six different tone selections achieved through simple capacitor networks, while the stereo wiring was simply a split

You can't fault the appeal of this Hawaiian-themed catalog cover, but Fender was now a long way from its roots as a lap-steel maker.

of each pickup to a different hot contact on a stereo output jack, to enable routing each to a separate amplifier. Despite their 'upgrade' status, each of these models is less collectable – and usually less desirable to players – than the standard ES-335. Some players do make use of the Varitone switching, but many simply bypass it, and rewire their guitars to mono while they're at it, to use their ES-345s and ES-355s as straight ES-335s.

After returning to the wider 1 $^{11}/_{16}''$ nut/neck width in 1968, the ES-335 went through a few other changes over the years that followed. Most were relatively minor component variations, such as a gradual change in the composition of humbucking pickups or fluctuations in the quality of wood stocks available to make the guitars. Along with the general decline in Gibson constructional quality noted by many players, these were factors that affected all of the company's guitars roughly equally. One more dramatic change included the use of a shorter center block for a time in the 1970s, which extended from neck to bridge, but left a free space at the bottom of the body. For a number of years around this time Gibson also used a trapeze tailpiece rather than the wrapover stop tailpiece mounted into the body/center block with inset studs. Both of these will of course change the guitar's sound slightly, too. Many players aren't even aware of the timber shortage, but examples from this era are among the less desirable Gibsons and perhaps the ES-335s that are furthest from the archetype. Otherwise, any of the above will get you quickly to the distinctive tone of the grandaddy of all semi-acoustics: a "warm, deep, woody glow?" Possibly not – but a voice blending a certain rich refinement with more snap, bite and midrange aggression than any fully hollowbodied electric before it, and just right for a surprisingly broad range of musical styles.

Just as the ES-335 is partly an amalgam of constructional elements of some of the Gibson guitars I have already covered, the building blocks of the 1964 Fender Super Reverb have largely been discussed in earlier chapters, but in considerably different forms. The blackface Super Reverb is very close to being a cross between the late-1950s tweed Bassman of Setup 3 and the Twin Reverb of Setup 9 – and arguably it achieves this blend in something closer to equal proportions than our ES-335 does to the Les Paul/ES-175 union. The amp has the old 5F6A Bassman's GZ34 tube rectifier, 40W output and 4x10″ alnico speaker configuration, and the Twin's approximate

Yet another maker uses the promise of sex to sell its impressive instrument.

preamp and PI format, and of course reverb and tremolo. You can tell already that this is an amp to beat, and many players feel the Super Reverb is the model that really carried the torch of Fender tone from the stunning larger models of the late 1950s into the revisions of the mid 1960s.

The Super Reverb arrived in late 1963, along with other blackface classics such as the Deluxe Reverb and Twin Reverb, and was just as radical and forward-looking an amplifier. These amps had the forward mounted controls that Fender had introduced in 1960, along with the businesslike black control panel and black Tolex covering with gray (later silver thread) grille cloth. They set the cosmetic tone for serious amps of the future more than any previous make.

Equally impressive were the refined reverb and tremolo (the latter dubbed 'Vibrato') that the Super carried, along with all but the bass and beginner models in the Fender range at this time. These onboard effects were appearing on other amps already, and had even arrived a year previous on Silvertone's similarly formatted model 1484 and 1285 Twin Twelve amps, for example, but the Fender versions sounded better than nearly all comers, and the amps were more powerful and better built to boot. Fender amps of this era contained some of the best components that the company ever used – from transformers right through to signal and filtering caps – and were rigorously hand wired in a sturdy, repair-friendly layout. These were the 'boutique-grade' amplifiers of their day when compared to most others available, and although they weren't cheap, they were built to last. A guitarist leaving the store with a Super Reverb in 1964 could head home not just with the salesman's pitch of this being "the best professional amplifier available today" ringing in his ears, but the firm understanding that it was true.

As mentioned above, the Super Reverb carried the same new big-blackface preamp circuit as the Twin, which was designed to yield excellent clean headroom and a crisp tonality. The Super lacked the Twin's Middle control on the Normal channel, which is really just a nominal difference (and of course the wide-body Twin had more room for bonus controls), but carried a Middle on the Vibrato channel and otherwise followed the same control layout exactly. Both amps run on very nearly the same voltages throughout, with high DC levels of between 250v and 270v on the first preamp tubes versus the more touch-inducing 170v-180v on the Deluxe Reverb of the same era or 150v-160v on the classic tweed amps. The two amps also carried identical PI circuits, and the output tubes ran on the same voltages – around 460v DC on the plates (anodes). So why the considerable difference in sound and performance?

A Quicker Road To The Crunch

Well, there are a few differences between the amps, too, and while you can count them on one hand, they make enough of an impact to change the Super Reverb's character. The Super of course has a tube rectifier, which just couldn't have kept up with the powerful Twin. Alongside this, it also has lower-value filter capacitors in the first stage of the power chain; the two are necessarily linked, as tube rectifiers just aren't happy with overly high levels of filtering, but these combined changes work to compound the differences between the amps. High filtering makes for tighter, firmer lows, but after a point it can also decrease some of the touch-sensitivity in the response of that portion of the frequency range. The Twin therefore gets the firm, fat bottom, but the Super gets the touchy-feely quality that many other players love. Tube rectification is liable to sag at high levels of power draw, inducing a compression effect that is felt as much as heard (although it should be noted that GZ34s and equivalent 5AR4s are pretty sturdy rectifiers, and less prone to sag than others), and this is another factor that softens the edge of the amp's response. Most obvious of all, though, is the fact that the Super only has two 6L6GC output tubes to the Twin's four. If the amps were otherwise entirely identical, this would still be enough to create a noticeable difference in performance. The smaller output stage is prone to a quicker onset of distortion and therefore easier access to that desirable edge-of-break-up sweetspot at any given volume level – a tone zone that finds most amplifiers at their most playable and best sounding. Of course, for players who want to push the taut, clean twang right to the ceiling, hey, that's what the Twin is there for.

Add these together, and the differences between the Twin and the Super are far more matters of touch and feel, married to a vary different onset of distortion, than they are anything to do with radically different voices. But as we have seen with other makes and models, players respond to the feel of an amp – best defined as the degree to which pick attack and playing style directly affect the amp's dynamics and distortion – as much as to its sound, and when the amp becomes a playable instrument to the extent that it is virtually inseparable from the guitar itself, the sound of the entire performance can be affected dramatically.

There are two more major differences between the Twin and the Super, one extremely obvious and the other probably less so: the speakers, and the type of output transformer (OT) that feeds them. The Super of course carried a smaller 40W OT versus the Twin's 85W OT, but it was still a heftier transformer than that on other mid-sized Fenders, such as the Bandmaster, Tremolux and Pro Reverb, and gave the Super a firmer low end and more volume overall than these other models. The relationship is comparable to the tweed Bassman's hefty 40W iron vs the smaller 28W OTs of the tweed Super and Pro, and further makes the Super Reverb the evolutionary successor to the tweed Bassman. As does, it almost goes without saying, the amp's 4x10″ speaker configuration.

By the early 1960s, Fender was clearly aware that this format had become more viable for the guitarist than for the bassist, and shifted its bass amps to piggy-back setups driving 12″ and 15″ speakers in closed-back cabs, but retained the vaunted open-back 4x10″ cab purely in its guitar combos. At first this configuration survived only in the brownface Concert Amp, which lacked the tube rectification and was quite a different amplifier besides, but it returned in 1963 for the Super Reverb, which was clearly the flagship model of the Fender 40-watters for guitar. Like the tweed Bassman, the Super had its 10″ speakers wired parallel for a 2-ohm load; also like the Bassman, it sometimes still used alnico drivers at this

The Super has plenty of kick-in-the-guts, even if its lows are slightly shaggier than a Twin's

time, when the speakers in most other Fenders now had the ceramic magnets that were fast becoming more common. Most of Fender's Jensens of the day were now ceramic units, such as the C10Rs that many Supers carried, but they would also sometimes have alnico CTS or Oxford types. Despite the alnico myth, however, players still often prefer the Jensens, which are crisp, sweet and bell-like, and can be driven into a distortion that is just about as juicy as that of their alnico-magnet forerunners. Note that the blackface amps have the more firmly fixed chipboard baffle versus the semi-floating plywood baffle of the tweeds – a change made in 1962, actually – so this also contributes to a tighter punch in the later amps.

With any of these speakers, the Super has plenty of kick-in-the-guts even if its lows are slightly shaggier than a Twin's, with a real bark in the upper mids and sharp, sometimes even glassy highs. With a Fender Stratocaster or Telecaster injected these are bright, cutting amps – still wailers when cranked, but you will find very few Fender players using the Bright switches on these models, and of course the Fender-Fender partnership offers greater headroom, too. Stick in a plummy Gibson ES-335, however, and the fatter frequency response of those humbuckers is going to drive the Super to even quicker crunch and sting, warm up the overall tonality, and add a little more midrange punch besides. This is blues city, a great combination of extremely playable dynamics and an eviscerating sting from the upper-midrange.

The Quest For Clean

Players who want greater headroom from a Gibson guitar run into a Fender of this size sometimes plug into the number 2 input, which has a lower sensitivity than number 1. This keeps the full frequency range of the Gibson humbuckers and the ES-335's broad voice on tap, but doesn't drive the preamp as hard, which in turn lets a cleaner signal through to the output stage. The less distortion you get happening before the output, the greater the output stage's potential proportion of distortion in the final brew. Many players understand that more output tube distortion rather than preamp tube distortion means mo betta mojo, so hey, these lower drive levels can be a good thing in some cases. Which takes us full circle back to the Fender-Fender setup: get that Super Reverb finally grinding with a Strat injected, and the overdrive sound can be rich, open and full-throated, a sound preferred by some to the thick, more saturated Gibson-driven breakup. Put the Gibson into input 2, however, and you've got all its thick, plummy tonality, little preamp distortion, and that rich, delicious output-tube distortion that we all love so much. So many sounds, so little time.

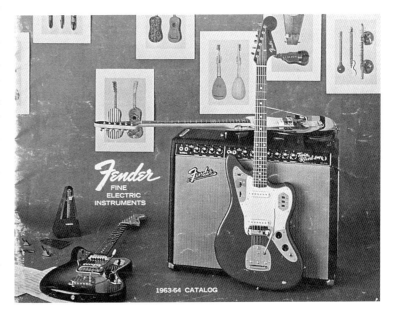

The cover of this 1963-64 catalog displays Fender's apparent roots in the pre-pre-pre-rock'n'roll age.

As with the Twin and Deluxe Reverbs, Fender changed the Super Reverb even further in the silverface years of the late 1960s and 1970s, partly in a quest for even greater headroom and partly in the name of the more efficient production of the CBS years. Many of these models can pretty easily be put back to pre-CBS specs by a good amp tech, and such 'blackfacing' modifications have become popular with more and more players over the years. This offers more affordable access to the great sound of the original AA763 and AB763 Super Reverb circuits than trying to locate – and pay for – a vintage blackface in good working condition. Fender's recent reissue of the model also offers a good approximation of the sound; it's not dead-on, but its components and constructional approach are very different, and of course it lacks some 40 years of aging, so it's not bad considering, and at least in the same ballpark.

It is hard to beat the original combination, but however you achieve an accurate ES-335-Super Reverb setup, there are plenty of fat, classy, singing tones to be tapped, and an extremely fun, playable rig besides.

With an SG Special into a Hiwatt, Pete Townshend whacked out a big, bold rhythm sound for The Who.

BRIT ROCK TO CLASSIC METAL

Much of what makes up the classic metal guitar sound of today evolved out of some heavy rockers' efforts to attain the loudest, gut-thumpingest, head-kickingest rhythm-guitar levels they could – largely achieved by taking a clean, bold signal and pumping it through an extremely powerful tube amplifier. This has been done with a range of guitars and amps over the past 35 years, but one of the pioneers of mega-volume punch was Pete Townshend of The Who, and he achieved the first of his truly huge sounds in the late 1960s with a Gibson SG Special plugged into a pair of Hiwatt Custom 100 full stacks. Compared to the Metallicas, Sepulturas or Slipknots of today, The Who might not sound especially 'metal,' and stylistically they weren't. But they were the first of the stadium-sized rockers to pursue that hyper-loud sound and bombastic stage energy, and for a long time they even held the *Guinness Book Of Records'* title as 'world's loudest rock band.' All done thanks – yes – to Keith Moon's thunderous drumming, John Entwistle's colossal bass sound, and Pete Townshend's guitar, the latter two through Hiwatt amps.

As far as the guitar is concerned, these massive volume levels were made possible by keeping the headroom up and achieving a driving, percussive sound, which of course carried a good dose of distortion because, well, that's just what any tube guitar amp does when you crank it up. But these levels were essentially far less overdriven than we think of most hard rock sounds being today. Listen to a lot of classic metal, though, from Black Sabbath, to Deep Purple to Iron Maiden, and the heaviest of the guitar sounds are achieved by reining in the oversaturation of distortion, and keeping that guitar relatively tight and pumping. Pete Townshend knew this lesson well; he was no great shakes as a lead guitarist, but he appreciated the power of loud rhythm guitar, and he wielded his like a weapon.

In Setup 6: British Blues we had a glimpse of the Gibson Les Paul's evolution into the SG in 1960, which marked the death of the most coveted production solidbody electric guitar ever made. The SG is a worthy rock instrument in its own right, however, and with hindsight it is difficult to understand Gibson's not bringing in the new model alongside its more staid single-cutaway predecessor, what with the numerous

At that time, the Les Paul was looking just a little too much like a shrunken-down, filled-in, f-hole-less Gibson archtop of old, and was selling in pretty small numbers

contemporary, 'classic reissue' and signature style versions of each model available today. At the time, though, the Les Paul was looking just a little too much like a shrunken-down, filled-in, f-hole-less Gibson archtop of old, and was selling in pretty small numbers. It wasn't captivating this bold new breed of guitarist out there, and something new was needed. And clearly, something pointy.

Gibson had tried to attack Fender's modernist solidbodies previously, and failed. The radical Flying-V and Explorer of 1958 proved just too out-there for guitarists, and didn't capture any of the magic that Fender had mustered up with its Stratocaster four years before, or even to some extent the Jazzmaster of the same year. They vanished in 1960 after only a very small production run, but Gibson clearly felt a modern rethink of the solidbody was called for – and judging by the success that the next model was to achieve, it was right.

By late 1960 the Les Paul Standard existed in name only. In place of the thick mahogany body with carved maple cap was a thinner all-mahogany design with angularly sculpted edges and two deep cutaways that each extended almost all the way to the neck's 22nd fret. This too was an all-new and quite futuristic design for its day, but at least retained a nod to traditional guitar lines with the curved waist and rounded and symmetrical lower and upper bouts, if slightly offset horn points. Gibson's Kalamazoo factory manufactured around 6,000 SG/Les Pauls in the first few years of the model's existence, compared to a total of fewer than 1,700 Les Paul Standards between 1958 and 1960, so this bid to join the modern era of the solidbody electric guitar finally seems to have been a successful one. With the cessation of Les Paul's deal with Gibson in 1962 these guitars became simply the 'SG' for 'Spanish Guitar,' and by 1963 the name of this important endorser no longer features on the company's guitars.

SGs have a slightly lighter, yet furrier core tonality but with a good range and plenty of body

The Les Paul-to-SG transition makes an excellent quick study of what a different body composition can do for a solidbody guitar's sound. SGs of 1961 carried the same PAF humbucking pickups; wiring layout; tune-o-matic bridge; Kluson tuners; and neck, nut and headstock composition as the last Les Pauls of 1960, and their bodies were made from the mahogany that comprised the majority of the Les Paul's, too. Of course the SG/Les Pauls were offered with a vibrato tailpiece as standard – first an odd side-to-side unit, later a more conventional up-down Vibrola – and this changes their sound some even when the wobbler isn't in use. Which is very often the case; many players disable it entirely or even install a replacement stop tailpiece. In this configuration, the Les Paul and SG sound similar, certainly, but very different too when you listen for the fine points. SGs have a slightly lighter, yet furrier, core tonality but with a good range and plenty of body. They are less full-throated but often possess a little more snap and sharpness.

Cracked Necks And Shifted Pickups

They sometimes had more snap in the literal sense, too, as the neck and headstock joints of these guitars were especially prone to breakage if the guitars were dropped or happened to slide off their amp-propped positions, as all too often happened. Players who liked to roam right up to the high end of the fingerboard appreciated SGs immediately, that double cutaway and less obtrusive neck heel giving easier access to the dusty end than almost any design before. But this configuration offered a lot less body wood at this crucial coupling zone, and the routing for the neck pickup meant that what was there was a lot thinner than most structural engineers would prefer. The necks' ultra-thinness at this time contributed to other weak points, especially at the headstock, which still had its severe 17 degree back angle in the early 1960s, and without the reinforcing wedge that later appeared behind the nut. Neck pickups were shifted slightly at different times through the 1960s to leave a little more wood at the body joint, and the necks themselves thickened up by the mid 1960s too, so the headstock became at least slightly less fragile. But many rock lead guitarists really loved the fast, thin SG necks from the model's first couple of years and the style has been turned to again and again for reissue models.

Of course, the SG Special of our main photo – and the one behind Pete Townshend's powerful late 1960s sound – was an example from later in the 1960s, and had another major difference from the Les Paul Standard. This model's P-90 pickups take it into entirely different territory. If the 1960 Les Paul Standard and 1961 SG/Les Paul are at least similar, the SG Special represents a more fully individual evolution of the model. Whereas Les Paul Specials and Juniors had more basic, slab-style bodies than the flagship Standards, SG Specials and Juniors shared the same bodies as their big brothers. They were differentiated only by pickups, some hardware alterations, and decoration, but these were enough to make them quite different guitars.

Pete Townshend used SG Specials between 1968-71, and they were usually 1966-1970 models (though occasionally pre-1965s too). These had standard trim, which means two P-90 single coil pickups, the usual Gibson two-each plus toggle-switch wiring, and a wrapover bridge/tailpiece. Some of his instruments originally carried Vibrola tailpieces, but Townshend removed these – as did many players – and anchored the strings at the wrapover bar unit alone. Of course this bridge was a somewhat downmarket piece of hardware compared with the tune-o-matic, but the fact that Gibson included it on a Vibrola-carrying guitar might have indicated the company's awareness that not all players would want to use their Vibrolas. The units were effective enough – a folded-back piece of bent steel that provided its own spring-like tension and offered a subtle vibrato travel akin to a Bigsby. But as ever they could contribute to some tuning difficulties, and also served to lighten the sound slightly, as do many vibrato tailpieces. Bypassed or removed, these SG Specials converted to the sturdy integral arrangement of the wrapover bridge; there was little useful intonation adjustment to be had here, but many players consider them to be among the most toneful pieces of hardware Gibson ever produced. On Townshend's guitar this certainly contributed to the solid, resonant sound he achieved, and helped to keep the tuning about as well anchored as an SG ever can be through all that on-stage windmilling, jumping and general Who-style larking about.

And with that notoriously unstable SG neck join, who needs a low-travel vibrato tailpiece anyway? Just hit a chord, jerk the neck around a little, and hey – instant vibrato! Townshend used this feature of the design to add depth and movement to his playing, and to give the occasional sustain-boosting jiggle that offered a more subtle trigger into feedback than walloping the strings again.

Gibson's P-90 pickups were always pretty hot for single coils, and could drive a tube amp as hard in terms of gain as the company's humbuckers. But their sonic signature was a little less fat-tending-towards-muddy (especially in the neck position) so there was more bright bite available here than on the humbucker-loaded SG. P-90s are also generally less refined than vintage-style humbuckers, but many players like that about them. Good examples are raw and just a little gritty sounding, with a midrange emphasis that really suits rock'n'roll, but plenty of sweetness, too. They have a silvery high end that is bright enough to cut through, but is less harsh than that of many other single coils.

Good P-90s are less refined than vintage-style humbuckers, but many players like that

Punch And Sizzle

These pickups' narrower magnetic window – which, it bears repeating, is still broader than that of a Fender-style pickup, and so offers a juicier sound than those, but certainly not as broad as a traditional humbucker – makes for a little more punch and sizzle in the guitar's overall tone, too. There's as much overall volume, and in some cases even a little more, as from standard humbuckers of around 7K-8K. But often the tighter, brighter frequency spectrum they present doesn't elbow an amp into saturation as quickly, so it's easier to tap the headroom of a big, clean design like the Hiwatt. Listen to this chapter's first two example tracks on the CD, and you hear how the P-90s of track 48 are easily as big sounding as the humbuckers of track 49, with a midrange nasal bark that works great for rock rhythm styles, too. This kind of voice often muddies a mix less than humbuckers (on stage or on record), yet somehow comes out sounding larger. All in all, these SGs offer a great example of what a good P-90 pickup can do, because they have less of the acoustic top vibrations of the many hollowbody electric models that also carry

Despite its outwardly 'Marshall-esque' appearance, the Hiwatt is a very different amp, designed for greater headroom and maximum punch. Faced with a Gibson SG Special with hot, raw P-90 pickups, the pair makes for a powerful, grinding rhythm assault and sharp, cutting leads.

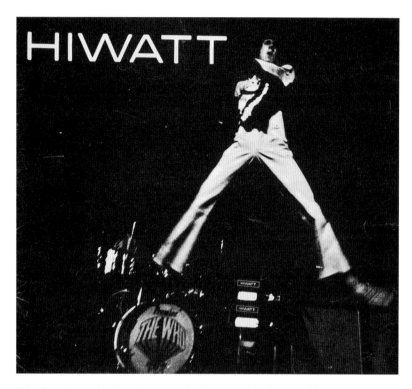

Peter Townshend clearly getting off on the heady combination of tight trousers and big, uh, amps.

Gibson's second most famous pickup, and are therefore less prone to the microphony that can sometimes plague these single-coil designs.

You never saw SG Specials in the hands of as many notable pros as the Standards, but they were the main guitar of Robbie Krieger of The Doors and Frank Zappa, who applied them to powerful yet entirely original work that was even further out on the fringes of rock convention than Townshend's playing. Humbucker-equipped SG Standards became a byword for big rock pyrotechnics, however, and propped up as many flamboyant solos through big, black British amp stacks as did Les Pauls through the late 1960s and 1970s. With humbuckers on board, that thin mahogany slab body exudes a creamier, more fluid lead sound, but still has plenty of brightness and even a little twang in its attack. It has understandably remained the SG model choice of the soloist. Get this into a big, bold amp with plenty of firm-bottomed output power – then stomp a germanium treble booster, silicon-transistor Fuzz Face, MXR Distortion+, or another early overdrive or distortion pedal, and you've got the classic heavy metal sound at your fingertips.

Pump that SG Special's sizzle and bark through a massive Hiwatt Custom 100 DR103, on the other hand, and the whole thing holds together amazingly well even near top volume. These amps are made to be driven, and sound far more girthsome and ominous pounding out the power chords than any over-saturated, cascading gain overdrive monster is ever going to manage, despite its considerable filth.

Hiwatt amps were never intended as a Marshall copy, despite their generally similar look, but were a design unto themselves from the start. Although many players have mistaken the amps for approximate copies of Jim Marshall's stacks, anyone who has played a good Hiwatt for any length of time knows better, as does any tech who has had the pleasure of opening one up. Hiwatt was founded in the mid 1960s by Dave Reeves, who had the intention of building the best big guitar amplifiers he could build, from considerations of components right through to wiring and cabinetry. The company used Partridge transformers that were bigger and better than most anything being used for guitar amplifiers at the time, partnered these with other military grade components, and even commissioned military-specification chassis wiring from Harry Joyce, who did other high-end contract electronics work, including wiring jobs for the Royal Navy.

Reeves was working for Arbiter's Sound City ampworks when the bug to build a better amp bit him, and early Hiwatt prototypes of around 1967 were essentially custom efforts that evolved out of that workshop. Before playing Hiwatts proper, Pete Townshend played Sound City amps in 1967-68, but these

L100 models were customized by Reeves to specs that would virtually define the DR103 circuit, and eventually they would even carry specially-made 'Hiwatt' name plates, despite their Sound City origins. When full-blown Hiwatts finally hit the market, they really raised the bar in terms of quality construction.

High-End Hiwatts

Look under the hood of a Hiwatt from the Dave Reeves era and the wire runs are truly breathtaking, like nothing seen until recent boutique builders started paying similar Joycean attention to details that only one out of 100 guitar players would ever notice. Grounding and shielding within the chassis is extremely well thought-out in order to keep noise and interference at a minimum, which extends to more shielded internal signal runs than other makers were using at the time, and even the use of an unusual metal shielding plate mounted vertically on the outside of the chassis to electronically separate the output tubes from the large filter capacitor cans. In addition, Hiwatt components are assembled on a single heavy-duty turret board that offers both extremely good electronic contact between points, and a fluid, logical signal flow that makes for quick assessment and easy repair, even by techs not necessarily familiar with the circuits.

And this raises what, even among all this quality workmanship, probably remains the main feature of Hiwatt amps: the circuits. These are very different from the juicy and gainy tweed Fender/Marshall, with cathode-following tone stacks and other features, and an advancement on either one if your goal is to move a full-frequencied yet bold and clean signal along to the output stage. They have this in common with the blackface Fender amps, and at first glance you could be forgiven for thinking you see certain similarities between these – or a Marshall/blackface Fender cross in the Hiwatts even – but in fact they are very different from either. The Hiwatt preamp and tone stages use a full four gain stages, one more than the most used by any of these Fender or Marshall topologies, plus very differently valued signal capacitors in almost every position.

Reeves's design features a shared three-knob tone-stack-plus-Presence control that appears, on the control panel, to duplicate the tweed Bassman's Marshall-inspiring format, but internally these functions occur in an entirely different part of the circuit. After each channel's first tube gain stage the signal hits a volume control, then runs straight to a second gain stage, with a Treble/Middle/Bass network configured between the plate (anode) output of this triode and the input of yet another ECC83 following (containing a further two gain stages to condition the signal prior to the phase inverter). This tone section lacks a little of the famous touch-sensitivity of cathode-follower design, but offers an efficient voice-shaping stage that also refuses to admit as much dirt as many more primitive tone stacks.

Like the post-1963 Fenders, however, the Hiwatts do use a 12AT7 (European ECC81) PI tube to offer a little less drive but, again, more headroom to the output tubes, which are EL34s. Get a muscular signal running to four of these beefy tubes, in turn pumping hard through a hefty Partridge OT, and you have a serious output going on. High filter capacitor values in the power supply also contribute to low-noise performance and a solid bass response without as much

If you push it, one of these amps will ease from tactile crunch into chewy roar

of the low-end flatulence that some Marshall Plexis exhibit. Unusually for an amp of this size and caliber, however, there is no choke in the power chain – but its absence probably helps this big rig keep from sounding too constipated, and otherwise is more than made up for by that high filtering and Reeves's low-

The guitar still carried his name – for a time – but it was a different beast entirely.

noise design.

I have perhaps overemphasized the 'cleanliness' of this amp up to now, but only to prove a point; garnering just a little more headroom out of the early stages of the Hiwatt circuits offers the 4xEL34 output stage – outwardly very similar to Marshall's – a bold, sumptuous signal that can then be taken to the limit for dynamics and output. But these amps are by no means distortion free, and if you push one they will certainly ease from tactile crunch into chewy roar. But the fact that less distortion artifacts seep into the signal chain up to the output stage means that the Hiwatts' tone and dynamics carries an even greater proportion of output-tube mojo than most, which results in one of the biggest, broadest soundstages going. More than one British recording professional has passed me the adage, "If you want a great Marshall sound, use a great Hiwatt," and although plenty of Marshall amps can certainly sound excellent, many guitarists are pleasantly surprised to find Hiwatts delivering a more consistent version of the tonal image they always held in their heads as 'the big British rock sound.'

But these are the stock Hiwatt Custom 100 DR103s. Townshend's amps were of course a little different...

Pete Townshend had used a wide range of amps with The Who up to the later mid 1960s, including models by Vox, Fender, Sound City, and Marshall, and in fact it was he who had leaned on Jim Marshall perhaps more heavily than most to get back to the drawing board and design a 100W amplifier. After playing the big new Marshall stacks for a time, Townshend found what he had been seeking all along in Dave Reeves's powerful designs, and these became his main amps through the bulk of his career with The

It is said that Townshend blames his tinnitus not on his Hiwatts, but on blasting his guitar through headphones for long periods of post-gig comedown – but maybe this is apocryphal

Who. On tour he usually used two heads with two Hiwatt SE4122 4x12″ cabs each for a total of four, although the bottom cabs of each stack were often 'dummy' units merely used to prop up the 'live' top cabs. A third head was also on hand as a spare... which was rarely needed. This was a lot of firepower, and when you went to a Who show in the late 1960s and early 1970s you really felt it – even more than heard it – and in fact if you stood too close you probably didn't hear much of anything for many hours, or even days, afterwards. Surprisingly, I have heard that Townshend blames his own tinnitus not on his Hiwatts, but on blasting his guitar through the headphones for long periods of post-gig comedown back in the years when his senses were usually comfortably numb by that stage of the evening. But maybe this is apocryphal.

Townshend's High-Gain Tweaks

In any case, Townshend's DR103 Hiwatts were modified by Reeves right at the factory, which is to say they were custom made. Changes from standard-issue included linking all four inputs, with a Volume control for each to make it easy to blend voices, and a 10dB gain boost at the first stage; disconnecting the Middle and Presence controls, so that only Bass and Treble remained; adding a Master Volume; and using four 12AX7/ECC83 preamp tubes rather than the three plus 12AT7/ECC81 in the PI. These Hiwatts pushed the front end a little harder for a crunchier sound right from the preamp, which in turn drove the output section harder too, especially with that extra 12AX7 in

the driver position. Townshend's amps were still nothing like the high-gain amps of the modern era, which achieve distortion primarily by cascading preamp stages, and still derived their huge, juicy sound largely from hard-pushed output tubes. But they were dirtier than stock Hiwatts, and helped to contribute to that massive Who sound. However much shred-certified OD saturation you can generate from a modern Boogie Rectifier model, Soldano, Bogner or what have you, an old Hiwatt Custom 100 DR103 still always sounds bigger to me – which is to say, enormous.

Hiwatt speaker cabs also followed the outward lines of the seminal Marshall 4x12″s, but they were similarly overbuilt, with thick plywood and ruggedized joints that stood the rigors of the road beautifully. They usually carried different drivers to the Marshalls, too, notably sturdy and powerful Fane 50W speakers, which Reeves considered upgrades on the Celestions that most other British amp-makers used at the time. These were powerful, efficient speakers, so they really blasted out the volume. Taken individually they were probably a little tighter and arguably colder than many single Celestion models of that era, but pushed hard – as they certainly were in a Hiwatt rig – they really roared. Their 50W rating also meant that a single 4x12″ cab could handle a full 200W, hence Townshend's ability to get away with having a dummy cab on the bottom of each of his stacks.

Hiwatts have also made major noises in the backlines of Pink Floyd, Rush, Family, Tommy Bolin and occasionally The Rolling Stones. But stick the gainy but not overly corpulent signal of a Gibson SG Special

Gibson's Custom Shop Pete Townshend SG Special is pre-soiled for your convenience, with greasy stuff smeared on the hardware to give just the right Live At Leeds patina

into Dave Reeves's unique preamp design feeding a gutsy power amp, and the resultant huge, thwacking rhythm assault and occasional wailing lead flurry that sums up the 'Townshend sound' is still a premier example of what these 100W amps do best. Townshend used his modified Hiwatts right up until 1981, which signaled the close of a packed decade of touring for The Who. The same year saw the passing of Dave Reeves, and Hiwatt itself passed into different hands. While the new caretakers continued to make decent amps, 1981 is widely seen as the start of a general decline in quality – or the end of the classic years of Hiwatt, at least.

Today, the Hiwatt brand has curiously wound up being split between two owners: Music Ground in the UK, and Fernandez in the USA. I have personally had more experience with Hiwatts from the former (marketed as Reeves amplifiers in the USA), and they appear to be extremely well built and great sounding amplifiers, with turret-board circuits and immaculate wire runs that even approach those of the great early 1970s Hiwatts. The company has reissued various DR103 Custom 50 and Custom 100 amps, including signature models for both Pete Townshend and David Gilmour. Often, however, original vintage examples are no more expensive than the new versions, since these Hiwatts never attained the collectability status of Marshalls from the same period. Most bigger Hiwatts probably would have been toured hard, but they were built to survive this. Aside from bagging an original 1960s Gibson SG Special to stick into either a new or vintage Hiwatt, you have a contemporary option to go for: Gibson has reissued a Custom Shop Pete Townshend SG Special; the couple I have tried have been fantastic guitars, but curiously they retailed when new for more than you would usually pay for a good vintage example of the real thing. They are beautifully made, though, and pre-soiled for your convenience, with impressively Townshendesque greasy stuff smeared on the hardware to give just the right *Live At Leeds* patina. Primed to rock, and rock big.

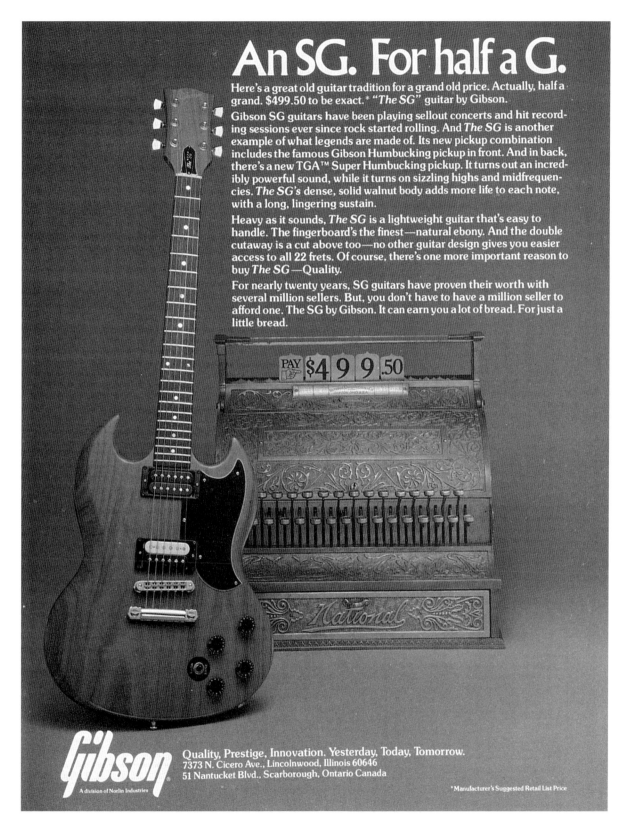

Even through Gibson's dark years, the SG soldiered on as a rock standard.

Stevie Ray Vaughan's favorite guitar was 'Number One,' a battered 1963 Strat.

AFTERWORD

This book has not been written to get you searching for expensive vintage equipment or to feed the already frenzied classic gear scene. If there is one point I would like readers to take away, it is that they can use the great range of equipment available – which, in combination, provides infinite variables – to create sounds all their own. Certainly fans of one great player or another can use these chapters to come close to emulating their hero's sound, but I think the information here is most valuable as a springboard to achieving your own tone and style.

It is important to recognize the wealth of outstanding contemporary gear available today, too, whether from the many independent 'boutique' makers, or from the very playable standard or reissue models from major brands. In real terms, the latter make good, usable instruments that are more affordable today than ever before in the history of the electric guitar. As for the boutique makers, well, I have played guitars, pedals and amps by many of these people that impress me as much as any rarified piece of vintage gear I have ever gotten my hands on. As a little taster in this direction, the last four tracks on the accompanying CD were recorded with guitars from Tom Anderson and John Suhr, through brand new amps from Carr and TopHat (both detailed more thoroughly in the CD track notes). Other amp-makers such as Bad Cat, Matchless, Mojave, Victoria, Clark, and so on are producing sounds that blend the best of vintage voicings with modern range, clarity and reliability, while luthiers such as Don Grosh, Rick Turner, Paul Reed Smith and plenty of others are building some of the best electric guitars ever played.

Your own 'classic sound' needn't necessarily come from a combination of gear played by a universally acknowledged artist. It might be that you find your own road to a sound that has been ringing in your head for years, or you might attain nuances of tone and style used by no one before, but which perfectly express your needs as a player.

Consider the nature of the whole 'classic sound' phenomenon. Most such 'classics,' though born decades ago, are still desired today because they are what we are familiar with; they have come to be perceived as great in themselves, but maybe there's nothing that makes them universally, intrinsically 'great' – they have been heard on hit records and in great live performances by top artists, and it's that greatness that defines them to this day. If Hendrix had played a hollow-bodied Gibson ES-125T through an Electro-Harmonix LPB1 and a little Gibson GA-30 amp, that would be the rig to die for today. If Eric Clapton had recorded the Blues Breakers' 'Beano' album with a Guild Starfire IV and a Selmer combo, well, yeah, Les Paul Standards would still cost a hundred grand today, but vintage Guilds and Selmers would probably have gotten a boost out of the deal, too. If a rig works for you – brings out the best in your playing and yields a tone that expresses the heart and soul of your efforts as a musician – then who cares if no 'classic' used it before you? Use the gear well, try to do more playing than tone chasing, and maybe future generations will be hunting down countless replications of your 2005 setup on the vintage market in 2030.

CD TRACK NOTES

Tracks on the accompanying CD were recorded with equipment that was as close to that of the chapter subjects as could be obtained. Although they were not always exactly the same pieces as appear in the photos (although indeed some were), they feature equivalent gear of the same type and era. No modeling amps or digital trickery of any kind was used at any time. Each track was also recorded free from studio compression or limiting or other enhancing processors, and no EQ was applied during recording or mixing. This was done in an effort to present the setups as they sound 'dry' in the average project studio, which can easily be replicated by many readers with basic home recording equipment available today, rather than as they would sound after undergoing the extensive studio processing that is a standard part of most professional recording. To that end, other than where noted, amps were close-miked with an ordinary Shure SM57 dynamic microphone. For some small rigs a vintage STC (Coles) 4038 ribbon mike was used in order to take advantage of its excellent 'in the room' sound. Either of these was fed straight into the Low-Z input of a MOTU 828 digital recording interface set at 24 bits and 44.1 KHz (converted to 16 bits for CD mastering) and recorded on a Macintosh lap top.

Riffs selected for the 54 examples here are not meant to be strictly 'in the style of' as so many training books offer, but are intended to display the equipment approximately as used in the genres for which they are most famous. The playing is occasionally unpolished, even a little sloppy in some places, but is intended to capture the gear in the hands of the 'ordinary guy' – to give a realistic picture of how it sounds in and of itself, rather than in the hands of a true guitar god. We have got those examples lining the shelves of every record store you care to walk into, but they don't usually go very far in showing you what guitar X will sound like plugged into amp Y if you take them home and try them out for yourself. In most cases, control settings are given in the universal 'o'clock' style, 9:00 being a quarter of the way up on the dial, 12:00 half way, and so on.

SETUP 1
EARLY JAZZ

Track	Equipment
1	Early 1940s Gibson ES-125 into Gibson EH-150 amp; amp Vol 11:00, Tone 1:00; flatwound pure nickel strings; STC 4038 ribbon mic at 18″ from cone.
2	Same amplifier settings, with a 1952 Telecaster set to bridge pickup.
3	Same setup as Track 1, but amp Vol & Tone 3:00.
4	Same again, Vol maxed.

Note how the first track screams 'late-1930s jazz,' where the second has the brighter, bouncier tonality of country swing, especially when the uptempo section kicks in – the only difference between the two being the guitar used. Track 3 shows how you just need to crank up the same gear to get the bite and tube distortion that defines the primitive electric blues sound, while Track 4 takes this a notch further, with a little more of a boogie styling.

SETUP 2
ROCK'N'ROLL

Track	Equipment
5	Pre-production 1954 Gretsch 6120 Chet Atkins Hollowbody guitar and Gretsch (Valco) 6160 amplifier. Guitar on bridge pickup; amp Vol 12:00, Tone 1:00.
6	Same, with slapback tape echo from an early Maestro Echoplex.
7	Same rig, guitar's pickup selector set at middle position for both pickups; amp Vol 10:00, Tone 12:00. Track 5 has a great raw, classic rock'n'roll sound, but the period rockabilly vibe really comes alive on Track 6, where the addition of an old tube-powered tape echo is the only change. Selecting a mellower but still lively guitar sound and toning down the amp's drive a little yields more of an early country tonality. Of course dropping the plectrum for some fingerpicking helps here, too.

SETUP 3
R&B

Track	Equipment
8	1964 Fender Stratocaster (rosewood fingerboard) into 1959 Fender Bassman (reconditioned, with reconed speakers). Guitar on neck pickup, pure nickel roundwound strings .010-.048. Amp set: Normal Vol max, Treble 3:00, Bass 10:30, Middle 3:00, Presence 3:00.
9	Same guitar and pickup into a thoroughly shagged-out 5F6A Bassman that reportedly once belonged to Buddy Guy. Amp set: Normal Vol max, Treble 2:00, Bass 12:00, Middle 1:00, Presence 0.
10	All the same as Track 9, with Strat set to bridge pickup.
11	Strat on neck pickup again, through 1957 Fender Super amp in virtually original condition, set: Vol max, Treble 1:00, Bass 1:00.
12	The 'good' Bassman with an original-spec 12AY7 tube in the first position.
13	The same, at same settings, but with a hotter 12AX7 in the preamp.

Track 8 displays a stinging, slightly scooped overdrive sound, with crackling highs and a really powerful, thudding low end, even if there's a little mush down there too. The tired out 'Buddy Guy Bassman' in Track 9 has lost a lot of its low-end oomph and maybe needs a good cap job and some speaker work (no, turning the Bass up didn't help – just made things muddier), but still has some real sizzle and magic to it. In Track 11, note how much harder the Super drives its two 10″ Jensen speakers than the Bassman drives its set of four. The sound isn't nearly as sparkling and full-frequencied, though. Tracks 12 and 13 speak for themselves: the difference in distortion is achieved with a simple preamp tube swap (both are good, tested US-made NOS tubes). Deciding which is preferable depends on the player, and the style of music the rig will be used for.

SETUP 4
BRITISH INVASION

Track	Equipment
14	1964 Rickenbacker 360/12 into 1964 Vox AC30 Top Boost. Bridge pickup selected on 360/12. AC30 set: Vol 10:00, all tone controls 12:00.
15	Same gear, but amp Vol set to 12:00 also.
16	Same guitar on middle switch position (both pickups). Blonde early 1960s Fender Showman amp set: Vol 9:30, all tones 12:00.
17	Same as Track 16, with compressor pedal added.
18	Same settings as Track 14.
19	Same again, with compressor pedal added.
20	Same amp (no comp this time), but with Fender Tele on bridge pickup.
21	The Rickenbacker 360/12 connected by DI straight to the recorder with the signal split 'Rick-o-Sound' style to two tracks: bridge pickup Left with medium echo, neck pickup Right with reverb.

These tracks take us through 20 years of the Ricky-into-Vox sound (with a Fender stop-off along the way), while also comparing the setup with and without comp. The approximate vibes here run: poppy Beatles, rocky Beatles, straight McGuinn, compressed McGuinn, straight indie/REM-ish jangle, compressed indie/REM-ish jangle, that jangle done on a juicy raw Telecaster, and finally the Rick-o-Sound stereo feature in all its glory. Often I find I prefer the ring and sustain of the compressed tracks, but the cleaner, thinner electric 12-string works great in some applications, too.

SETUP 5
SURF'S UP

Track	Equipment
22	1960 Jazzmaster into 1961 Fender Showman 12 amplifier. Guitar on bridge pickup. Amp Vol 1:00 with tones at 12:00; amp tremolo set fast, medium depth; original JBL D120F speaker.
23	Same rig and settings, with Fender Reverb Unit added, set: Dwell 10:30, Mix 10:30, Tone 1:30.
24	Same as Track 23, with 1964 Fender Stratocaster on bridge pickup.
25	1963 Fender Jaguar into 1961 Showman 12 amplifier. Guitar set first for bridge pickup only, then neck pickup added for the middle break, then bridge-only again. Amp Vol down to 10:30. Fender Reverb Unit set: Dwell 12:00, Mixer 11:00, Tone 7.
26	Same as Track 25, but with the Jazzmaster again, played bridge pickup, then neck pickup for the middle break, then bridge again.

Dick Dale has always claimed, contrary to most commonly held convictions, that the splashy spring reverb sproing isn't in fact the 'true sound of surf music,' rather it's the dry but intensively played instrumental, with speed and pick attack simulating the roll of the waves and a little amp tremolo thrown in for dimension. Controversial stuff in some surf circles, perhaps, but on Track 22 you can easily hear how the atmospheric tremolo chop and the speed picking (sloppy though it occasionally may be) create a moving, energetic instrumental guitar sound, even without the otherwise ubiquitous reverb. When that great vintage Fender outboard reverb joins the party on Track 23, however, there certainly is another dimension to the sound, and many people will agree it really ups the surf vibe a notch. On Track 25, note the choked, plonky, sustainless sound of the Jaguar vs the fatter growl of the Jazzmaster on Track 26. That said, the Jag still gushes with fantastic surf sounds, if perhaps of a tamer breed.

SETUP 6
BRITISH BLUES

Track	Equipment
27	Gibson Les Paul Standard (Custom Shop 'burst reissue, I'm afraid) into 1966 Marshall 1962 model 'Bluesbreaker' combo. Guitar set to neck pickup. Amp set: Vol 4:00, Treble 3:00, Bass 1:00, Mid 3:00, Presence 2:00.
28	Same as Track 27, but Les Paul set to bridge pickup.
29	Same as Track 27 (neck pickup again), but with a germanium-transistor Treble Booster added.
30	Same amp settings again, Fender Telecaster on bridge pickup (no booster).
31	Same settings as Track 28, but amp Vol down to 9:30.

Track 27 really bags that fat, chewy, compressed 1960s British blues sound, and adding the sweet, smooth germanium-based treble booster in Track 29 pushes it all right over the top. Note how the Marshall's Celestion Greenbacks strain to reproduce all the low frequencies in the first example, and go pretty mushy in the mids as well with the treble booster added, but the whole package sounds great. Flick to the bridge pickup, as on Track 28, and the brighter, edgier sound takes you right out of 'Beano' territory. Along these lines, the Tele sounds very cool too, and not as 'twangy' as you might imagine; a great rock'n'roll voice. You never hear the clean settings of these Marshalls talked about much, so Track 31 gives us a taste of that – well, clean going on crunch really. Compare this to the tweed Bassman set clean-ish with a 12AY7 in Track 12. Different guitar, different amp, different settings and a different riff, but the sound has some similarities.

SETUP 7
CLUB JAZZ

Track	Equipment
32	Late 1960s Gibson ES-175 into mid-1970s Polytone Mini Brute MkII. Guitar set to neck pickup. Amp set: Vol 9:00, Treble 12:00, Bass 12:00, Reverb 12:00, Emphasis switch Normal (middle).
33	ES-175 on neck pickup again, into silverface Fender Deluxe Reverb set: Vol 10:00, Treble 11:00, Bass 9:00, Reverb 9:30.

Forgive me Joe Pass, Wes Montgomery, Kenny Burrell et al. Still, you gotta' dig that smooth, warm, coctail-lounge vibe. The only difference between these two tracks, gearwise, is the amps. Many people would call Track 32 'warmer,' despite the fact that this is one adjective so often applied to tube equipment. The all-tube Fender Deluxe Reverb in Track 33, on the other hand, has just as full and round a low-end response when you listen carefully, but its upper-mid and high frequencies have more second-harmonic action going on there, too, and hence a more complex voice.

SETUP 8
THE JIMI RIG

Track	Equipment
34	1964 Fender Stratocaster into late-1960s Marshall 'Plexi' JTM50 1987 Lead amp with Celestion G12H-loaded 4x12″ cab. Guitar on bridge pickup. Amp Normal Channel set: Vol 4:00, Treble 1:00, Middle 2:00, Bass 1:00, Presence 1:00.
35	Same again, with a vintage Vox Wah-Wah and Dallas-Arbiter Fuzz Face chained between guitar and amp, in that order. Fuzz on for first half of the track, wah-wah added to it for second half.
36	Same amp tone settings, but Vol down to 11:00. Strat first set to 'notched' bridge/middle pickups position, then neck pickup, then bridge.
37	Amp set as for Track 36, Strat on neck pickup played through a modern Roger Mayer Octavia.
38	1968 Gibson SG Custom through 1971 Marshall JTM50 'Metal-panel' 1987 Lead Amp, with germanium treble booster added second pass. Guitar on bridge pickup.

Amp High Treble channel set: Vol 3:00, Treble 12:30, Bass 1:00, Middle 11:00, Presence 12:00.

39   Amp as Track 38 except Vol down to 12:00, silicon Fuzz Face added for lead passages. Guitar/fuzz settings: bridge pickup dry for first pass rhythm, fuzz added for first leads; neck pickup second pass rhythm, fuzz added for second pass leads; back to bridge/fuzz for outro.

When I listen to Track 34 I always think, 'Yeah, this has got some happening tone going on.' Then Track 35 rolls along, and the Fuzz Face and Vox Wah-Wah just lift things so much. It's raw and filthy, but also very soulful, bluesy and rocky at the same time. Yeah, this is a JTM50 instead of a JTM100 as was more central to Hendrix's rig, but the 50-watter is easier to record at high drive levels, and offers a good glimpse of the same tonality. Track 36 runs us through different Stratocaster pickup selections on a cleaner amp setting – something Hendrix made the most of – while Track 37 gives a sampling of that crazy Octavia sound. Tracks 38 and 39 take the Marshall stack beyond Hendrix's day to visit a couple stadium rock sound of the 1970s. The first a more evil rock riff and lead sound, the second a classic crunchy power-chord rhythm, with a later-era fuzz sound for solos.

SETUP 9
COUNTRY

Track   Equipment

40   1952 Fender Telecaster into 1965 Deluxe Reverb, with compressor pedal added. Amp set: Vol 10:30, Treble 1:00, Bass 2:00, Reverb 0, Speed 11:00, Intensity 1:00. Recorded with STC 4038 mike set 18″ away. On-the-fly effects and pickup setting changes according to track timings:
0:00–0:18 Tele neck pickup with amp tremolo on.
0:20–0:40 Tele switched to bridge pickup.
0:41–1:04 amp tremolo switched out, compressor pedal switched in.
1:05–end tremolo switched back in.

41   Tele on bridge pickup, same Deluxe but set: Vol 1:00, Treble 1:30, Bass 12:00. Ibanez TS9 Tube Screamer set for crunchy boost added for solo.
Recorded with STC 4038 mike set 24″ away.

42   Tele on bridge again, this time through a 1960 tweed Fender Tremolux amp set: Vol 2:00, Tone 3:00. Ibanez TS9 Tube Screamer set for crunchy boost added for solo. Recorded with STC 4038 mike set 24″ away.

Track 40 runs us through some of the changes of the country

sound, though more in an alt-twang style than in pure classic Nashville session style. Within the sample we here the range of the Telecaster on neck and bridge pickup, with and without compression (pedal) and tremolo (amp). Note the big, plummy clean sound you can get from the Deluxe Reverb by keeping the volume down fairly low, which enables you to use a more sensitive recording mike. Track 41 exhibits the same amp cranked up to crunch levels vs its 18W 6V6-based predecessor of some five years before, for a raw slab of hillbilly roots-rock. Note the slightly scooped blackface tonality of the Deluxe Reverb, compared to the Tremolux's pronounced midrange bark, which is classic Fender tweed.

SETUP 10
AMERICAN GARAGE

Track   Equipment

43   Late 1950s Silvertone U-3 guitar into Silvertone Medalist amplifier. Guitar on middle pickup. Amp set: Vol 10:30, Bass 12:00, Treble 2:00.

44   Same rig, U-3's bridge and middle pickups on full. Amp set: Vol max, Bass 1:00, Treble 11:30.

45   Amp set as Track 44, with 1960 Les Paul Jr.

For Track 43, our catalog-bought garage band rig is set clean for what is intended to be a wiry, clean-with-bite tone, but thanks to the tired output tubes and and overworn speakers, there's a little dirt in here already. Simply stir in one cod-funk rhythm progression with even heavily cheddar-strewn turnaround riffs, and... well, no great tone by any definition, but potentially very cool in the right context. Crank this thing to max, though, and you really start to get some depth and motion going on. You can hear this tone really breathing, the speakers pumping and shaking in their interaction with the overloaded tubes and OT – even when there's not a lot of signal going through – and plenty of sparkly, crackly overtones, thanks to that Silvertone's thin, bright lipstick pickups, which really come into their own here. On Track 45, our protagonist – thinking himself a real guitar hero now – has received a new Gibson Les Paul Jr guitar for his 18th birthday to replace the 'cheapo' Silvertone he had received in the guitar/amp set for his 16th two years before (but 'an amp's just an amp, right?' So the Medalist stays.) The P-90 pickups on this guitar are still single coiled, but note how much harder they drive the amp. (No, you're not hearing things. The LP Jr is tuned down a semitone from the U-3... before lunch/after lunch takes, with no tuner in the shop.)

SETUP 11
CHICAGO BLUES

Track   Equipment

46   1964 Gibson ES-335 and 'blackfaced' 1969 Fender Super Reverb with CTS alnico speakers. Guitar on neck pickup. Amp set: Vol 12:00, Treble 1:30, Bass 12:00, Reverb 9:00, Speed 0, Intensity 0.

47   Amp as Track 46 with 1964 Fender Stratocaster on neck pickup.

These are both great blues tones. More oomph and guts in Track 46, more snap and sting in Track 47 – but I think it's impossible to say, objectively, that one is better than the other. Whether you prefer the ES-335 or the Stratocaster is really down to a matter of taste.

SETUP 12
BRIT ROCK

Track   Equipment

48   1967 Gibson SG Special into stock early 1970s Hiwatt Custom 100 DR103 with single 4x12″ with Fane speakers. Amp set: Vol 12:00, Bass 1:00, Middle 12:00, Treble 12:30, Presence 2:00. Guitar on bridge pickup.

49   Amp set the same, with 1968 Gibson SG Custom on bridge pickup.

50   Same amp/guitar settings as Track 48, with Ibanez TS9 Tube Screamer set to high gain for lead sounds.

No Townshend-modded DR103 here I'm afraid, just the standard model, but it's a pretty huge sound nonetheless. To my ears, the P-90s make Track 48 sound fatter than the humbuckers in virtually the same guitar in track 49; Gibson's single coils don't drive the early stages of the amp quite as much as the fat-frequencied humbuckers, so there is less mush, more thud. Track 50 exists merely to show what this rig does when you stick a signal booster in front of it. This is a thick, bass-heavy electric sound that segues easily from classic rock to early metal.

AFTERWORD
BOUTIQUE SETUPS

Track   Equipment

51   Recent John Suhr S-style guitar with h/s/s pickups, set to bridge humbucker into Carr Mercury amp, set: Vol 12:00, tones 1:00, Hi Cut, half Boost at full 8W output.

52   Same Suhr guitar and pickup selection, into TopHat Club Royale (tube rectified) set: Vol 10:00, Treble 10:00, Middle 1:00, Bass 11:00, Master max, Fat Boost.

53   Recent Tom Anderson T Drop Top guitar set to neck pickup, into Carr Mercury set: Vol 1:30, tones 1:00, Hi Cut, Rev 9:00, no boost.

54   Same guitar and pickup selection, into TopHat Club Royale set as per Track 52 but with Boost switch set to Off.

A sample of the future in classic guitar and amp combinations, as available today. Suhr and Anderson guitars should need no introduction – both are first-class updates of classic styles, which yield some of the most playable and best sounding electric instruments available today. The Carr Mercury is an amazing little 8W single-ended 1x12″ combo that comes standard with a single KT66 output tube. It has a built in output attenuator that lets you switch down from full output to 2W, 0.5W or even 0.1W. A big sound from a compact little amp. TopHat's Club Royale is a 20W 1x12″ based on a pair of EL84 output tubes and a cleverly modified version of the Vox-style Top Boost preamp. These little screamers have been popular for recording and club-sized gigs for a few years now, and deservedly so.

GLOSSARY

Abalam Trade name for abalone laminated to thin plastic sheet, the result of a new cutting technique which yields more of the useable shell and less waste.

abalone Shellfish used for inlay material on guitars. Comes in many iridescent hues, most prized being the green heart. Becoming rare.

AC Short for "alternating current," an electric current that can change the direction in which it flows. This is the type of electricity that flows from common domestic wall outlets (commonly 120V in the US, 230-240V in the UK). See also *DC*.

acrylic Paint containing acrylic resin, widely used in guitar finishes as a more eco-friendly substitute for cellulose lacquers.

action Often used to describe only the height of the strings above the tops of the frets; thus "high action," "low action," "buzz-free action" etc. In fact, the term can refer to the entire playing feel of a given instrument; thus "good action," "easy action" etc.

active (active electronics, active circuit) Circuitry in some guitars that boosts signal and/or widens tonal range with necessary additional (usually battery) powering. Refers to a pickup or circuit that incorporates a preamp. See also *preamp*.

active crossover See *crossover*.

active powered Not necessarily amplified, but using (active) electronics to assist or improve functioning.

ADAT Type of multi-track digital audio tape.

ADT Artificial (or automatic) double tracking. Used to reinforce an existing signal, for instance making one singer sound like two.

alder Medium weight hardwood commonly used for solid guitar bodies, for example some of those made by Fender.

alnico Magnet material used for pickups and speakers (generally of more "vintage" design). It is an alloy of aluminum, nickel, and cobalt. Also, a nickname for a single-coil Gibson pickup with flat-sided polepieces.

alternating current See *AC*.

amp(lifier) Electrical circuit designed to increase the level of a signal; but more usually, an audio system for boosting sound before transmission to a loudspeaker. The system could be a power amp, or backline instrument amplifier, or line amp.

amplification Making a signal bigger (may refer to voltage, analogous to signal level and loudness, or current). General term for amps, speakers and associated gear.

analog (UK: analogue) System which reproduces a signal by copying its original

amplitude waveform. Examples include the groove of an old vinyl recording, the electrical signal on a magnetic tape recording, or the voltage levels of an analog synthesizer. As opposed to digital, where the signal is recorded as a series of numbers.

anode (plate) Part within a vacuum tube (UK: valve) which collects current.

anti-surge "Delayed" fuse (body marked "T") that withstands brief current surges without breaking. Note that it doesn't prevent current surges.

archtop Guitar with arched body top formed by carving or pressing. Usually refers to hollowbody or semi-acoustic instruments; thus "archtop jazz guitar". As opposed to the other principal type of acoustic guitar, the flat-top.

arpeggio Broken chord in which the notes are played sequentially rather than together.

ash Medium to heavy hardwood commonly used for solid guitar bodies, for example by Fender.

atonal Type of composition, usually of the 20th century, which has no allegiance to a tonal center.

attack Speed at which a sound (or filter, or envelope) reaches its maximum level. For instance, percussive sounds usually have fast attacks, while smooth, liquid sounds have slow attacks.

attenuate Reduce in strength.

attenuator Electronic circuitry that reduces level, usually in fixed steps of useful round-figure amounts, such as -10dB, -20dB. Also the knob or switch that controls such a setting.

baby blue Popular (unofficial) name for Fender's early Sonic Blue Custom Color.

backlash Any "give" in a tuner's operation where the string-post does not immediately move when the tuner button is turned.

backplate Panel fitted over a cavity in the rear of a guitar body, allowing access to pots and wiring or vibrato springs.

baffle Front panel or baseboard of a speaker cabinet onto which direct-radiating drivers and smaller horn flares are mounted.

Bakelite First plastic, invented 1909. Used for some guitars, parts and components from the 1930s to the 1950s.

ball-end Metal retainer wound onto the end of a guitar string and used to secure it to the anchor point at the bridge.

banjo tuners Rear-facing tuners found on some guitars, notably on some early Martin OM and Gibson reverse-body Firebird models.

bass pickup See *neck pickup*.

B-bender String-pulling device giving a

pedal-steel effect on regular electric guitar. The best known models are by Parsons-White, and Joe Glaser.

bias For a tube (valve) guitar amp, a critical "tune-up" setting (and also of a tape machine or other piece of equipment), generally involving some auxiliary voltage or current that helps the circuitry to work properly.

Bigsby Simple single-spring non-recessed vibrato device developed by Paul Bigsby. Now sometimes used as a generic term for similar designs by other makers.

binding Protective and decorative strip(s) added to edges of the body and/or fingerboard and/or headstock of some guitars.

birdseye Type of maple with small circular figure.

blade pickup (bar pickup) Pickup (humbucker or single-coil) that uses a long single blade polepiece for each coil, rather than the more usual individual polepieces for each string.

block markers Square-shape or rectangular-shape position markers in the fingerboard.

blond (blonde) Natural finish, usually enhancing plain wood color; or (on some Fenders) a slightly yellowed finish.

Bluesbreaker Nickname for the Marshall 2x12 combo used by Eric Clapton on the John Mayall album of the same name. Originals are highly sought after, and the model was re-issued by Marshall in the late 1980s.

board (UK: desk) Mixer, mixing console, mixdown unit.

boat neck Alternative name for V-neck (describes shape). See *V-neck*.

bobbin Frame around which pickup coils are wound.

body Main portion of the guitar, onto which are (usually) mounted the bridge, pickups, controls etc. Can be solid, hollow, or a combination of the two.

bolt-on neck Describes a (usually solidbody) guitar with neck bolted rather than glued to the body. Typified by most Fender electric guitars. In fact, such a neck is most often secured by screws.

bookmatched Wood split into two thin sheets and joined together to present symmetrically matching grain/figure patterns.

bottleneck Style of guitar playing using a metal or glass object to slide up and down the guitar strings instead of fretting individual notes. The broken-off neck of a bottle was originally used, hence the name.

bound See *binding*.

bout Looking at a guitar standing upright, the

bouts are the outward curves of the body above (upper bout) and below (lower bout) the instrument's "waist."

boutique amp High-end, generally hand-built and hand-wired guitar amplifier produced usually in limited numbers by an independent craftsman.

box Slang term for (usually hollowbody "jazz") guitar.

BPM Beats per minute – the tempo of the music.

Brazilian rosewood Hardwood derived from the tropical evergreen Dalbergia nigra and used in the making of some guitar bodies, necks and fingerboards. Now a protected species, meaning further exportation from Brazil is banned.

bridge Unit on guitar body that holds the saddle(s). Sometimes also incorporates the anchor point for the strings.

bridge block On acoustic guitars, this refers to the drilled section of a bridge through which the strings are threaded.

bridge pickup Pickup placed nearest the bridge. At one time known as the lead or treble pickup.

bridgeplate On electric guitars, this is the baseplate on to which bridge components are mounted; on acoustic guitars, the reinforcing hardwood plate under the bridge.

bullet Describes the appearance of the truss-rod adjustment nut visible at the headstock on some Fender and Fender-style guitars.

burst Abbreviation of sunburst (finish), but often used specifically to refer to one of the original sunburst-finish Gibson Les Paul Standard models made between 1958 and 1960.

button Knob used to turn tuners (machine heads).

cable Another name for a cord (lead) to supply mains power, or to connect amps and speakers, or to connect instruments and amplifiers. Can also be used generally for the sheathed connecting wires, with or without connectors.

camber See *radius*.

cans Slang term for headphones.

capacitor (cap) Frequency-dependent electrical component. Within an electric guitar tone control, for example, it's used to filter high frequencies to ground (earth) making the sound progressively darker as the control is turned down. Used similarly in guitar amplifiers, as well as for filtering noise from power supplies by passing AC signal to ground.

capo (from capo tasto or capo dastro)

Movable device which can be fitted over the fingerboard behind any fret. It shortens the strings' length and therefore raises their pitch. Used to play in different keys but with familiar chord shapes.

carbon graphite Strong, stable, man-made material used by some modern electric guitar makers. Has a very high resonant frequency.

cathode biased In a tube amp, an output stage which is biased according to the voltage drop across a resistor connected to the cathode of the power tube(s). Often considered a source of "vintage" tone, it is a feature of the tweed Fender Deluxe, the Vox AC-30 and others. See also *fixed bias*.

cavity Hollowed-out area in solidbody guitar for controls and switches: thus "control cavity."

cedar Evergreen conifer of the Mediterranean; the timber is used particularly in the making of classical guitar necks. In flat-top and other building the term often refers to "western red cedar," which is not a cedar at all but a North American thuya or arbor vitae.

cellulose See *nitro-cellulose*.

center block Solid wooden block running through the inside of a semi-acoustic guitar's body.

chamfer Bevel or slope to the edges of a guitar's body.

chassis Steel or aluminum casing that houses the electronics of an amp or an effects unit.

checkerboard binding Binding made up of small alternate black and white blocks running around the circumference of a guitar body. Normally associated with high-end Rickenbacker guitars.

cherry Shade of red stain used in translucent guitar finishes and most commonly associated with Gibson who used it extensively from the 1950s onwards. Hence often referred to as Gibson Cherry Red.

choke Small transformer within some guitar amps which helps to filter AC noise from the circuit.

choking String colliding with a higher fret as the string is played and/or bent.

class A Amplifier with output tubes set to operate throughout the full 360-degree cycle of the signal. Class A is sometimes considered "sweeter" sounding harmonically, but is less efficient power-wise than class AB. (The term is often incorrectly used to describe guitar amps which are in fact cathode-biased class AB circuits with no negative feedback, and therefore share some sonic characteristics with class A amps.) See *class AB*.

class AB Amplifier with output tubes set to cut off alternately for a portion of the signal's 360-degree cycle, thereby sharing the load and increasing output efficiency. (In reality, this is the operating class of the majority of guitar amps, and certainly of many classics by Marshall, Fender, Mesa/Boogie and others.) See *class A*.

clay dot Refers to the material used for the dot inlays on Fender guitars from circa 1959 to 1963.

coil(s) Insulated wire wound around bobbin(s) in a pickup.

coil-split Usually describes a method to cut out one coil of a humbucking pickup, giving a slightly lower output and cleaner, more single-coil-like sound. Also known, incorrectly, as coil-tap.

coil-tap (tapped pickup) Pickup coil which has two or more live leads exiting at different percentages of the total wind, in order to provide multiple output levels and tones. Not to be confused with coil-split.

comping Playing style, usually associated with jazz, which sustains the tempo and rhythm of a piece while simultaneously stating its chord changes.

compound radius See *radius*.

compressor Sound processor that can be set to smooth dynamic range and thus minimize sudden leaps in volume. Overall perceived loudness is in this way increased without "clipping."

conductor wires Wires attached to the start and finish of a pickup coil which take the output signal to the controls. A four-conductor humbucker, for example, actually has five output wires: four conductor wires and a fifth (bare) wire which comes from the pickup's grounding plate and/or cover and must always be connected to ground (earth).

conical radius See *radius*.

contoured body Gentle curving of the front and/or back of a solid guitar body, and usually designed to aid player comfort.

control(s) Knobs and switch levers on outside of guitar activating the function of electric components that are usually mounted below the pickguard or in back of the body.

control cavity See *cavity*.

cord (cable, UK: lead) Cable to supply unit with power, or to connect amplifiers and speakers, or to connect instruments and amplifiers.

counterpoint Music that consists of two or more independent melody lines.

coupling Exchange of mechanical energy between an instrument's string(s) and soundboard.

cross-head screw Screw that has two slots in a "cross" shape in its head.

crossover Circuit, sometimes built into amps and/or speakers, that splits a signal into two or more complementary frequency ranges.

current Flow of electrons in an electrical circuit, measured in amps.

cutaway Curve into body near neck joint, aiding player's access to high frets. A guitar can have two ("double," "equal," "offset," "twin") cutaways or one ("single") cutaway. Sharp ("florentine") or round ("venetian") describe the shape of the horn formed by the cutaway.

cypress Conifer native to southern Europe, east Asia and North America and widely planted for decorative purposes and for wood. Used in the 19th century for the bodies of cheaper guitars taken up by the flamencos.

damping Deadening of a sound, especially by stopping the vibration of a string with, for example, the palm of the hand.

DC Short for "direct current." Electric current flowing only in one direction. Tube (valve) amps utilize DC voltages for the vast portion of their internal operation.

DC resistance "Direct current" resistance: a measurement (in ohms) that is often quoted in pickup specs to give an indication of relative output.

dead string length Portion of the string beyond the nut and behind the saddle.

desk See *board*.

digital System of recording or processing which stores and processes analog information by converting it into a series of numbers (binary 1s and 0s).

digital modeling See *modeling amp*.

diode Electronic component used within some guitar amps as a solid-state rectifier to convert AC current to DC. Also occasionally used in solid-state overdrive circuits. See also *rectifier*.

dissonance Perceived sonic clash between two or more notes that are sounded together.

distortion Signal degradation caused by the overloading or intentional manipulation of audio systems (such as guitar amplifier). Often used deliberately to create a harsher and grittier or sweeter and more compressed sound.

dive-bomb See *down-bend*.

dog-ear Nickname for some P-90 pickups, derived from the shape of the mounting lugs on the cover. See also *soap-bar*.

dot markers Dot-shape position markers in fingerboard.

dot-neck Fingerboard with dot-shape position markers; nickname for Gibson ES-335 of 1958-62 (and reissues) with such markers.

double-locking vibrato See *locking vibrato*.

double-neck (twin-neck) Large guitar specially made with two necks, usually combining six-string and 12-string, or six-string and bass.

down-bend Downward shift in the strings' pitch using a vibrato. In extreme cases this is known as dive-bombing.

down-market See *low-end*.

DPDT switch Double-pole double-throw switch, usually miniature or sub-miniature variety used for guitar coil-tap or other such switching.

dynamics Expression in music using a range of volume (intensity) shifts.

earth (UK term; also known as ground, especially in US) Connection between an electrical circuit or device and the ground. A common neutral reference point in an electrical circuit. All electrical components (and shielding) within a guitar (and amplifiers, signal processors, etc) must be linked to earth as the guitar's pickups and electrics are susceptible to noise interference. See also *shielding*.

ebonized Wood darkened to look like ebony.

ebony Dense, black hardwood used for fingerboards and bridges.

effects (effects units, FX) Generic term for audio processing devices such as distortions, delays, reverbs, flangers, phasers, harmonizers and so on.

effects loop Patch between the preamp and power amp (or sometimes within preamp stages) of guitar amp, processing unit or mixer for inserting effects that will operate on selected sound signals.

electron tube See *tube*.

electronic tuner Typically battery-powered unit that displays and enables accurate tuning to standard concert pitch.

end-block Thick wooden block used to join sides of guitar at the lower bout.

EQ See *equalization*.

equalization (EQ) Active tone control that works by emphasizing or de-emphasizing specific frequency bands. General term for tone control.

European spruce Sometimes called German spruce, picea abies tends to come from the Balkans. Spruce originally meant "from Prussia." Used for soundboards.

face See *plate*, *soundboard*.

Farad Measure of electrical capacitance, and usually (for electric guitar capacitors) quoted in microfarads (μF) or picofarads (pF).

feedback Howling noise produced by leakage of the output of an amplification system back into its input, typically a guitar's pickup(s).

f-hole Soundhole of approximately "f" shape on some hollowbody and semi-acoustic guitars.

figure Natural pattern on surface of wood; thus "figured maple".

fingerboard (fretboard, board) Playing surface of the guitar that holds the frets. It can be simply the front of the neck itself, or a separate thin board glued to the neck.

finish Protective and decorative covering on wood parts, typically the guitar's body, back of neck, and headstock.

five-position switch See *five-way switch*.

five-way switch (five-position switch) Selector switch that offers five options, for example the five pickup combinations on a Strat-style guitar.

fixed bias In guitar amps, a technique for biasing output tubes using a pot to adjust negative voltage on the tube's grid as compared to its cathode. (Note that the name is somewhat misleading as "fixed-bias" amps generally have a bias which is adjustable, whereas cathode-biased amps are set and non-adjustable.) See *cathode biased*.

fixed bridge Non-vibrato bridge.

fixed neck See *glued neck*.

flame Dramatic figure, usually on maple.

flame-top Guitar, often specifically a Gibson Les Paul Standard, with sunburst maple top.

flat-top Acoustic guitar with flat top (as opposed to arched) and usually with a round soundhole.

floating bridge Bridge not fixed permanently to the guitar's top, but held in place by string tension (usually on older or old-style hollowbody guitars).

floating pickup Pickup not fixed permanently to the guitar's top, but mounted on a separate pickguard or to the end of the fingerboard (on some hollowbody electric guitars).

floating vibrato Vibrato unit (such as the Floyd Rose or Wilkinson type) that "floats" above the surface of the body.

flowerpot inlay Describes an inlay depicting a stylized vase and foliage used by Gibson on, notably, its L-5 model.

14-fret/12-fret Refers to the point at which a flat-top acoustic guitar's neck joins the body.

frequency Number of cycles of a vibration occurring per unit of time; the perceived pitch of a sound. See also *Hertz*.

fretboard See *fingerboard*.

fretless Guitar fingerboard without frets; usually bass, but sometimes (very rarely) guitar.

frets Metal strips positioned on the fingerboard of a guitar (or sometimes directly into the face of a solid neck) to enable the player to stop the strings and produce specific notes.

fretwire Wire from which individual frets are cut.

FX Abbreviation for effects. Also known more formally as signal processors – boxes that can be used to alter sound in a creative and/or artistic manner.

gain Amount of increase or change in signal level. When dBs are used, increased gain is shown as +dB; reduction is shown -dB; and no change as 0dB.

gauge Outer diameter of a string, always measured in thousandths of an inch (.009", .042" etc). Strings are supplied in particular gauges and/or in sets of matched gauges. Fretwire is also offered in different gauges, or sizes.

gig Live musical event.

glued neck (glued-in neck, set neck, fixed neck) Type of neck/body joint popularized by Gibson which permanently glues the two main components together.

greenback Describes a particularly desirable Celestion 12" guitar speaker that had a green magnet-cover.

ground (also known as earth, particularly in the UK) Connection between an electrical circuit or device and the ground. A common neutral reference point in an electrical circuit. All electrical components (and shielding) within a guitar (and amplifiers, signal processors, etc) must be linked to earth as the guitar's pickups and electrics are susceptible to noise interference.

ground wire Wire connected from vibrato, bridge, tailpiece, switch, pickup cover, grounding plate etc to ground (earth).

grounding plate Metal baseplate of pickup that is connected to ground (earth).

grunge tuning Tuning all strings down one half step (one semitone) for a fatter sound.

hardtail Guitar with non-vibrato bridge (originally used primarily to distinguish non-vibrato Fender Stratocasters from the more common vibrato-loaded models).

hardware Separate components (non-electrical) fitted to the guitar: the bridge, tuners, strap buttons, and so on.

harmonic Usually refers to a ringing, high-pitched note produced by touching (rather than fretting) strategic points on the string while it is plucked, most noticeably at the fifth, seventh and 12th fret. In fact, "harmonics" also occur naturally during the playing of the acoustic or electric guitar (or any stringed instrument) and are part of any guitar's overall voice.

harmonic distortion "Ordinary" distortion occurring in analog (audio) electronics, speakers and mikes, involving the generation of harmonics.

headstock Portion at the end of the neck where the strings attach to the tuners. "Six-a-side" type (Fender-style) has all six tuners on one side of the headstock. "Three-a-side" type (Gibson-style) has three tuners on one side, three the other.

heel Curved deepening of the neck for strength near body joint.

herringbone Describes a black-and-white decorative inlay for acoustic guitars, as popularized by the Martin company.

Hertz (Hz) Unit of frequency measurement. One Hertz equals one cycle per second. See *frequency*.

hex pickup Provides suitable signal for an external synthesizer.

hook-up wire Connecting wire (live or ground) from pickup to pots, switches etc.

horn Pointed body shape formed by cutaway: thus "left horn," "sharp horn," etc. See also *cutaway*.

hot In electrical connections, means live. Also used generally to mean powerful, as in "hot pickup."

hot-rodding Making modifications to a guitar, usually its pickups and/or electronics.

HT Symbol denoting high voltage in amplifier circuits (short for High Tension) and particularly used in the UK. See *B+*.

humbucker (humbucking) Noise-canceling twin-coil pickup. Typically the two coils have opposite magnetic polarity and are wired together electrically out-of-phase to produce a sound that we call in-phase. See also *phase*.

impedance Electrical resistance to the flow of alternating current, measured in Ohms (Ω). A few electric guitars have low-impedance circuits or pickups to match the inputs of recording equipment; the vast majority are high impedance. Impedance matching is important to avoid loss of signal and tone. Also commonly encountered with speakers,

where it is important to match a speaker's (or speaker cab's) impedance to that of the amplifier's speaker output (commonly 4Ω, 8Ω or 16Ω).

Indian rosewood Hardwood from tropical evergreen tree, known as East Indian rosewood or Dalbergia latifolia. Used for acoustic guitar bodies, fingerboards or necks, especially now that Brazilian rosewood is not freely available.

inertia block See *sustain block*.

inlay Decorative material cut and fitted into body, fingerboard, headstock etc.

insulation Plastic, cloth or tape wrap, or sheath (non-conductive), around an electrical wire, designed to prevent wire(s) coming into contact with other components and thus shorting the circuit.

intonation State of a guitar so that it is as in-tune with itself as physically possible. This is usually dependent on setting each string's speaking length by adjusting the point at which the strings cross the bridge saddle, known as intonation adjustment. Some bridges allow more adjustment, and therefore greater possibilities for accurate intonation, than others.

jack (UK: jack socket) Mono or stereo connecting socket, usually ¼" (6.5mm), used to feed guitar's output signal to amplification.

jackplate Mounting plate for output jack (jack socket), usually screwed on to body.

jack socket See *jack*.

jewel light Fender-style pilot light with faceted cut-glass "jewel" screwed on over a small bulb.

Kluson Brand of tuner, originally used on old Fender, Gibson and other guitars, and now reissued.

lacquer See *nitro-cellulose*.

laminated Joined together in layers; usually wood (bodies, necks) or plastic (pickguards).

lead Shorthand for lead guitar: the main guitar within a group; the one that plays most of the solos and/or riffs. Also (UK) term for cord; see also *cable*, *cord*.

lead pickup See *bridge pickup*.

leaf switch See *toggle switch*.

LED Abbreviation of light emitting diode, a small light often used as an "on" indicator in footswitches, effects and amplifier control panels. Sometimes also used as a component within circuits.

ligado Left-hand technique involving hammering-on and pulling-off. Especially important in flamenco playing.

linear taper See *taper*.

locking trem See *locking vibrato*.

logarithmic taper See *taper*.

logo Brandname and/or trademark, usually on the headstock.

lower bout See *bout*.

lug Protruding part or surface. On electrical components, a lug (sometimes called a tag) allows a connection to be made.

machine head See *tuner*.

magnetic pickup Transducer using coils of

wire wound around a magnet. It converts string vibrations into electrical signals.

mahogany Very stable, medium weight hardwood favored by most guitar makers for necks, and by many for solid bodies.

mains Term for high AC voltage (particularly in the UK) as supplied by domestic wall socket – that is, the "main" domestic supply.

maple Hard, heavy wood, often displaying extreme figure patterns prized by guitar makers. Varying kinds of figure give rise to visual nicknames such as quilted, tigerstripe, curly, flame.

master volume/tone Control that affects all pickups equally. In amplification, a master volume control governs the output level – or operating level of the power section – when partnered with a gain, drive or volume control that governs the level of the individual preamp(s).

microfarad See *Farad*.

MIDI Abbreviation of Musical Instrument Digital Interface. The industry-standard control system for electronic instruments. Data for notes, performance effects, patch changes, voice and sample data, tempo and other information can be transmitted and received.

mod Abbreviation for modification. Any change or after-market customization made to a guitar, amplifier or effects pedal.

modeling amp Guitar amplifier using digital technology (though occasionally analog solid-state circuitry) to emulate, or model, the sounds of classic tube amps.

mother-of-pearl Shell of some molluscs, for example abalone, used for inlays in decoration of rosettes, fingerboards, headstocks, tuning pegs etc.

mounting ring Usually plastic unit within which Gibson-style pickups are fitted to the guitar body.

mustache bridge Describes the shape of a flat-top acoustic guitar bridge plate, typically found on the Gibson J-200 model.

neck Part of the guitar supporting the fingerboard and strings; glued or bolted to the body, or on "though-neck" types forming a support spine to which "wings" are usually glued to form the body.

neck block In acoustic guitars, the end of the neck inside the body where it is built up to meet the top and back of the guitar.

neck pickup Pickup placed nearest the neck. At one time known as the rhythm or bass pickup.

neck pitch Angle of a guitar's neck relative to the body face.

neckplate Single metal plate through which screws pass to achieve a bolt-on neck fixing (Fender-style). Some bolt-on neck-to-body joints use separate washers for each screw.

neck pocket Rout, or recess, into which the neck fits on the body of a bolt-on-neck guitar.

neck relief Small amount of concave bow in a neck (dipping in the middle) that can help to create a relatively buzz-free action.

neck-tilt Device on some Fender (and other) neck-to-body joints that allows easier adjustment of the neck pitch.

nickel Major component of most metal guitar strings.

nitro-cellulose (US: lacquer) Type of finish used commonly in the '50s and '60s but now rarely seen on production guitars.

noise Any undesirable sound, such as mains hum or interference.

noise-canceling Type of pickup with two coils wired together to cancel noise, often called humbucking. Any arrangement of pickups or pickup coils that achieves this.

nut Bone, metal or (now usually) synthetic slotted guide bar over which the strings pass to reach the tuners and which determines string height and spacing at the headstock end of neck.

nut lock See *locking nut*.

Offset Contour Body Fender trademark used to describe the distortion of a conventional solidbody shape to aid the player's comfort and present the neck at a more comfortable angle. Fender's Jazzmaster and Jaguar models were the first with this design.

offshore Made overseas; more specifically and often used to mean outside the US.

ohm Unit of electrical resistance.

open tuning Tuning the guitar to a chord or altered chord, often for slide playing.

out of phase Audible result of the electrical linking of two coils or two pickups in either series or parallel in such a way as to provide at least partial cancellation of the signal. Usually the low frequencies are cancelled so that the resulting sound is thin, lacking in warmth, and often quite brittle. To create an audible result that is in-phase (for example of two coils within a humbucker) the coils must be linked electrically out-of-phase. Phase relationship also depends on polarity of magnets. See also *humbucker*.

oxblood Describes the color of the woven grille cloth used on Fender amps in the early 1960s.

PAF Gibson pickup with Patent Applied For decal (sticker) on base – as was the first, vintage version of the Gibson humbucker.

parallel Electrical circuit that has all the positive points joined together and all the negative points joined together. If we consider that a single-coil pickup has a positive (live, hot) and negative (ground, earth) output, when two single-coil pickups on a Stratocaster (position two and four on a five-way switch), for example, are selected together, they are linked in parallel. Can also apply to the parallel linking of resistors or capacitors in a circuit, etc. See also *series*.

passive Normal, unboosted circuit.

PCB Abbreviation for printed circuit board, a mass-produced fiber board with copper "tracks" making connections between components. It is now the most common circuit board in modern consumer electronics,

and is employed in the majority of guitar amplifiers, other than those that use expensive hand-wired designs.

pearl See *mother-of-pearl*.

pearloid Fake pearl, made of plastic and pearl dust.

pentode Tube (valve) containing five functional elements. Most output tubes in guitar amplifiers are pentodes. Also see *triode*.

phase Relationship of two waveforms with respect to time. See also *out of phase*.

Phillips screwdriver See *cross-head screwdriver*.

pick (plectrum, flat pick) Small piece of (usually) plastic or metal – and in olden times tortoiseshell – that is used to pluck or strum a guitar's strings.

pickguard (UK: scratchplate) Protective panel raised above body or fitted flush on to guitar body.

pickup Any unit mounted on a guitar (or other stringed instrument) which transforms string vibration to an electrical signal to be passed along to an amplifier. See *magnetic pickup*, *piezo pickup, transducer*.

pickup switch Selector switch that specifically selects pickups individually or in combination.

pin bridge Acoustic guitar bridge that secures the strings by pins rather than by tying.

pitch Frequency of a note: the perceived "lowness" or "highness" of a sound. See also *neck pitch*.

plain strings Plain steel guitar strings with no outer windings. See *wound strings*.

plectrum See *pick*.

plexi Nickname for Marshall amplifiers of the mid to late 1960s that used gold-painted "plexiglas" plastic control panels. Also used to refer to the sound produced by Marshall amps of this era, or the reproduction of such a tone.

P-90 Model name for early Gibson single-coil pickup.

point-to-point Method of constructing hand-wired amplifier circuits where individual components are connected directly to each other, without the use of a circuit board.

polarity Relationship of positive and negative electrical currents (or north and south magnetic poles) to each other. The magnetic polarity of a pickup refers to the north or south orientation of the magnetic field as presented to the strings.

pole Simultaneously-switched circuit within an electrical switch; thus "two-pole."

polepieces Non-magnetic (but magnetically conductive) polepieces are used to control, concentrate and/or shape a pickup's magnetic field. Can be either adjustable (screw) or non-adjustable (slug) as in an original Gibson humbucker. Magnetic polepieces are those where the magnet itself is aimed directly at the strings, as in an original Stratocaster single-coil.

polyester Type of modern plastic finish used on some guitars.

polyphonic Music made up of several independent lines, each of which is known as a voice.

polyurethane (urethane) Type of modern plastic finish that is used on some guitars.

position markers Fingerboard inlays of various designs; visual clues to the player of fret positions.

pot (potentiometer) Variable electrical resistor that alters voltage by a spindle turning on an electrically resistive track. Used for volume and tone controls, etc.

power amp Output stage of a guitar amplifier that converts the preamp signal to the signal capable of driving a speaker. In a tube (valve) amp, this is where the big tubes live.

preamp (pre-amplifier) Circuit designed to boost low-level signals to a standard level and EQ them before they're sent toward the power amp (hence "pre-amplifier") for full amplification. Guitar circuit usually powered by battery that converts the pickup's output from high to low impedance (preamp/buffer) and can increase the output signal and boost or cut specific frequencies for tonal effect. Also, the first gain stage in a guitar amp, which generally also includes the EQ circuitry and any overdrive-generating stages.

pre-CBS Fender guitars and amps made before CBS takeover in 1965.

pressed top Arched top (usually laminated) of hollowbody guitar made by machine-pressing rather than hand-carving.

purfling Usually synonymous with binding, but more accurately refers to the decorative inlays around the perimeter of a guitar alongside the binding.

push-pull Power amplifier in which output tubes (valves) operate on alternate cycles of the signal. (This is the most common power amp format in guitar amps that contain more than one output tube.)

pyramid bridge Flat-top acoustic guitar bridge having pyramid shaped "bumps" at each side. Common to early Martins.

quarter-sawn Wood cut on radius of tree so that "rings" are perpendicular to the surface of the plank. Structurally preferable to flat-sawn wood for guitar building.

quilted Undulating figure seen on surface of wood, usually maple.

rectifier Component within a guitar amplifier which converts electrical current from AC to DC; can comprise solid-state diodes or a tube (valve) rectifier.

reissue Instrument or amp based on an earlier and usually classic model, reintroduced at a later date.

relief See *neck relief*.

resistor Electrical component which introduces a known value of resistance (measured in ohms) to the electrical flow in a circuit.

resonant frequency Frequency at which any object vibrates most with the least stimulation.

reverb (reverberation) Ambience effect

combining many short echoes; can be imitated electronically, generally by the installation of a spring unit in guitar amps, or digitally in pedals and studio effects units.

rhythm pickup See *neck pickup*.

rosewood Variegated hardwood traditionally used for acoustic guitar backs, sides and fingerboards. Brazilian or Rio is the most highly prized; Indian is more common.

rout Hole or cavity cut into a guitar, usually into the body. Cavities of this kind are thus said to be routed (rhymes with "shouted") into the body.

saddle(s) Part(s) of a bridge where the strings make contact; the start of the speaking length of the string; effectively the opposite of the (top) nut.

sag Slight drop in power supply of a guitar amplifier (particularly noticeable in designs comprising tube rectifiers) when a powerful note or chord is played, producing a compression-like softening and squeezing of the signal.

scale length (string length) Theoretical length of the vibrating string from nut to saddle; actually twice the distance from nut to 12th fret. The actual scale length (the distance from the nut to saddle after intonation adjustment) is slightly longer. See *intonation*, *compensation*.

scratchplate See *pickguard*.

scratch test To verify if a pickup on a guitar plugged into an amp is working by gently rubbing ("scratching") the tip of a screwdriver on the pickup's polepieces and listening for sound.

selector Control that selects from options, usually of pickups.

semi See *semi-acoustic*.

semi-acoustic (semi-solid, semi) Electric guitar with wholly or partly hollow thin body. Originally referred specifically to an electric guitar with a solid wooden block running down the center of thinline body, such as Gibson's ES-335.

semi-solid See *semi-acoustic*.

serial number Added by maker for own purposes; sometimes useful for determining the period of the instrument's construction.

series Electrical linkage of positive and negative points within an electrical circuit with additive effect – for example, the two pickup coils within a series-wired humbucker. In this instance, the total resistance of a series-wired humbucker is the sum of the resistance of each coil. Parallel linkage of the same two coils results in the resistance being one quarter of the sum total. Generally, the higher the resistance the "darker" the resulting tone. Also applies to method of linkage of capacitors or resistors within an amplifier or other electrical circuit. See *parallel*.

set neck (glued neck, glued-in neck, fixed neck) Type of neck/body joint popularized by Gibson which permanently "sets" the two main components together, usually by gluing.

set-up General term including but not restricted to a broad and complex combination of factors (string height, saddle height, intonation adjustments, fret condition, neck relief, etc) required to get the guitar playing to its optimum level.

shellac Natural thermoplastic resin made from secretions of lac insect, which lives on trees in India and Thailand. Dissolved in alcohol, it creates a finish that is applied to guitars by French polishing.

shielding (screening) Barrier to any outside electrical interference. Special paint or conductive foil in the control or pickup cavity to reduce electrical interference. See also *ground*.

signal Transmitted electrical information – for example between control circuits, or guitar and amplifier, etc – usually by means of a connecting wire or cord (lead).

single-coil Original pickup type with a single coil of wire wrapped around (a) magnet(s).

single-ended Amplifier in which the power tube (valve) – usually just one – operates through the entire cycle of the signal. Such amps are necessarily, therefore, class A. Classic examples include the Fender Champ and Vox AC-4.

skunk-stripe Walnut strip inserted in back of one-piece Fender maple necks after truss-rod is inserted.

slab board (slab fingerboard) Fender type (circa 1959-62) in which the joint between the top of the neck and the base of the fingerboard is flat. Later this joint was curved.

slot-head screw Type with a single slot in its head.

slush lever See *vibrato*.

snakehead Headstock shape that is narrower at the top than the bottom. Usually refers to early Gibson type.

snot green See *mint green*.

soapbar Nickname for P-90 pickup with a cover that has no mounting "ears". See *dog-ear*.

solid General term for any solidbody guitar.

solid-state Circuitry using transistorized components rather than tubes (valves).

soundboard Vibrating top of a guitar body. See *top*, *plate*.

SPDT switch Single-pole double-throw miniature switch.

speaker (loudspeaker, driver) Component consisting of a ceramic or alnico magnet, voice coil, and paper cone, driven by an amplified signal to reproduce sound waves in moving air.

speaking length Sounding length of a guitar's string: the part running from the nut down to the bridge saddle.

splice-joint One method of fixing a guitar head to its neck when each has been carved from a different section of wood.

splined Grooved surface of potentiometer shaft that assists tight fitting of a control knob.

spring claw Anchor point for vibrato springs

in body-rear vibrato cavity. Adjusting the spring claw's two screws will affect the position and potential travel of the vibrato.

spruce Soft, light hardwood used for the soundboard on many acoustic guitars.

stop-tail Slang for the style of wrapover bridge fitted to low and mid-priced Gibson solidbodies. See *wrapover bridge*.

stop tailpiece See *stud tailpiece*.

strap button Fixing point on body to attach a guitar-strap; usually two, on sides (or side and back) of guitar body.

Strat Abbreviation of Fender Stratocaster, so universally used that Fender have trademarked it and use it themselves.

string block In classical-guitar terminology, this is the drilled section of a bridge through which the strings are threaded.

string length Sounding length of string, measured from nut to bridge saddle (see also *scale length*).

string post Metal shaft on tuner with a hole or slot to receive the string and around which the string is wound.

string winder Device to assist in the speedy winding of a string onto the tuner's string-post.

stud tailpiece (stop tailpiece) Type of tailpiece fixed to solid or semi-acoustic guitar top, either as a single combined bridge/tailpiece unit, or else as a unit separate from the bridge.

sunburst Decorative paint finish in which (usually) pale-colored center graduates to darker edges.

sustain Length of time a string vibrates. Purposeful elongation of a musical sound, either by playing technique or electronic processing.

sustain block (inertia block) Metal block under the bridgeplate of a floating vibrato (vintage-style Fender, for example) which, because the vibrato is not permanently fixed to the body, replaces the body mass necessary for sufficient string sustain.

sympathetic resonances Sounds produced by open strings that are not struck.

syncopation Displacement of the normal beat.

synth access Guitar type with a built-in pickup to enable connection to an external synthesizer unit.

system vibrato See *vibrato system*.

table See *plate*, *soundboard*, *top*.

tailpiece Unit on body separate from bridge that anchors strings. See also *trapeze tailpiece*, *stud tailpiece*.

taper Of a potentiometer: determines how smoothly the resistance is applied as the control is turned down. Most modern pots use a logarithmic taper as opposed to a linear taper.

tapped pickup See *coil-tap*.

thinline Hollowbody electric guitar with especially narrow body depth; term coined originally by Gibson for its Byrdland model introduced in 1955.

three-position switch See *three-way switch*.

three-way switch (three-position switch) Selector switch that offers three options.

through-neck (thru-neck) Neck that travels the complete length of a guitar, "through" the body, and usually with "wings" added to complete the body shape.

tigerstripe Dramatic figure, usually on maple. See *flame*.

timbre Tone quality or "color" or "flavor" of a sound.

tin To apply solder to a wire before making the soldered joint.

toggle switch Type of selector switch that "toggles" between a small number of options. It is sometimes called a leaf switch.

Tolex Trade name of vinyl covering manufactured by DuPont corporation and commonly used by Fender (and some others) on guitar amps and hardshell cases. (Often generically – if incorrectly – used to refer to any vinyl amp covering.)

top Vibrating face of the guitar. See *soundboard*, *plate*.

top nut See *nut*.

tranny Short for "transistorized." Nickname given to solid-state circuitry or equipment.

transducer Unit that converts one form of energy to another; the term is sometimes used generically for piezo-electric pickups, but technically applies to any type of pickup or loudspeaker, etc. See *magnetic pickup*, *piezo pickup*.

trapeze tailpiece Simple tailpiece of trapezoidal shape.

treble-bleed cap Simple circuit where capacitor (sometimes with an additional resistor) is attached to volume control potentiometer and thus retains high frequencies when the volume control is turned down.

treble pickup See *bridge pickup*.

tremolo (tremolo arm, tremolo system, trem) Erroneous but much-used term for vibrato device/system. The musical definition of tremolo is the rapid repetition of a note or notes. Perhaps this is why Fender applied the name to its amplifier effect, which is a regular variation in the sound's volume.

triode Tube (valve) containing three functional elements, and most common in the preamp circuits of guitar amplifiers in the form of "dual triodes" – tubes which contain two triodes in a single glass bottle.

truss-rod Metal rod fitted inside the neck, almost always adjustable and which can be used to control neck relief.

truss-rod cover Decorative plate covering truss-rod access hole, usually on headstock.

tube US term for the electrical component that the British call a valve; an abbreviation of electron(ic) vacuum tube. In a guitar amp, a tube amplifies the input signal by regulating the flow of electrons.

Tune-o-matic Gibson-originated bridge adjustable for overall string height as well as

for individual string intonation.

tuner Device almost always fitted to the headstock, one per string, that alters a string's tension and pitch. Also called machine head or (archaically) tuning peg. See also *electronic tuner*.

tuner button Knob that the player moves to turn the tuner mechanism in order to raise or lower a string's pitch.

12-fret/14-fret Refers to the point at which a flat-top acoustic guitar's neck joins the body.

twin-neck See *double-neck*.

two-pole See *pole*.

unwound string See *wound string*.

up-bend Upward shift in the strings' pitch brought about by using a vibrato.

up-market See *high-end*.

upper bout See *bout*.

upscale See *high-end*.

valve Short for "thermionic valve;" the British term for electron tube. See *tube*.

vibrato (slush lever, trem, tremolo, tremolo arm, vibrato bridge, vibrato system, wang bar, whammy) Bridge and/or tailpiece which alters the pitch of the strings when the attached arm is moved. Vibrato is the technically correct term because it means a regular variation in pitch. Also used to define this effect when contained within a guitar amp.

virtuoso Instrumental performer with excellent technical abilities.

V-joint One method of fixing head to neck, or neck to body. More complex than normal splice-joint.

V-neck Describes shape of cross-section of neck on, typically, some older Strats, Teles, and Martins.

waist In-curved shape near the middle of the guitar body, usually its narrowest point.

wang bar See *vibrato*.

Watt Unit of electrical power, commonly used to define the output of guitar amps, the power-handling capabilities of speakers, etc. Technically, the rate that energy is transferred (or work is done) over time, equal to a certain amount of horse-power, or joules per second. Named for James Watt, British pioneer of steam power.

whammy See *vibrato*.

wolf note (wolf tone, dead note) Note with a sound unpleasantly different from or less resonant than those around it. The phenomenon is much affected by instrument construction, and can be indicative of a minor flaw in a guitar.

wrapover bridge Unit where strings are secured by wrapping them around a curved bar.

zero fret Extra fret placed in front of the nut. It provides the start of the string's speaking length and creates the string height at the headstock end of the fingerboard. In this instance the nut is simply used to determine string spacing. Used by some manufacturers to make the tone of the open string and the fretted string more similar.

INDEX

Page numbers in *italics* indicate pictures.

THANK YOU

Copious thanks once again to Charlie Chandler, Paul and Ian, and the Guitar Experience shop in Hampton Wick, SW London for loaning or procuring a huge proportion of the fine gear used in the recording of this CD.

Thanks to Adam, Barrie, Joe and all the staff at Vintage & Rare Guitars on Denmark Street, London, for allowing us to photograph much of their precious stock (and even record a few rigs), for attacking the mammoth case mountain without a safety net, and for pointing us to the best coffee in central London. Also to Scott, Glenn, Rick Harrison and all at Music Ground's store on Denmark St, London, for letting us pilfer their vintage gear closet.

Further thanks to Rod Fogg for the loan of his fine jazz rig, Aspen Pittman for the use of some of his own photographs, Bjorn Gladwell and Rosetti/Rickenbacker, and to Neil Whitcher of Fender GBI.

I would also like to thank my publishers Nigel Osborne and Tony Bacon for their constant support, Miki Slingsby for his outstanding photography, John Morrish for his attentive editing and Paul Cooper for the look of the book. Finally, thanks to Jess, Freddie and Florence for putting up with a poor man's Hendrix after breakfast, and a woozy Dick Dale in the afternoon.